Simon G
Plays :

Butley, Otherwise Engaged, The Rear Column,
Quartermaine's Terms, The Common Pursuit

This volume includes five of Simon Gray's best-known plays. *Butley* ('could well join that distinguished gallery of human debris represented by Willie Loman, Jimmy Porter and Bill Maitland in post-war drama' *Evening Standard*); *Otherwise Engaged* ('adult and literate, scathingly funny but ultimately disturbing' *Sunday Telegraph*); *The Rear Column* ('Gray's best play and one of the most interesting—and least facile—studies of the skeletons in our cupboards' *Times Literary Supplement*); *Quartermaine's Terms* ('Mr Gray's selection of details and exchanges is immaculate: he achieves drama and mystery in mundane lives' *The Times*); and *The Common Pursuit* ('Mr Gray is still the master of elegantly clenched despair . . . the most carefully and acerbically crafted dialogue in town' *Punch*). The volume opens with a characteristically laconic introduction by the author.

SIMON GRAY was born on Hayling Island in 1936 and educated at Portsmouth Grammar School and Westminster, then at universities in Canada and France before reading English at Cambridge. For twenty years he was a lecturer in English Literature at Queen Mary College, London. He has written a number of novels and television plays including *Sleeping Dog, Death of a Teddy Bear*, for which he won the Writers' Guild Award, *Pig in a Poke, Man in a Side-Car, Two Sundays* and *Plantiffs and Defendants*. Since his first stage-play, *Wise Child* (1967), he has written *Dutch Uncle* (1969), an adaptation of *The Idiot* for the National Theatre (1970), *Spoiled* (1971) and *Butley*, which won the *Evening Standard* Best Play award for 1971. *Otherwise Engaged* won both the *Evening Standard* and *Plays and Players* Best Play awards for 1975. Subsequent stage plays have been *Dog Days* (Oxford Playhouse, 1976), *Molly* (Watford Palace, 1977; Comedy Theatre, 1978), *The Rear Column* (Globe Theatre, 1978), *Close of Play* (National Theatre, 1979), *Stage Struck* (Vaudeville Theatre, 1979), *Quartermaine's Terms* (Queen's Theatre, 1981, the only play ever to win the Cheltenham Prize for Literature), a version of Molière's *Tartuffe* (Kennedy Center Washington, 1982) and *The Common Pursuit* (Lyric Theatre, Hammersmith, 1984 and Long Wharf Theatre, Newhaven, U.S.A); a revised version was performed at the Matrix Theatre, Los Angeles in 1986.

The front cover shows 'Scholars at a Lecture' by William Hogarth, courtesy of the Hogarth House, Chiswick. The photograph of Simon Gray on the back cover is reproduced by courtesy of the *Sunday Telegraph*.

SIMON GRAY

Plays : One

Butley
Otherwise Engaged
The Rear Column
Quartermaine's Terms
The Common Pursuit

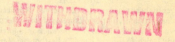
A Methuen Paperback

METHUEN'S WORLD DRAMATISTS
This collection first published in Great Britain as a paperback original in 1986 by
Methuen London Ltd., 11 New Fetter Lane, London EC4P 4EE and in the
United States of America by Methuen Inc., 29 West 35th Street, New York,
NY 10001.

Reproduced, printed and bound in Great Britain by
Hazell Watson & Viney Limited,
Member of the BPCC Group,
Aylesbury, Bucks

Butley first published in 1971 by Methuen & Co. Ltd.
Reprinted in 1975, 1977 and 1979 by Eyre Methuen Ltd. and in 1984 by Methuen
London Ltd.
Copyright © 1971 by Simon Gray
Otherwise Engaged first published in 1975 and reprinted in 1977 and 1978 by Eyre
Methuen Ltd.
Reprinted in 1984 by Methuen London Ltd.
Copyright © 1975 by Simon Gray
The Rear Column first published in 1978 by Eyre Methuen Ltd.
Copyright © 1978 by Simon Gray
Quartermaine's Terms first published in 1981 by Eyre Methuen Ltd.
Revised edition published in 1983 by Methuen London Ltd.
Copyright © 1981, 1983 by Simon Gray
The Common Pursuit first published in 1984 by Methuen London Ltd.
First published in this revised edition in this collection 1986.
Copyright © 1984, 1986 by Simon Gray
This collection and introduction © 1986 by Simon Gray

British Library Cataloguing in Publication Data

Gray, Simon
Plays : one. — (Methuen's world dramatists)
I. Title
822'.914   PR6057.R33

ISBN 0-413-40420-X

Contents

Simon Gray

A Chronology of Performed Plays

PLAY	FIRST PERFORMED	
The Caramel Crisis	1966	tv
Wise Child	1967	
Death of a Teddy Bear	1967	tv
Sleeping Dog	1968	
Pig in a Poke	1969	tv
Dutch Uncle	1969	
The Idiot (from Dostoievsky)	1970	
Spoiled	1971	
Butley	1971	
Man in a Side Car	1971	tv
Otherwise Engaged	1975	
Two Sundays	1975	tv
Plaintiffs and Defendants	1975	tv
Dog Days	1976	
Molly	1977	
The Rear Column	1978	
Close of Play	1979	
Stage Struck	1979	
The Rear Column (from the stage play)	1980	tv
Quartermaine's Terms	1981	
Tartuffe (from Molière)	1982	
Chapter 17	1982	
The Common Pursuit	1984	

Introduction

Some years back, in that halcyon age when Bernard Levin was theatre critic of *The Sunday Times*, I was invited to write a programme note for a play of mine, *Dog Days*, that was being given its first production at the Oxford Playhouse. I was glad to do so. The play had an eccentric history, having been finished about a month before *Otherwise Engaged*, to which it was distinctly a sibling, coming out of the same impulses, with similar situations here and there, and similar relationships if not similar characters. It had taken me years, on and off, to write, and for various personal reasons I couldn't quite fathom, I'd never felt at ease with it. I'd refused to allow any production until the Oxford Playhouse one, and now – halfway through rehearsals with everything going ostensibly quite well – I was again full of doubts. The programme note seemed an admirable opportunity, therefore, to make my apologies to the audience. It's a worried, not to say fretful piece of writing, expressing not only a clear lack of confidence in the play, but in myself as a writer, and possibly even as a human being. In fact, the director was so disturbed by it that he suggested we dispense with it. After all, he pointed out, why should we expect an audience to want to sit through a play that the author himself publicly insisted wasn't up to much? He was right, of course, but I stuck to my guns, even though I'd aimed them directly at myself. The programme note duly appeared. Among those to read it on the first night was Bernard Levin, who duly (the following Sunday) pulled the trigger. Now I could argue – and did at the time – that Levin had either misread the piece or deliberately chosen to misrepresent it (he described my little bout of grovelling as evidence that I thought myself as great a playwright as Shakespeare). I still had to admit that there was an important lesson to be drawn from the experience. Don't, if you can avoid it, write anything about your own work. So it's only on the over-riding principle that nothing one has learnt from experience applies to the present case, however similar it may be to all past cases, that I've undertaken to write the introduction to this collection of five of my plays. What follows is, in fact, five programme notes.

Butley, the first play in this collection, was the fifth of my plays to be produced. Of the previous four, the first, *Wise Child* is best remembered, when remembered at all, as the piece that brought Alec Guiness back to the theatre disguised so heavily as a woman that in the second interval one evening, I overheard a couple of elderly ladies angrily wondering when he was going to make an appearance, or had they come to the wrong play? Actually they had probably come to the wrong play, if their sensibilities were anything like that of the retired Colonel figure, who led out wife and grown-up children halfway through the first act, with an anguished cry of 'Oh, Sir Alec, I thought you were above this sort of thing'. *Wise Child* got by, in other words, as something of a *succès de scandale*, and I followed it a year later with a flop de scandale at the Aldwych called *Dutch Uncle*, which is best remembered as the play everyone connected with it wanted to forget, even before it was performed in public. Once, in a small Greek restaurant in Watford, it was mentioned glancingly by someone passing himself off as a friend, and I was promptly and publicly sick. After that came *Spoiled*, which was done at the Haymarket by an American producer, got one or two decent reviews but no audiences, and closed in the traditional six weeks. After which came an adaptation of *The Idiot* for the National, which pleased some of the audience but none of the critics, and died young. And then *Butley*, at the Criterion, which received as many bad reviews as good ones, along with quite a few predictions of early closure. But the Monday after one of the Sunday critics gave us only six weeks at the most (and he felt we didn't deserve even that much) there was standing room only, and so it was to remain for month on month until we closed over a year later, still playing to packed houses. I'd like to salute across the years that crafty young playwright who, if he didn't give the world a major work, at least delivered a starring vehicle to the likes of Alan Bates, and so managed to hitch a ride for himself. The set, by the way, was taken, down to details, from my office at Queen Mary College, London, which made the experience of sitting at my own desk in private more disorientating even than seeing Alan Bates do it in public. There was a period when people asked me whether I'd based Butley on myself. I now realize that it was far more likely that, for a time at least, I based myself on Butley – or more precisely, Alan Bates's performance in it.

In the five years after *Butley*, I was working on three stage plays and two television plays, and had completed none of them when I wrote, very quickly, *Otherwise Engaged*. This, as I've already hinted, was probably written as a briskly snubbing answer to the problems I hadn't yet been able to formulate properly in *Dog Days*. While the hero of *Dog Days* is unable to stop talking, the hero of *Otherwise Engaged* only prefers brevity when he can't have complete silence – or rather a silence filled with music. Everything in the play flows from that simple fact, which can be confusing on the page unless the reader remembers that, though not uttering, the hero would be visible – highly visible, I like to think – on the stage. This treacherous relationship between stage presence and page absence can be illustrated by the response of the play's producer who, on first reading it nearly rejected it on the grounds that there was no main part. What lines the hero had I pared down in rehearsal, then to the bone in Oxford. In previews in London I chipped away at the bone, until we were left with what I fondly assumed was the merest, if not the purest, marrow. Again it was suspected in some quarters that (as I'd given the hero my Christian name), I'd based his character on my own. The truth here, however, is that, out of a combination of laziness and a desire to get on with the writing, I stuck down the first name that came into my head, with the intention of changing it when I got to the last draft. The reason I didn't finally change it was that, by the end of the writing, Simon Hench seemed to me to have as much right to his name as I to mine. The play ran for two years at the Queens, with Alan Bates, then Michael Gambon, then Hywel Bennett, in the lead. The first night would have been a completely agreeable experience if the director hadn't been hounded out of town a few days before by a pack of gossip columnists, some of whom I actually found hiding behind the seats at the last dress rehearsal.

The Rear Column was an exhausting ordeal in the writing – on and off it took me eight years to get from my first researches to the final version. It was an exhausting ordeal, too, in the production – the lighting never seemed to work properly, the sound was either too loud or inaudible, there were interminable problems over costumes. It was all made endurable, however, by the patience and devotion of the director and the cast, and then made unendurable all over again by the critics, who got the play off the stage in six weeks (of course). As will be quite evident to any reasonably attentive reader, *The Rear Column* deals with a group of late Victorian officers and gentlemen going to pieces physically, emotionally and finally, morally, when trapped for over a year in the Congo. One of them becomes a sadistic murderer, another a drug addict, a third practises cannibalism, a fourth degenerates into hysterical hypochondria, and the fifth – the ironist and intellectual – retreats into an ineffectually sarcastic self-disgust. Most of the London critics saw it as an out-dated celebration of Victorian virtues – five *Boys' Own* (the reference was used in several newspapers) adventurers heroically holding out against adversity. I find this a more perverse but less interesting reading than that of the American critic who analysed it into a story about five Victorian queens going up the Congo in order to come out of the closet. On the whole, though, the American critics liked the play, and had no trouble working out what it was about. One or two of them actually advanced to the central point, which is not an assertion that the five Victorians had behaved badly, but an implicit question about whether you or I or he could have behaved better. Reports of Vietnam atrocities lay – distinctly, I thought – in the background, and it is perhaps worth mentioning that the play is based on a true event which was the source not only of Conrad's *The Heart of Darkness*, but also of a recent film about Vietnam, *Apocalypse Now*.

On the other hand, the source of *Quartermaine's Terms* was my own history as a teacher in language schools in Cambridge, during my eight or so years there as first undergraduate, and then fraudulent post-graduate. I used some of what I experienced in the last section of a novel I wrote, *Little Portia*, some sixteen years before I sat down to the play. In the novel the setting is contemporary, and therefore was found ridiculous, while the play is set in the past, which therefore has about it some aspects of the sublime. I have to admit to a deep personal attachment to Quartermaine himself, who embodies for me aspects of a world that vanished so poignantly before I'd even finished making fun of it. It took me a long time – as long as usual, anyway – to get through all the irrelevant drafts and into the final one, of which I recall only the moment when I wrote the last lines of dialogue. Perfect, they seemed to me, in their elegaic conclusiveness – I was sure they'd haunt me down my remaining years. At the first read-through, however, they embarrassed me so deeply that I cut them on the spot, and can no longer remember even what they were. The first language school I taught at still had flourishing branches across the country when we went into rehearsal. The director, the designer and I visited one of the London ones when doing research into atmosphere, the set, etc., and I asked the accommodating young principal whether the school's founders ever visited his building – I'd never seen them in Cambridge in my day, I said. He replied that the founders were long retired, probably dead, and that the schools, in which foreigners were taught both our language and our customs, were now owned by a Swiss consortium. This seems to me a reasonable metaphor for the state of the nation.

I can't remember too much about the production – a sign that all went well – but do recall that the rehearsal room was in Kennington, in walking distance of the Oval, and that on several evenings the director and I dropped in to check on the progress of a test match.

The last play in this collection, *The Common Pursuit*, is still unfinished as I write this, although it's already received two handsome productions, the first at the Lyric, Hammersmith, the second at the Long Wharf theatre, in New Haven, over in the States. The next production is, as I write this, in rehearsal at the Matrix theatre, Los Angeles. After the production at the Lyric, the suspicion grew (in me, anyway) that I hadn't got the text quite right, and so I found myself re-writing parts of it for the Long Wharf production. The text there seemed to be distinctly better, but after the production the suspicion grew that it still hadn't quite worked, and so when the Matrix production loomed, I found myself re-writing other parts of it, then abandoned that method (if local patchwork can be called a method), and settled down to re-write the play from beginning to end. I finished the draft a day or so before we began casting, and heard it for the first time when the company gave a read-through. It seemed to me distinctly better, but not quite right – too long and explanatory in the first act, too elliptical (i.e. skimpy) in the crucial scene in the second act – so I spent the two days before proper rehearsals began editing and re-writing. The script the director finally took into rehearsal seemed to me distinctly better, but I can't be sure as I had to fly back to London (for Christmas) without having heard it. I go back to Los Angeles in a few days time, for the last stretch of rehearsals. No doubt I'll find myself making further changes, but these, I've promised myself, will result, if not in a perfect text, then the final one.

As I wrote a whole book – *An Unnatural Pursuit* – about the vagaries of the Lyric, Hammersmith, production, I've so far avoided that aspect in this note to the play. Nevertheless, it might be of mild interest to the reader (it's of intense interest to me) to learn that I've just been telephoned from Los Angeles with the news that the actor playing Nick has left the cast; the actor playing Humphry has left the cast; the actor playing Stuart is to take over the part of Humphry; a new actor has been introduced, to play the part of Nick; and the director himself is playing the part of Stuart. A new director has been found. Under the circumstances, they should all be in exactly the right mood for any revolutionary changes I propose in the text.

SIMON GRAY
London, January 1986

P.S. As it turned out I did a great deal of work on the text during one of the most fraught rehearsal periods I have ever experienced, with further changes of cast and one or two incidents in the Green Room of the kind usually described as 'serious' when they take place on the football pitch. Nevertheless, or perhaps I should say therefore, the production when it finally emerged went well and will be shown with some alterations – but not too many, I trust, to the text – in New York in the autumn of this year. I don't propose, however, to send in any bulletins from that experience.

Acknowledgements
In *Butley*, the lines from T.S. Elliot's *Collected Poems* 1909–1962 quoted on pages 29–30 and 72–73 are reprinted by kind permission of Messrs Faber and Faber Ltd. The lines by Beatrix Potter, from *Cecily Parsley's Nursery Rhymes* and *Appley Dappley's Nursery Rhymes*, quoted on pages 6, 7, 12, 41 and 73 are reprinted by kind permission of Messrs Frederick Warne & Co., Ltd.

Butley

To the staff and students, past, present and future, of the English Department, Queen Mary College, London

BUTLEY was first presented on 14th July 1971, at the Criterion Theatre by Michael Codron with the following cast:

BEN BUTLEY	Alan Bates
JOSEPH KEYSTON	Richard O'Callaghan
MISS HEASMAN	Brenda Cavendish
EDNA SHAFT	Mary Wimbush
ANNE BUTLEY	Colette O'Neil
REG NUTTALL	Michael Byrne
MR GARDNER	George Fenton

Directed by Harold Pinter

Act One

*An office in a College of London University. About 10 in the morning.
The office is badly decorated (white walls, greying, plaster boards)
with strip lighting. There are two desks opposite each other, each
with a swivel chair.* BEN's *desk, left, is a chaos of papers, books,
detritus.* JOEY's *desk, right, is almost bare. Behind each desk is a
bookcase. Again,* BEN's *is chaotic with old essays and mimeographed
sheets scattered among the books, while* JOEY's *is neat, not many
books on the shelves. On each desk there is a table lamp and in front of
each desk a hard chair. There is one telephone, on* BEN's *desk, the
flex of which is long enough to reach* JOEY's *desk. There are a few
hard-backed chairs around the walls, and one armchair, in* BEN's
*corner of the room. On the wall is a blown-up picture (photograph)
of T. S. Eliot, with a smear across it and one of its corners curled.
The panels to the office door are frosted glass, behind which people,
when they approach, are dimly seen.*

BEN *is a heavy smoker, and should smoke more frequently than the
text indicates.* JOEY *does not smoke.*

As the curtain rises, BEN *enters, in a plastic raincoat, which he takes
off and throws into his chair. He has a lump of cotton wool on his
chin, from a particularly nasty shaving-cut. He goes to his chair, sits
down, looks around as if searching for something, shifts uncomfortably,
pulls the plastic mac out from under him, searches through its pockets,
takes out half a banana, a bit squashed, then throws the raincoat
over to* JOEY's *desk. He takes a bite from the banana, removes it from
the peel and drops the last piece onto his desk. Then he throws the
peel onto* JOEY's *desk. He slumps into his chair – a long pause – the
telephone rings.*

BEN. Butley, English. Hello, James, have a nice break? (*A pause –
he mouths a curse.*) Sorry, James, I can't talk now – I'm right in the
middle of a tutorial – 'bye.

Then he touches the cottonwool and tries to pull it off. He lets out an exclamation. Touches his chin, looks at his finger.

(*In an undertone*). Bugger!

He gets up, looks under his desk, drags out a bulging briefcase from which he pulls an opened bag of cotton wool. He delves into his briefcase again and takes out a tin of Nescafé. He shines the base on his sleeve, then holds it to his chin as if it were a mirror. He tries to put the cotton wool on, then switches on the light. It doesn't come on. He sticks the cotton wool on. He shoves the Nescafé tin back into his briefcase and stuffs the cotton wool into his jacket pocket. He goes across to the main switch and flicks it on. The strip lighting flickers into brilliance. He checks the cotton wool using the glass door of his bookcase as a mirror, then, unable to bear the striplight, flicks it off again. He goes across to JOEY's *desk and tries the lamp. It comes on. He wipes stray wisps of cotton wool from his fingers with the banana skin, then drops it into the clean ashtray on* JOEY's *desk. He switches off* JOEY's *lamp and carries it across to his desk. There is a shape at the door, then a knock.*

Bugger! Just a minute!

He carries his lamp across to JOEY's. *The door opens cautiously.*

A minute I said. (*He goes to the door and checks it with his hand.*) Hello.
STUDENT (*off*). Hello.
BEN (*after a pause*). Can I help you?
STUDENT (*off*). Well, it's my tutorial. On Wordsworth. 'The Prelude'.
BEN. Oh. No, I can't give tutorials during the first week after the break I'm afraid. Too much administration.
STUDENT (*off*). Oh? When should I come then?
BEN. Come at the same hour of the same day of next week.
STUDENT (*off*). Next week?

BEN. Next week. If we keep to our time-table we'll know where we are, won't we? All right? (*He closes the door.*)

He goes back to his desk, sits down and takes out of his pocket a copy of 'Cecily Parsley'.

'The Prelude'.

He shudders, then turns a page, reaches for the light, clicks it. Nothing happens. He gets up and goes over to JOEY's *desk, tries the light, it comes on. He sighs. He sits down in* JOEY's *chair, opens one of his drawers, props his feet in it, and settles down to read.*
JOEY *comes in with a briefcase. He puts it down on his desk, clears the banana peel into the waste-paper basket, picks* BEN's *raincoat up, carries it over to the peg, puts the desk lamps back on their respective desks. He turns on his table light – it comes on.*

Good morning.
JOEY. Good morning.
BEN. Nice to see you.
JOEY. Nice to be seen. What's the matter with your chin?
BEN. I'm trying to cultivate cotton wool on it. Your own is shining pleasantly, what did you have to work with, a razor?
JOEY. What did *you* use?
BEN. Anne left one behind. Behind the fridge, to be exact. So either mice have taken up shaving, or that stubble was sheared from her calves. I thought of mounting a tuft in a locket. You needn't have taken the only one we have.
JOEY. It also happens to be the only one I have.
BEN. Couldn't you have shared Ted's? It's no pleasure slicing open my chin with my estranged wife's razor blade. The symbolism may be deft, but the memory still smarts.
JOEY. I didn't mean to take it, in point of fact. I put it in the bag without thinking.

BEN. Lust is no excuse for thoughtlessness. And where is your bag? (*He stands up and peers round for it.*)

JOEY. What? Oh, I left it with Reg.

BEN. Reg? Who's Reg? (*He perches on the front of his own desk with his feet up on a chair and lights a cigarette.* JOEY *hastily occupies the vacated desk chair.*)

JOEY. Reg is his name.

BEN. Whose name?

JOEY. Ted's.

BEN. Reg is Ted's name?

JOEY. The one you call Ted is the one I call Reg. He calls himself Reg too.

BEN. How sweet.

JOEY. In fact, everybody calls him Reg except you. You call him Ted.

BEN. Why do I do that, I wonder.

JOEY. To embarrass me.

BEN. Oh yes, that must be it. (*Pause.*) Did you have a good week-end?

JOEY. It was all right. (*Pause.*) Have you seen James this morning?

BEN. Ah! Our Professor! He's just been hounding me on the telephone. He and Hazel spent most of the break in bed recovering from one of Hazel's gastric goulashes.

JOEY. Did he say anything? I mean, are there any details yet?

BEN. You want details of James' diarrhoea?

JOEY. You know what I mean. About my board.

BEN. Ah. About your board. Now when is that, exactly?

JOEY. A fortnight tomorrow.

BEN. Indeed? A fortnight tomorrow? Mmmm. Where the hell is it? (*He begins to search in his desk drawers –* JOEY *comes over to him.*)

JOEY. What?

BEN. It's no real advance. (*Sits.*) But it's got some interesting things in it. Damn! Anyway –

'How do you do, Mistress Pussy?

Mistress Pussy, how do you do?'
'I thank you kindly little dog,
I fare as well as you!'

JOEY. Did he say anything?

BEN. You're genuinely interested in this promotion of yours,
aren't you? Why? (*Little pause.*) No, he didn't say anything.
Your name didn't come up, and there's no reason that it should
until, in the normal course of events and strictly according to
the rules, the board is rigged, the strings are pulled, and it's
passed over for that of someone more closely related to the
Principal, or with more distinguished qualifications. I should
warn you that there are almost as many of the latter as of the
former.

Cecily Parsley lived in a pen,
And brewed good ale for gentlemen;
Gentlemen came every day.

(*Joey goes to his shelves and takes down a book.*)

Till Cecily Parsley ran away.
Why? (BEN *crosses to* JOEY.) Why has he got your bag?

JOEY. He happened to pick it up for me when we got off the train.

BEN. Not many young men are as gallant these days. You haven't
been home yet then?

JOEY. To the flat. No? (*He sits at his desk.*)

BEN. Ah. Why not?

JOEY. Because I didn't have time, obviously. (*He begins to correct
a set of essays from his briefcase.*)

BEN. I waited for you.

JOEY. Did you? Sorry.

BEN (*watches him*). You had a nice little mid-term break then, did
you?

JOEY. It was all right.

BEN. Well, are you going to tell me about it, or shall I probe and
pry?

JOEY. I'd rather let it slip out naturally, if I may?

BEN. But you're much more charming under interrogation. My natural force plays excitingly with your natural submissiveness. Or has your holiday changed you, as we say in the trade, radically? (*He opens* JOEY's *briefcase.*) Ah-hah! I thought so! (*As* JOEY *looks up.*) Blake! Why is your briefcase bulging with Blake? (*He opens one of the books and takes out a piece of paper.*) What's this?

JOEY. I happen to be lecturing on him this half. (*He tries to take the book and notes from him.*) Kindly don't mess my notes up. Can I have it back, please?

BEN. Notes to whom? Reg?
> What immortal hand or eye
> Could frame thy fearful symmetry?

Ted is certainly quite symmetrical – in a burly sort of way.
> Did he who made the lamb make thee?

Laughs.

JOEY. All right, all right, let's *be* infantile. (*He goes across to* BEN's *desk and picks up his briefcase.*)

BEN (*drops* JOEY's *book and notes, lunges across and grabs his own briefcase*). No, bags first go. I haven't unpacked it for weeks.

He opens it, as JOEY *returns to his marking. He pulls out an empty scotch bottle, then a red-covered manuscript.*

It's laid out like a film script. It must be an American M.A. thesis – Ah – 'Henry James and the Crucified Consciousness' – aaah.

BEN *wanders over to* JOEY's *desk, pulls out a blue sock, puts the thesis down on* JOEY's *desk, along with a few more papers, files, crumpled newspaper, the Nescafé tin and the briefcase itself.*

Now where's the other – there must be a pair –

JOEY (*picks up the thesis*). You mean you forgot to give his thesis back?

BEN. Not yet. So far I've forgotten to read it. Forgetting to give it back will come later. Failing Americans is a slow and intricate ritual and that's what they come here for – the ritual – aaah, here it is.

> BEN *takes out another sock. It is red. He picks up the blue. Looks at them.*

JOEY. Those are mine. Naturally.

BEN. Naturally you're very welcome. (*He tosses the socks at* JOEY.) Personally I wouldn't be caught dead wearing a pair like that. (*He lifts up his trousers, studies his socks.*)

JOEY. Those happen to be mine, too.

BEN. You really must give up buying cheap socks. I can feel a hole growing around the toe.

JOEY (*savagely*). Perhaps if you bothered to cut your toe-nails – (*He picks up the thesis and essays* BEN *has dropped.*)

BEN. Are we going to have a tantrum?

JOEY. The thing is to stop your rubbish creeping across to my side of the room.

> *He makes as if to stack them neatly, then crams them savagely into* BEN'*s shelves.*

Here, anyway. (*He goes back to his desk and continues marking.*)

BEN. *Are* we? I'd quite enjoy one.

JOEY. Would you?

BEN. Then I'll know you're back, you see. You've been a little thin on presence so far.

JOEY. There's not enough room.

> BEN *sits down cross legged on the top of* JOEY'*s desk and watches* JOEY. *He clears his throat delicately. He smiles genteely.*

BEN (*genteel*). I was just wondering if I might enquire as to how your friend is, may I?

> JOEY *smiles.*

Hoh, h'I'm so glad.

JOEY *continues transcribing marks.*

May h'I hask, done all those, 'ave we?

He takes the essay JOEY *is holding.*

Ho, but you 'adn't done them last week 'ad you? Did you do them on the train, going h'up with your friend?

Shape at the door, BEN *doesn't notice.*

H'I h'always say that h'if h'a job's worth doing h'it's worth h'ignoring.

Knock on the door. BEN *turns, starts to move rapidly to it. When it opens,* MISS HEASMAN, *a pretty, competent-looking girl steps in.*

MISS HEASMAN. Oh, sorry, I was just wondering when my tutorials are.
BEN. Same as last term, except of course for this week.
MISS HEASMAN. You didn't take me last term. My name is Heasman, Carol Heasman. I'm replacing Mrs Grainger.
BEN. Mrs Grainger?
MISS HEASMAN. Yes. She said she didn't get to see you often, owing to administrative tangles.
BEN. Mrs Grainger got into administrative tangles?
MISS HEASMAN. No, you were busy with them.
BEN. If only they'd let us get on with it and teach. (*Laughs.*) Anyway, you'd better come at the same hours as Mrs Grainger, all right?
MISS HEASMAN. I expect so. What were they?
BEN. Could you find out from Mrs Grainger, please?
MISS HEASMAN. I'll try.
BEN. Thank you. (*He holds the door wider.* MISS HEASMAN *goes out.* BEN *returns to his desk.*) I didn't care for that one at all, there was an air of mad devotion about her that reminds me of my wife's mother, the mad monk. (*Looking at* JOEY, *who is still*

transcribing marks. JOEY *tries to go on working. In a normal tone after a pause.*) You're in trouble, Joey.

JOEY. What? (*He looks up.*)

BEN. I'm sorry. I've been wondering how to tell you. But as you've still got a fortnight before the board. (*Sits. Pause.*) A member of the department has his knife out.

JOEY. Who?

BEN. That pre-break meeting we had – the one you had to leave early – to meet Reg?

JOEY. Yes. Well?

BEN. The contemporary books list?

JOEY. Yes. Well, go on.

BEN. On the face of it, you were very adroit. You didn't actually support me, but you indicated a certain, attitude shall we say? By coughing into my speeches with dialectical authority. You wouldn't have thought that so genteel a rhetorical device could give offence. On the face of it. Eh?

JOEY. But who – who did I offend?

BEN (*gets up and perches on the front of his desk again*). First of all who proposed that a contemporary novels list – Burroughs, Genet, Roth, etc. – be added to our syllabus?

JOEY. You did.

BEN. And who opposed it?

JOEY. Everybody else. Except – me.

BEN. Who won?

JOEY. We – you did. They gave way in the end – didn't they?

BEN (*sinisterly*). Oh yes, it was passed unanimously – but I happen to know that one person – one powerful person there – resented *our* victory and blamed you – yes, you – for it.

JOEY. But this is ridiculous! It's absolutely – I scarcely said anything anyway.

BEN. Exactly. But this person was hoping – was *relying* – on you to oppose that book list with every cell in your body.

JOEY. Ben, please – eh?

BEN. Think, child, think! Who had most to lose by that list being passed? Who is *most* affected?

JOEY. Nobody. Nobody at all. You're the one who's going to teach it, they'll be *your* lectures, *your* seminars, *your* tutorials . . .

BEN (*after a long pause, as* JOEY *realizing, looks at him*). Exactly. Precisely. Absolutely. Fool! Imbecile! Traitor! Lackey! – I wouldn't be caught dead reading those books. And you know how it exhausts me to teach books I haven't read. Why didn't you oppose me?

JOEY. It's your own fault. Your instructions were quite clear.

BEN. Haven't you heard of a sub-text? It's very fashionable now, In fact, I remember advising you to use the word twice in every paper when I was guiding you through your finals. (*He goes to examine him.*) But what's the matter, dear? You're looking a little peaky around the gills, wherever they are? Were you frightened, a trifle? You needn't be – you played the toad to perfection. (*He returns to his desk.*)

JOEY. Is there a sub-text to that? Or can I take it as straight abuse?

BEN. It's straight abuse. Can you take it?

JOEY (*trembling slightly*). No, not any longer. (*He gets up, and begins to pack his briefcase.*)

BEN. Where are you going?

JOEY. To the library.

BEN. Why?

JOEY. I've got a lecture at twelve.

BEN. But you're not running away from me so soon?

JOEY. And there are a few things on my Herrick I've got to dig up. (*He goes to the door –* BEN *cuts him off.*)

BEN. Dig up! (*Laughs.*)

Diggory, diggory Delvet
Little old man in black velvet
He digs and he delves
You can see for yourselves
The holes dug by Diggory Delvet.

It is velvet, isn't it, this jacket? (*Fingering it.*)

JOEY *tugs his sleeve away.*

No, don't flounce.

They stand staring at each other.

You were due back last night, remember?
JOEY. Did it make any difference?
BEN. In that I spent the evening expecting you.
JOEY. In point of fact, I said I'd be back either last night or this morning.
BEN. Also you didn't phone.
JOEY. I was only in Leeds for four days. Of course I didn't phone.
BEN. Why not? Language difficulties? I reserved a table at Bianchi's. I was going to take us out.
JOEY *(after a pause).* I'm sorry.

BEN *shrugs. They each return to their desks.*

It just didn't occur to me –
BEN. It doesn't matter.
JOEY. I'm sure I said –
BEN. Yes, yes, I expect you did. I assumed you were coming back, that's all. And as I spent four days on the phone to people who weren't there – bugger! *(He sits down at his desk.)* I'm sorry. All right? And if that doesn't satisfy you, Edna thinks well of you, and James is more than happy.
JOEY. How do you know?
BEN. These things slip out. Under my persistent questionings.
JOEY. Edna's actually very important, isn't she? *(He goes across to* BEN *and sits on the hard chair in front of* BEN's *desk.)*
BEN. It depends rather on the context.
JOEY. I mean in terms of influence –
BEN. You mean in terms of promotion?
JOEY. Well – *(Grins.)*

BEN. She'll certainly sit on your board, yes. Don't worry. You'll get your lectureship. Then you'll be safe for ever.

JOEY. I like Edna, in point of fact. No, really. We came in on the tube together this morning. She was telling me about her Byron –

BEN. Can we actually – do you mind? – not discuss either Edna or Byron but most of all Edna on Byron, for purely private reasons just at the moment. The thought of them weighs on my spirit. (*Pause*.) Tell me, while you were amusing yourselves in Leeds, I saw a film on television about a publisher who hates himself. I've been meaning to ask you – does Ted hate himself?

JOEY. He quite likes himself, actually.

BEN. I don't blame him. He seemed an amiable sort of chap the one time I met him, even though his mouth was full of symbolic sausage and his fist around a tankard of something foaming symbolically. I had the impression that most people would like him. And as he seemed exactly like most people, only from the North, ergo, he'd be favourably disposed towards himself only more so, or not? (*Smiles*.)

JOEY *also smiles*.

Tell me, does he ever discuss his work with you? Or does he leave it behind him at the office? When you go around for one of those little dinners, does he put his feet up, perhaps, while you slave away over a hot stove, or does he do the cooking? No, I don't mean to probe – or am I prying? For instance, in our Professor's ménage Hazel rips the meat apart with saw-edged knives while James brews up sauces from *Guardian* headlines. In my ménage, when I had one – remember? – Anne under-grilled the chops and over-boiled the peas while I drank the wine and charted my dropping sugar count. Now that you and I are sharing my life again I open the tins and you stir the Nescafé again, just as we always used to do, those evenings, at least, when you're not cooking for Reg or Reg isn't cooking for you –

which, arriving where we began, does it happen to be? and if it's the former, why, now I think of it, have you never cooked for me, do you think?

JOEY. He does the cooking, in point of fact.

BEN. Christ I feel awful. (*Pause.*) Do you know, all the time you were away, I didn't have one telephone call. I consider that very frightening. Not even from Tom.

JOEY. Oh. (*Pause.*) I thought you found his company intolerable.

BEN. But one likes, as they say, to be asked. Also one likes people to be consistent, otherwise one will start coming adrift. At least this one will. (*Stands up.*) Also how does one know whether Tom is still the most boring man in London unless he phones in regularly to confirm it. This is the fourth week running he's kept me in suspense. He and Reg have a lot in common, haven't they? (*Pause. He sits on the desk.*)

JOEY (*drily*). Really?

BEN. Didn't Ted do his National Service with the Gurkhas?

JOEY. I really can't remember. I've never been very interested in Ted's – Reg's – military career, which was anyway about a decade ago. (*He goes back to his own desk.* BEN *follows him.*)

BEN. Oh, but the experience lives on for us through our born raconteurs – and Ted is something of a raconteur, isn't he? That magnificent anecdote of his – surely you remember?

JOEY. No. (*He picks up his briefcase and moves towards the door.*) I really must get to the library –

BEN. No, wait. (*Blocks his way.*) You repeated it to me. About the Gurkha and the bowl of soup. (*He holds up two fists.*) I don't know if I can do your imitation of his accent – woon day Chef was in ta kitchen – is that close? – stirring ta soup wi' his elbows – wan in coom a little tyke –

JOEY. I remember.

BEN. I was sure you would. Your imitation of Reg made me laugh so much that I was prepared to overlook its cruelty. Anyway my point was simply that Tom's a great National Service bore, too. There's that six volume novel he's writing about it – that's something else. Yes. He's stopped showing me his drafts. (*He goes back to his desk.*)

JOEY. The last time he brought one around you dropped it in the bath.

BEN. It! He brought around seventeen exercise books, of which I dropped a mere three into the bath. No, I don't like his silence. It's sinister.

JOEY. Well, you could always phone him up. (*He starts for the door again.*)

BEN. I haven't finished. (*He comes over, takes* JOEY's *briefcase from him and sits in* JOEY's *desk chair.*)

JOEY. I must do something on this bloody lecture.

BEN. Why? You're looking furtive. Why are you looking furtive?

JOEY. I'm not looking at all furtive.

BEN. Have you seen Tom recently?

JOEY. No. No I haven't.

BEN. When did you last hear from him?

JOEY (*shrugs*). Perhaps he's busy.

BEN. Of course he's busy. He's too dull to be anything else, the question is, why has he stopped being busy with me? (*He returns to his own desk and sits on the hard chair.*) Do you think he's dropped me. His attentions have been slackening since my marriage broke up, now I come to think of it.

JOEY (*carefully*). He's very fond of Anne, isn't he?

BEN (*laughs*). That's an idea. I must find out whether he's been hounding *her*.

JOEY. But Anne – (*Stops.*) She likes him, doesn't she? I mean, I always thought – had the impression that she was fond of him?

BEN. Oh, I expect she became addicted. She took up all my vices except drinking, smoking and you. She never cared for you. Did you know that?

JOEY. I had my suspicions. Thank you for confirming them.

BEN. She said that Tom became a school teacher because he had to prove, after three years of being taught by me at Cambridge, that education was still a serious affair. Whereas you wanted to get back to your old college here and with me because you were incapable of outgrowing your early influences. Nursery dependence. This analysis was based crudely on the fact that you are homosexual. She also said you were sly and pushing, and that she didn't trust you an inch.

JOEY. You never told me this before.
BEN. You never asked me before.
JOEY. I didn't ask you now, either.
BEN. I know. But I got tired of waiting. (*Pause*.) Do *you* like *her*?
JOEY. I thought we were friends.
BEN. I'm sure you still are. (*He sits in the armchair*, JOEY's *briefcase tucked under his arm*.) She just can't stand you, that's all. Something about you gives her the creeps, was her word. Creeps. (*Laughs*.) What's the matter? Are you upset?

JOEY *shakes his head*.

You shouldn't be. It was just her way of getting at me. Don't you see how I emerge? As someone whose protégé is a creep? But *I* didn't take offence. I don't see why you should. (*Pause*. JOEY *tries to take his case* – BEN *clutches it to him*.) Tell me, what does he do, Reg's dad?

JOEY *looks at him*.

(*Smiles*.) But we're not ashamed, are we?
JOEY (*pause*.) He owns a shop.
BEN. What sort of shop?
JOEY. Just a shop. (*He walks away from him*.)
BEN. Just a shop? Just a shop like Harrods, for example. What does he sell?
JOEY (*after a pause*). Meat, I think.
BEN. You think. Did you ever see the shop?
JOEY. Of course. Why?
BEN. Was there meat on display?
JOEY. Yes.
BEN. In that case he either owns a meat museum or if it was for

sale you're quite right, he owns a shop that sells meat. He's what's called a butcher.

JOEY (*sits on the hard chair in front of* BEN's *desk*). That's right, he's a butcher.

BEN. Mmm huh. And do they live over their shop?

JOEY (*hesitates*). No. They live in um, in a place just outside Leeds, in point of fact.

BEN. In Point of Fact? And what sort of place is it, a Georgian terraced house, a Chippendale-style flat, a dug-out, a rural cottage; a bungalow!

JOEY. Yes. A bungalow.

BEN. A bungalow, eh? Now let's see, starting with the garden, do they have, say, plaster gnomes in the garden?

JOEY. And also much to your satisfaction, say, an electric fire with coals in it, and a sofa decorated with doilies and a revolving bookcase with the collected works of Mazo de la Roche –

BEN. In the garden? How witty!

JOEY. And their front door-bell plays a tune, can you believe that? (*Pause.*) They happen to be very nice people, nevertheless.

BEN. Nevertheless what?

JOEY (*emphatically*). Nevertheless they happen to be very nice people.

BEN (*sits on the edge of his desk, leaving* JOEY's *briefcase in the armchair*). What tune? (*Pause.*) Does Reg's mother work in the shop too?

JOEY. No.

BEN. Oh. Where is she then, in the day-time?

JOEY. Out.

BEN. Out where?

JOEY. Just out.

BEN. She has a job then?

JOEY. Yes.

BEN. And where does she do this job? On the streets?

JOEY. You could put it like that, yes.

BEN. What does she do? Sweep them?

JOEY. No.

BEN. She walks them?

JOEY. Yes, in point of fact.

BEN. The precise suburb is irrelevant. (*Pause.*) So Reg's mother is a prostitute.

JOEY *giggles, checks himself.*

JOEY. No, she's a – traffic warden.

BEN. She isn't! But what on earth did you do?

JOEY. Nothing in particular.

BEN. You went to a football match?

JOEY. Football match?

BEN. Hasn't it caught on there? Here in the South we place it slightly below music and well above theatre, in the cultural scale. Did you?

JOEY. What?

BEN. Go to any football matches?

JOEY. Well done. Yes we did. We went to a football match – and furthermore we wore rosettes, coloured scarves and special hats and carried rattles.

BEN. You didn't! (*Laughs.*) Rattles and rosettes? You didn't! You poor old sod. Why in Christ did you stay? (*Pause.*) All right then, why did he take you there? Is it like bringing one's latest girl back to the folks –?

JOEY. His friends back. He doesn't like people to know he's queer. A lot of the time he doesn't like me to know. But I suppose he probably took me there as a kind of compliment – and perhaps as a test.

BEN. To see if you could take him *au naturel*?

JOEY. That sounds reasonable, yes.

BEN. And could you?

JOEY. He's much more natural as a London publisher who knows all about food, and cooks marvellously. Much more natural and much more convincing.

BEN. But tell me – the butcher and the traffic warden – do they *know* –

JOEY. Know what?

A shape appears at the door. BEN *charges out as* MISS HEASMAN *knocks.*

BEN. Oops! Sorry!

MISS HEASMAN. Sorry!

BEN (*off*). Just dashing up to the Registrar's – some administrative tangle. Mrs Grainger isn't it?

MISS HEASMAN (*off*). Miss Heasman! I can't find Mrs Grainger but I'm very anxious for a session on *A Winter's Tale.*

BEN. Good God! Are you really? Well keep trying and perhaps by next week . . . I go up here. Goodbye.

BEN *dodges back and surprises* JOEY *as he tries to leave.*

. . . that you and Reg have it off together?

JOEY. Of course not. (*Shuts the door.*) And now I think I'd like to stop talking about it if you don't mind. I'm beginning to feel queasy.

BEN. Recollections of tripe and stout?

Guilt Lord, I pray
Answer thy servant's question!
Is it guilt I feel
Or is it indigestion?

Don't worry, *rognons au vin* at Bianchi's will calm the unsettled soul. (*He sits on his desk – lights a cigarette.*)

JOEY. Tonight you mean? For dinner?

BEN. I hardly fancy them for tea.

JOEY. Um, the thing is, I'm um going around to Reg's tonight. (*Pause.*) I – I didn't – I'm sorry, it just seemed impossible not to go, under the circumstances.

BEN. Mmm huh. (*Little pause.*) I'm willing to treat Reg if necessary.

JOEY. Well, you see Reg has already got our dinner.

BEN. Oh? And what's he got for your dinner?

JOEY (*laughs*). Well, kidneys, as a matter of fact. His father gave him some special – English kidneys. As a treat. Lamb's kidneys.

BEN. Mmm huh. (*Little pause.*)

JOEY. Sorry.

BEN. There's no problem. I'll get some more and Ted can cook them for me. (JOEY *goes back to his desk. Pause.*) What's the matter?

JOEY. I'd rather you didn't.

BEN. Mmm huh. May one ask why?

JOEY. It might be awkward.

BEN. Oh? May one wonder why?

JOEY. Perhaps he doesn't like you very much.

BEN. You surprise me. I thought he'd taken rather a fancy, on our one meeting.

JOEY (*sits*). On your one meeting you pretended you thought he was an Australian and addressed him as 'Cobber'. You also pretended you thought he was an interior decorator, in order to remind him of Ted, whom he knew to be his predecessor. You were also sick over his shoes. It was a terrible evening. He hated you.

BEN. You never told me this before.

JOEY. You never asked me before.

BEN. *That* was creepy. (*Pause.*) Anyway you exaggerate. The confusion over his national identity and profession lasted a mere twenty minutes at the beginning of the evening. It took me some twenty seconds to be sick over his shoes at the evening's end. The intervening hour was an unqualified success, in spite of the odd misunderstanding that developed into the occasional quarrel. Also you know very well that I'd taken up drinking again because I was still brooding over Anne's departure. I had what is called a drinking problem. I no longer have it.

JOEY. Let's face it Ben, you drink every night. Very heavily.

BEN. Exactly. There's no problem. I'm used to it again. (*Pause.*) Well, Joey?

JOEY *shrugs awkwardly.*

I might also be glad of a chance to make it up. I enjoy being on terms with your chaps. (*Pause.*) Also I don't fancy a fifth night of eating alone. (*Pause.*) Well?

JOEY. He won't want you to come.

BEN. Have you asked him?

JOEY. No.

BEN. Then why don't you? Come on. Let's find out. (*He picks up the telephone, and hands it to him.*) Well?

JOEY. He's not there.

BEN. How do you know, unless you try?

JOEY. He said he wouldn't be there until after lunch.

BEN *stares at him.*

He told me he had some things to do.

There is a shape at the door, not noticed by BEN *and* JOEY, *followed by a knock, and simultaneously* EDNA *comes in. She is in her late forties and carries a small pile of folders.*

EDNA. Hello, Ben. Joey.

BEN. Hello, Edna.

JOEY. Hello.

EDNA. Am I barging in on something?

JOEY. No, not at all, in fact I was just on my way to the library. (*He picks up his briefcase and stands up.*)

EDNA. Oh, it's no good going there. It's closed while they install a new security device. It won't be opened until this evening.

JOEY. Oh. (*He sits down again.* BEN *goes back to his desk.*)

EDNA. Isn't that a comment on our times? Do you know I found a couple of students in the canteen. They actually pretended to have heard from some source or another that there were no tutorials during the first week of the half. What do you think of that?

BEN (*sits at his desk*). *Folie de grandeur*. They must learn to leave such decisions to us.

EDNA. Exactly. I wonder what they'd have to say if we started putting them off for any nonsensical reason that came into our heads.

BEN. Yes, I often wonder that. There's so much about them one never finds out. I mean they come, they go away –

EDNA (*sits opposite* BEN). Do you know anything about my particular black sheep, by the way? His name's Gardner.

BEN. Gardner? Gardner, Gardner.

JOEY. Yes, he comes to the odd lecture, aloof in feathers.

BEN. Feathers?

JOEY. He wears a kind of hat with feathers in it.

EDNA. Yes, that dreadful hat. I wish there was some action we could take about that, too. You don't remember him, Ben?

BEN. I certainly can't place the hat.

JOEY. Isn't Gardner the one you had a conversation with just before the break? In a pub? You mentioned –

BEN. A feathered youth? In a public house? Certainly not.

EDNA. Actually, the reason I asked whether you remember him, Ben, is that you interviewed him for his place here. I've just looked him up in the files. (*She hands* BEN *Gardner's open file.*)

BEN. Possibly. I only remember the ones we manage to reject, like Father O'Couligan.

EDNA. I must say, Ben, his headmaster's report was very unfavourable.

BEN. I'm not surprised. Father O'Couligan was in his forties. The Headmaster must have had him in the sixth form for a couple of decades at least. And frankly five minutes of O'Couligan was as much as I –

EDNA. No, I was talking about Gardner. I simply can't help wondering what made you take him.

BEN. Well Edna, I suppose I must have decided he wasn't fit for anything else.

EDNA. A university isn't a charity, you know.

There is a silence.

BEN. Do you mean for me, Edna? Or for the students?

EDNA. I'm not in the mood to be flippant about the more loutish of our students today. Not with the committee's report on the Senate House fresh in my mind.

BEN. Sorry, what report?

EDNA. It was in *The Times* this morning.

JOEY. I read it. In *The Guardian*. It was very disturbing.

BEN *looks at him.*

EDNA. Disturbing! They completely destroyed the Velium Aristotle. Completely destroyed it. *That* was their way of protesting about South Africa.

JOEY. I thought it was about Rhodesia. The University maintaining relationships –

EDNA. Well, one excuse is as good as another, of course.

BEN. James said it was the Greek Colonels. But perhaps we're underestimating their capacity for direct logical connections. Perhaps they were protesting about the Velium Aristotle.

EDNA. It wouldn't surprise me. I had one or two last term who were mutinous about *The Faery Queen.*

BEN. You mean the Principal? He really should learn discretion.

EDNA (*after a short pause, releases a burst of ghastly laughter*). No Ben, you mustn't say things like that. (*Laughs again.*) Besides the Velium Aristotle is no laughing matter. But I intend to nip Gardner in the bud before he gets completely out of hand. I'm not having any bomb-throwing hooligan skipping *my* seminars!

BEN. Any bomb-throwing hooligan has permission to skip mine. (*He gets up and moves towards the door.*)

EDNA (*retrieves* GARDNER's *file from* BEN's *desk*). Well there's no point in my haranguing you. I suppose I'd better take it to James.

BEN. To James?

EDNA. Certainly. Gardner is ripe for a Dean's Report. Oh, I meant to say, you and Anne must come around soon, if you could bear an evening in my poky little flat. And Joey, of course.

BEN. Thanks.

JOEY (*enthusiastically*). I'd love to.

EDNA. How's the baby?

BEN. Oh, very well. As far as one can tell. With babies, I mean.

EDNA. Yes, they are indecipherable, aren't they? How old is he now?

BEN. He's (*thinks*) six or seven months about.

EDNA. It's wretched of me, but I've forgotten his name. Though I do remember him as a bonny little thing.

BEN. Miranda.

JOEY. Marina.

BEN. Yes. (*Laughs.*) Marina. He's called Marina.

EDNA. Oh dear, oh Ben, I'm sorry. I always think of babies as 'hims' or 'its'.

BEN. Well, it's probably safer these days. Our ends never know our beginnings.

EDNA. Any teeth yet?

BEN. Just the – uh – (*Wags his finger around his mouth*) – gums you know and a few wisdom . . . or whatever they're . . .

EDNA. That sounds most satisfactory. Are you all right for baby-sitters?

BEN. Baby-sitters. (*Laughs.*) Oh, no problem. Marina's mother is a marvellous baby-sitter. Anne has simply added a contemporary skill to Goethe's ideal woman. (*After a pause.*) I'm afraid we are going through what we professionals know as a sticky patch.

EDNA. Oh dear. Ben, I'm sorry. I don't know what to say. You must both be desperately unhappy. (*Pause.*) I do hope she's not in that flat all by herself.

BEN. Oh, we sorted that out. She told me that if I was half a man

I'd leave. But on discovering that *she* was, she left herself. She's with her mother. Together they make up two pairs. I imagine Marina is the odd man out.

EDNA. I see. Oh dear. (*Pause.*) It's always so sad for the children.

BEN. Yes, we do suffer the most.

EDNA. Where are *you* now, Joey, are you still in that bedsitter?

JOEY (*little pause*). No. (*Another pause.*) I've moved back in with Ben again, in point of fact.

EDNA. Oh, so you're both back where you were then.

BEN. Exactly.

EDNA. By the way, did I mention that the little office next to mine's going begging at last? So if either of you wants a place of your own . . .

BEN. Thanks, Edna, but we're used to roughing it down here.

EDNA. It's up to you, of course . . . Well I must leave you two to get on with it. (*She goes to the door.*) If you should clap eyes on young Gardner, please send him straight up to me on pain of a Dean's report. (*She goes out.*)

There is a silence.

BEN. I enjoyed that. It was so graceful. In a little office next door to Edna. Christ. What does she want him for? (*He returns to his desk.*) She's got her own coterie – all those boys and girls that look as if they've got the curse permanently. (*Little pause.*) Her obsession with Byron is one of the more triste perversions. But she shouldn't be allowed to practise it with students. She's got her bloody book for therapy.

JOEY. She's finished her book. That's what she was telling me on the tube this morning.

BEN. Well done, Edna. I suppose it means another two decades while she finds a publisher.

JOEY. She's found one.

BEN. She never did understand her role. Which is not to finish an unpublishable book on Byron. Now the centre cannot hold. Mere Edna is loosed upon the world. (*Pause. Sits in the arm-*

chair.) Bloody woman! (*Pause.*) Bugger! (*Pause.*) Bugger!
The Dean's Report!

JOEY. It *was* Gardner you told me about then? The boy who complained about Edna's seminars in a pub.

BEN. Edna holds her seminars in a pub? I shall have to report this.

JOEY. The one you said was interesting.

BEN. I don't find anything interesting about a student who com-
plains of Edna's seminars. You did it yourself years ago, and
you're as dull as they come.

JOEY. Did you encourage him?

BEN. As far as I remember, which is frankly nothing, we had a
perfectly respectable conversation about Edna's vagina, its
length and width.

JOEY. Oh God!

BEN. You mustn't be jealous, Joseph. The young are entitled to
the importunities that you once enjoyed.

JOEY (*gets up and walks towards* BEN). I can't afford to quarrel with
Edna. Besides, I've got to like her.

BEN. Because you've got to, doesn't mean I've got to.

JOEY. She thinks of us as allies. If you upset her, she'll blame me
too.

BEN. What the Hell are you doing here anyway? You're not
lecturing until later. You could have gone straight home and
tidied up your room. It's in a disgusting state.

JOEY. The only room in the flat that isn't in a disgusting state is
mine.

BEN. Really? Then can you explain why it looks as if a large, dignified and intelligent man has been going to seed in it?

JOEY (*after a pause*). Did you have to use my room?

BEN. Do you think I could put up with the mess everywhere else?
You're out most evenings, it's easy for you to keep your room
clean. I don't see why you shouldn't learn what it's like to stay
at home and fret your way into a drunken coma.

JOEY *after a moment, goes back to his desk and sits down.*

Is *that* your tantrum? How piffling.

JOEY. Look, Ben, I've got this lecture. Can I do some work, please? As I can't go to the library – Please?

BEN (*goes to him*). When will you phone Reg up then?

JOEY. I told you. After lunch.

BEN. Why are you lying about his being out? (*He points* JOEY's *desk lamp directly into his face in interrogation.*)

JOEY. I don't make a habit of lying.

BEN. Which is why you go on being so bad at it.

There is a shape at the door. BEN *looks towards it, hurries to his feet, as there is a knock. He goes over to the door, opens it a fraction.*

(*Jovially.*) Good morning, good morning, good morning.

STUDENT (*off*). I just wanted to find out about my tutorials.

BEN. Good. Good. Have you got an essay, please!

STUDENT (*off*). Well no, I mean you haven't set one.

BEN. Well do me one for next week, all right?

STUDENT (*off*). Well, what on?

BEN. You must decide for yourself, can't expect spoon feeding. Righto. (*He shuts the door, comes back rubbing his hands.*) I think that's the lot –

As a shape comes to door, there is a knock. The door opens as BEN *spins around.*

MISS HEASMAN. I found Mrs Grainger, she says she would have come to you on Tuesdays at two if you'd been able to see her.

BEN. So be it. Tuesdays at two with our fingers crossed. (*He crosses them.*)

MISS HEASMAN. Today is Tuesday.

BEN. Ah well, I wouldn't have been able to see her again today, I'm afraid, as she would have needed a week in which to do me an essay.

MISS HEASMAN. Poor Mrs Grainger. But I'm all right as I've

ACT ONE 29

done one. (*She takes one out of her file, and hands it to* BEN, *who takes it reluctantly.*) I haven't put a title on, but I thought 'Hate and Redemption in *A Winter's Tale*'.

BEN. Needs work. (*He hands the essay back.*) That title.

MISS HEASMAN. Don't you want to read it before the tutorial?

BEN. No, you'll have to read it aloud to me. Unless, I tell you what, give it to me now and I'll do my damnedest to get it read before next week.

MISS HEASMAN (*her eyes go to* BEN's *desk*). No, I'll read it aloud. Two o'clock then. (*She turns and goes out.*)

BEN (*imitates her walk and slams the door*). Bugger! (*He comes back to his desk.*) 'Hate and Redemption' – I told you she was mad. She must be a secret agent, in Edna's employ . . . (*He picks up a handful of essays from the desk then drops them one by one on the floor.*) Hate and Redemption, Pity and Terror, Sin and Salvation. (*Dropping more essays onto the floor.*) Faith and Despair in *Pride and Prejudice*, The Mill on the Floss, Appley and Dappley, Cecily Parsley. (*Liturgically, as he is dropping essays. He looks at his desk.*) Why don't those cleaning women do their job properly? Standards are declining everywhere. Ruskin's char threw Carlyle's history of the French Revolution out with the other rubbish. But then they took a pride in their work in those days. (*He picks up another essay, looks at it, laughs and sits down.*) I should think Reg would enjoy cooking my kidneys. It sounds worse than settling my hash. Anne's mother the mad monk settles the hash of bus-conductors, milkmen, postmen, anyone stupid enough to waste their time insulting her. 'Oh, I settled his hash all right.' She probably got the taste for it after she killed off her husband. I wonder if there was any reference in the coroner's report to the state of his hash. This hash, my life . . . this long disease my . . . (*He begins to read, then lets it slip from his fingers, leans back, picks reflectively at the cotton wool.*) Why the hell did we call her Marina?

I made this, I have forgotten
And remember.

The rigging weak and the canvas rotten
Between one June and another September.
Born in June, May . . . April . . . February . . . November . . .
Conceived in September . . . So sometime in early September
there was what you might call a seminal fuck . . . Where? In
the park once we . . . let me think, beneath the trees.
Beneath the trees there is no ease
For the dull brain, the sharp desires
And the quick eyes of Woolly Bear.
It must be have been our last, we were already fallen into the
sere, the yellow leaf, a flash of thigh in the yellow leaf,
What seas what shores what granite islands towards my
timbers
And woodthrush calling through the fog
My daughter.

JOEY. You do miss her then?

BEN (*goes over to* JOEY). You know, what marks you out as a
repressed as well as a practising pervert is your sentimentality
over children. Marina doesn't need a mother or father, she
needs a pair of hands, to pick her up, change her, put things to
her mouth, put her down again.

JOEY. But later on she might need a father.

BEN. You generally have the taste to let *me* raise the subject of my
ruined marriage.

JOEY. I can't help wondering whether you miss it.

BEN. Only the sex and violence. And these days one can get those
anywhere.

JOEY. So there's absolutely no chance . . .

BEN. Chance of what?

JOEY. Of your marriage reviving. You don't want it to?

BEN. Reviving? It's never died. I consider it inviolate. I'm a one
woman man and I've had mine, thank God.

JOEY. But things can't just go on as they are.

BEN. Can't they. Why not? (*He takes the telephone directory from
his desk and begins to look up a number.*)

JOEY. But supposing she wants to marry again.

BEN. Good God! Who would want to marry *her*?

JOEY. You did.

BEN. That was before she'd been through the mill . . . (*He begins to run his finger down the column.*)

JOEY (*standing up*). Listen Ben, you could be making a mistake about Anne. If you really don't want to lose her –

BEN (*goes to the telephone on* JOEY'S *desk*). Your conversation is beginning to sound as if it's been stitched together from song titles of the fifties. (*He begins to sing.*) Making a mistake about Anne – . . . If you really don't want to lose her . . .

JOEY. Look Ben, I'm trying to tell you something.

BEN. Haylife and Forlings . . . (JOEY *looks at* BEN. BEN *sings as he dials.*) Three four eight – owe seven two owe.

JOEY. What are you doing?

BEN (*sits down and speaks into the telephone*). Ah hello – can I speak to Mr Nuttall, Reg Nuttall please.

JOEY (*hurrying over to the telephone*). He's not there.

BEN. Thank you. (*He waits, humming and smiling at* JOEY.)

JOEY *seizes the telephone, they wrestle over it,* BEN *hangs on to it.*

(*Into the phone, crouched away from* JOEY.) No, I'm waiting for Mr Nuttall please.

JOEY. All right. All right. I'll do it.

BEN *hands him the receiver.* JOEY *puts the receiver down and holds onto telephone. There is a pause.*

BEN. Well?

JOEY. Do you intend to stay in the room while I find out if he'll have you to dinner?

BEN. Certainly. But *you* needn't stay while I find out. (*He goes to pick up the telephone.*)

JOEY (*shouts*). I said I'd do it!

BEN (*a long pause*). But what *are* you afraid of? He can only say
no, in which case I'll only make your life a living hell.

JOEY. Perhaps I'm afraid he'll say yes.

BEN. Well, you do worry for him, don't you, dear?

JOEY. Why do you think it's him I'm worried for?

BEN. Oh, we all know how you worry for yourself. (*He reaches for
the telephone.*)

JOEY *holds it tight, and looks at* BEN. BEN *laughs and reaches
for it.*

JOEY (*runs away with it followed by* BEN). You're a fool, Ben. A
bloody fool!

BEN *stops.*
The telephone rings.

BEN (*takes the telephone and puts the base down on his desk.* JOEY *sits
down at his desk*). Butley, Nursery. (*Laughs.*) Oh hello James,
what? Ah, well I was just pondering those lines –

His rhythm was present in the nursery bedroom,
In the rank ailanthus of the April dooryard –

(*Pause.*) No, no, I'm quite free. (*Little pause. He mouths a curse.*)
Gardner? Gardner, Gardner, Gardner. No I don't recall a
student called Gardner – What year is she? Ah! *He!* (*He
grimaces at* JOEY. *A shape appears at the door.*) Oh God. Poor
Edna.

There is a knock on the door.

(*He claps his hand over the mouth-piece. To* JOEY.) Block that
student! (*Into the receiver.*) He says I *what*? No he must have
misunderstood me. I don't recall telling a student . . .

JOEY *has gone to the door, opens it, then steps back.*
ANNE *comes in.*
BEN *sees* ANNE, *gapes at her and turns back to the telephone.*
Look, I appear to have miscalculated, I've got a student after all,
speak to you later, eh? 'Bye. (*He hangs up.*)

There is a silence.

How are you?

ANNE. Thank you. And you?

BEN. Coping with Edna. Do you remember Edna? The one you called a human contraceptive? Do you remember?

ANNE. Actually, I called her a pill.

BEN. Well, I updated you. (*He laughs.*)

Another silence.

ANNE. How are *you*, Joey?

JOEY. Oh. Um, very well thanks. Um, how's Miranda?

ANNE. Marina. She fills her belly and her nappy. She grows the odd tooth. She cries.

BEN. How adult. Except for the odd tooth, one loses that. (*Pause.*) Actually, I've been thinking of finding a new dentist. I know you dote on Tonks, darling, but he's terribly camp. One sits in that chair with one's whole body at his mercy. (*To* JOEY.) Who do you go to?

JOEY. A man in Pimlico.

ANNE. Joey's teeth are always in marvellous condition.

BEN. Are they? Let's see.

JOEY. What?

BEN. Let's see your teeth.

JOEY *grimaces.*

(BEN *goes close, inspects them.*) You're quite right. (*To* ANNE.) They sparkle. Although from time to time I've noticed – (*He hums* 'Christ the Lord is risen today.')

ANNE (*laughs to* JOEY). One of Ben's marriage jokes. I'm surprised you haven't heard it.

JOEY. Well, I haven't.

ANNE. How flattering for me.

JOEY (*after a pause*). Well, I think it'd be better if I – I'd better get along. (*He picks up his briefcase.*)

BEN. Why?

ANNE. Because he's embarrassed.

BEN. Are you?

JOEY. I've got a lecture.

BEN. He has. On Blake.

ANNE. Ahh. Then he'd better go.

JOEY *goes out.*

BEN. He's very sensitive. You frighten him.

ANNE. Because he's creepy, and he knows I know it.

BEN. Yes. I've told him. He took it surprisingly badly.

ANNE (*pause*). You've settled down nicely together again, then, have you?

BEN. We have our ups and downs.

ANNE. That's all right then. May I sit? (*She sits on the hard chair in front of* BEN'S *desk.*)

BEN. I went to see you over the weekend, as arranged, but you were out.

ANNE. Yes, I'm sorry.

BEN. Grounds for a scene though, don't you think?

ANNE. Oh, I should wait. (*Little pause.*) I had to see Tom's head-master about a job.

BEN. And did you get one?

ANNE. Yes.

BEN. Good. (*He stares at her.*) But you look a trifle peaky around the gills – wherever they are. I can never locate them on Joey. Are you all right?

ANNE. I'm fine.

BEN. Good. I saw Marina instead. I expect your mother the mad monk told you.

ANNE. She said it was very quick. Like a visit from the post-man.

BEN. I was there for twenty minutes. You'd better check on the postman. Ah! (*He sits at* JOEY's *desk.*) Well, this is almost as delightful as it's unexpected, to what is it owed?

ANNE. I came to find out whether you wanted us back.

BEN (*after a pause*). Is that an offer?

ANNE. No. It's a question. I'd like the truth please. *Do* you want us back?

BEN. Frequently. (*Little pause.*) But not permanently. Do you want to come back?

ANNE. No.

BEN. We've cleared that up then. I think we're going to get on very well from this time forth, don't you?

ANNE (*pause*). Joey hasn't told you, then?

BEN. Told me what?

ANNE. He's known for weeks. His – what's his name – friend Reg must have told him.

BEN. Reg?

ANNE. Tom told him. At least, he told me he had.

BEN. Tom? Tom and Reg? What on earth have Tom and Reg got to do with us?

ANNE. He's asked me to marry him.

BEN (*after a pause*). Which one? (*Pause.*) You're not. (*Laughs.*) You can't be.

ANNE. Yes I am. Do you mind?

BEN. Yes, yes, I mind very much.

Pause, he pulls himself together.

After all, a man's bound to be judged by his wife's husband. The most boring man in London – you said yourself he was the dullest man you'd ever spent an evening with.

ANNE. That was before I got to know him properly.

BEN. And what do you call him now?

ANNE. The dullest man I've ever spent the night with. But I don't mind. Why should you?

BEN. Because – because I shall miss old Tom, that's why. I'm too old to make mature new friendships with bores, far too impatient. (*He walks round to his own desk.*) They have to grow on you steadily, hours by hours through years on years, until they're actually doing their bit towards holding you together.

Like ivy around crumbling walls. (*Little pause.*) Is that why you want him?

ANNE. Are you going to make difficulties?

BEN. What?

ANNE. About the divorce?

BEN. Divorce?

ANNE. You see, I'm not allowed to marry him until I'm divorced from you. It's the law of the land. Are you going to make difficulties?

BEN. This is humiliating.

ANNE. But deserved. By both of us.

BEN (*laughs*). I'll bloody make difficulties all right. After all, this is liable to be the only phase of our marriage that I shall enjoy. At least since the moment in the registry office when the clerk who handled our contract was under the impression that he was supposed to bind me for a year or two to the mad monk your mother. (*He gets up and faces her across his desk.*) I'll have to have my fun somewhere, won't I? Because after all one moment of pleasure isn't much out of a whole year, is it?

ANNE. It's a moment more than I had.

BEN. And how many moments do you expect from your next?

ANNE. I shan't count them. I'm not in it for fun, you see. I never was. And nor were you.

BEN. Oh. What *was* I in it for?

ANNE. Perhaps you wanted a break.

BEN. Well, I'm certainly getting one, aren't I?

ANNE. Or perhaps you were frightened. But it doesn't matter any more because you're not any more. And I suppose you needn't ever try again, now that you've found out whatever it is you were determined to learn. (*Pause.*) I don't care. Not at all.

BEN. Then you're half-way there. And Tom will certainly teach you to sit still. (*He walks round behind her and comes to face her.*) If you must get married again, surely we can do better for you than that. After six weeks you'll be the two most boring men in London. There are signs already. You're developing a new tone –

a combination of the didactic and the enigmatically stoic – that's more than half-way towards Tom's prose style. By the way, does he know that you greet spring and its signs of life with wheezings and sneezes from your hay-fever? Tom endorses spring. He admires it for its moral exuberance. (*Pause.*) Do you still make little popping sounds when you drink your coffee? No, it's your nose – your nose I've always taken exception to, or is it your mouth? You can't marry Tom.

ANNE. I can.

BEN. All right, you probably can. You can probably do a lot of hideous things. You're tough, versatile and brutal. What I mean is, don't.

ANNE. Why not?

A shape appears at the door.

Well?

A pause.

EDNA (*knocks, steps in*). Can I have a word? (*She is obviously distraught.*)

BEN. By all means. (*He gestures to* ANNE.)

EDNA. Oh, I'm sorry, I didn't realize – I'll look back later, if I may. (*She goes out.*)

ANNE. He's asked me to live with him until we get married. Are you going to make trouble?

BEN. Tell me, when did we last have it off? Was it that time in the park, beneath the trees, or did we have a quick go subsequently, in bed or under the kitchen table, Joey and I were trying to work it out –

ANNE *rises.*

(*He jumps away, as if expecting a blow, shields his face, then laughs, shakily.*) You're going to live with him *until* you get married, did you say? At least that's a realistic prospectus. (*He calls out, as* ANNE *leaves.*) 'Bye, darling. 'Bye bye, sweet princess, goodbye . . . (*He closes the door behind her and stands pulling at the cotton wool on his chin. He pulls it off.*) Ahh, Butley is himself again. (*Hums 'Christ the Lord', then sings.*)

   Christ your breath is bad today

   Haa-aa-al-it-osis. Haa-aa-

(*He breaks off, trembling. He sits down at his desk, puts his hand to his face, takes it away, looks at it, touches his chin, inspects his fingers.*) Bloody woman! Bloody woman! (*He feels in his pocket and takes out more cotton wool*).

Curtain

Act Two

The office as before. It is shortly after lunch.
When the curtain rises MISS HEASMAN *is sitting on the hard chair
by* BEN's *desk, reading from her essay.* BEN *is apparently asleep in the
armchair a cigarette in his hand.*

MISS HEASMAN (*a pause – she looks at* BEN). 'Hermione's re-
    awakening – the statue restored to life after a winter of sixteen
    years' duration – is in reality Leontes's re-awakening, spiritually,
    and of course the most moving exemplification of both the re-
    vitalization theme and thus of forgiveness on the theological as
    well as the human level.'

BEN. Level?

MISS HEASMAN. Yes.

BEN. The human *level*?

MISS HEASMAN. Yes. Um, shall I go on?

BEN. Mmm.

MISS HEASMAN. 'The central image is drawn from nature, to
    counterpoint the imagery of the first half of the play, with its
    stress on sickness and deformity. Paradoxically, *A Winter's Tale*
    of a frozen soul –'

BEN. Bit fish-mongery, that.

MISS HEASMAN (*laughs mirthlessly*). '– is therefore thematically
    and symbolically about revitalization.'

BEN. Sorry. Re-whatalization?

MISS HEASMAN. Re-*vit*alization.

BEN (*gets up and goes to* MISS HEASMAN). Thematically and sym-
    bolically so, eh?

MISS HEASMAN. Yes. (*She looks towards him challengingly.*)
    'The central image is drawn from' – no, we've had that – um. 'In
    this context –'

BEN. Can you see?

MISS HEASMAN. What?

BEN (*aims his desk light at* MISS HEASMAN's *essay, forgets to turn it on, goes to a hard chair in the corner of the room and sits down out of view.*) There.

> MISS HEASMAN *after a moment, leans over, turns on the light.*

Sorry. No irony intended. (*Pause.*) 'Context.'

MISS HEASMAN. Um, yes. 'In this context it might be sɪ ͗ that Leontes represents the affliction that is a universal, and so contingently human evil, and in this sense, the sense of a shared blight...'

BEN (*lets out a noise like a laugh, pretends to be coughing*). Sorry. Yes, a shared blight – yes, look, how much longer is it exactly?

> MISS HEASMAN *fumbles through the pages* – BEN *goes over to his desk.*

I'll tell you what, as our time together's drawing to a close, read the last two or three sentences, so we can get the feel of your conclusion.

> MISS HEASMAN *looks pointedly at her watch, riffles through her pages.*
> BEN *picks at the cotton wool on his chin, drums his fingers, checks these movements, smiles attentively when* MISS HEASMAN *looks at him.*

MISS HEASMAN. Ready?

BEN. Please, please.

MISS HEASMAN. 'So just as the seasonal winter was the winter of the soul, so is the seasonal spring the spring of the soul. The imagery changes from disease to floral, the tone from mad bitterness to joyfulness. As we reach the play's climax we feel our own – spiritual – sap rising.'

BEN (*after a long pause*). Sap?

MISS HEASMAN. Sap.

BEN. Sap. Sap. Yes, I think sap's a better word than some others that spring rhymingly to mind. Good. Well, thank you very much. What do you want to do – I mean, after your exams?

(*He sits on the hard chair opposite* MISS HEASMAN.)

MISS HEASMAN. Teach.

BEN. English?

MISS HEASMAN. Yes.

BEN. Well, I suppose that's more radical than being a teacher of exams, for which I think you're already qualified, by the way. I hope you'll take that as a compliment.

MISS HEASMAN. It isn't meant to be one, is it? But whatever you think of my essay, if I don't do well in the exams, I might not be able to be a teacher.

BEN. Teacher of whom?

MISS HEASMAN. Sixth forms, I hope.

BEN. Isn't it more exhilarating to get them earlier? Sixth-form teachers are something like firemen called in to quench flames that are already out. Although you can never tell – recently I've enjoyed reading almost as much as I did when I was twelve. I do hope I didn't slip through their net – it makes one lose confidence. But I'm sure *you'll* be all right. Perhaps books are just my *madeleines*, eh?

> Gravy and potatoes
> In a big brown pot
> Put them in the oven
> And cook them very hot.

MISS HEASMAN. I'm sorry?

BEN. And so am I. I'm not really myself this afternoon, what do you want to do next week?

MISS HEASMAN. We have to cover at least six Shakespeares.

BEN. From what I've heard already, Shakespeare's as good as covered. (*He opens the door.*)

MISS HEASMAN (*holds out her essay*). Could you please write some comments on this?

BEN. It's a good thing to be merciless. (*Taking the essay.*) It comes in useful when dealing with the young.

MISS HEASMAN. Believe it or not, you can be as rude as you like. I don't take it personally.

BEN. That's another good way of taking the fun out of teaching. Good afternoon, Miss Heasman.

MISS HEASMAN. Thank you. (*She goes out.*)

> BEN *stands at the open door, gestures obscenely after her. Then, aware that he is holding her essay, pinches his nostrils, holds the essay at a distance, makes gagging sounds, pantomimes gas-poisoning as he goes back to his desk.*
>
> MISS HEASMAN *has come back to the door, stands watching him.*
>
> BEN *drops the essay onto his desk, stiffens, turns slowly.*
>
> *He and* MISS HEASMAN *stare at each other.*
>
> MISS HEASMAN *turns and goes quickly from the room.*

BEN (*makes as if to hurry after her, stops*). Oh Christ! Bloody girl!

> *He stands for a moment, then takes out an address book, looks up a name, goes over to his desk and dials the number.*

Hello, Kent Vale Comprehensive? Headmaster please. (*Little pause.*) Ben Butley. (*Aside.*) Friend to Education. (*Into the telephone.*) Thank you. (*He puts the telephone on the desk, runs over to a carrier bag, extracts a quarter of Scotch, runs back, clamps it under his chin, unscrews the cap as he talks in a Scottish accent.*) Ahh, hello Headmaster, sorry to trouble you on a trifling matter, but I've been trying to make contact with one of your staff, Tom Weatherley, and it's proving to be a tricky business. (*Pause.*) Ben Butley, Friend to Tom Weatherly, a member of your staff. Do you ken him? (*Little pause.*) Oh, naturally I don't want to disturb him if he's teaching, but I've got a rather delicate message for him, I'd rather entrust it to someone of authority like yourself, if I may? (*Listens.*) Thank you. It's just that could he and I have a little chin-wag – (*Little pause.*) – chin-wag some time about the proceedings – solicitors, alimony, maintenance, custody, visiting rights – always so sad when there are wee bairns to consider – we always say – property, so on, so forth. (*Pause.*) Oh, I'm Tom's fiancée's husband. I've only just heard the news. By the way, H.M., quite a coincidence, my wife that was, Tom's wife to be, Ann Butley that is, might be coming to teach in your school, I believe, do keep an eye out for her, I'd be most obliged. (*He takes the telephone away from his chin feels his chin, makes a face.*) Oh, and there is one other thing, could you tell Tom that he'll have to foot the bill for any ops; this time unless he can get it on the National Health, I've got enough blood on my hands – (*Looks at his fingers.*) – at the moment, and it's all my own, ha ha ha, if you see what I mean. (*Little pause.*) Oh you don't, well never mind, H.M., I don't really think we educationalists should be expected to see anything but the clouds into which we thrust our heads eh?

There is a shape at the door. BEN *looks towards it.*

Love to Tom and Anne when you see them, eh? Goodbye.

He puts down the telephone, stares towards the door, then takes a swig of Scotch, goes to the door, peers through the frosted glass. He drops the Scotch into his pocket and knocks gently against the glass.

Tap tappit, tap tappit, he's heard it before.
But when he peeps out there is nobody there

Opens the door.

But packets and whimsey put down on the stair.
(*He walks over to his desk.*) Or is something frightening him again? Is that why he's peeping through the frosted glass with his whiskers twitching and his paws to his nose, eh?

JOEY *after a pause, enters – goes to his desk, puts down his briefcase and turns on the desk lamp.*

If it's Anne you were hiding from, she's gone. If it's Edna, she hasn't arrived.

JOEY. I heard voices. I thought perhaps you and Anne were still –

BEN. What? Thrashing it out? Having it off? What would Anne and I still be doing, together in a small room, after two hours? She was always succint, even with her knickers down.

JOEY. I saw Edna in the common room. She was just leaving when I went in.

BEN. And how did she seem? Jovial?

JOEY. No, very upset.

BEN. Ah.

JOEY. Was that Miss Heasman I passed in the corridor?

BEN. How did she look? Jovial?

JOEY. She had her face averted. As if she were in tears.

BEN. Then that was certainly Miss Heasman, yes. Everything seems to be running smoothly, doesn't it? (*He stares at* JOEY.) Tell me, what did you make of old Anne turning up in that enterprising fashion?

JOEY. I don't know.

BEN. You don't?

JOEY *looks at him.*

She was under the impression that you've known for some time.

JOEY (*a pause*). I did try to warn you.

BEN. Yes and thank you. But tell me, how come that you've known for some time?

JOEY. Well actually I got it from Reg.

BEN. From Reg? Yes? (*Pause.*) You know I think we're building up a case here for a conspiracy theory of personal relationships. Go on.

JOEY (*sits*). Tom's meeting Reg had nothing to do with me. It was something professional, I don't know what, but they got on very well and Tom told Reg and Reg told me, and then Tom phoned Reg and told Reg not to tell me or if he *had* told me to ask me not to tell you until he or Anne had told you.

BEN. Yes, I recognize Tom's delicate touch there in your sentence structure. It must have been amusing to hear me chatter mindlessly on about my marriage, eh?

JOEY. I tried to warn you.

BEN. But was it amusing? Was it fun? (*Pause.*) Are you going to answer me?

JOEY. Sorry. I took the question to be rhetorical.

BEN (*going over to him*). All right. Let me ask you, then, *why* you promised not to mention to your best friend – is that presuming? – that his wife was being screwed by, while contemplating marriage to, the most boring man in London? Is that question sufficiently unrhetorical?

JOEY. Because I didn't think it was my business.

BEN. Not your business? And how many personalities and dramas over which we've gossiped and whinnied in the past years have been our business? There have been some pretty sticky silences between us recently, and here you were, my dear, in possession of a piece of information that was guaranteed to raise at the very least an amused eye-brow?

JOEY. All right, because I'm a coward, that's why. I'm sorry. (*Pause.*) I *am* sorry, in point of fact.

BEN. Matters of fact and points of fact have been cluttering your syntax since you started going steady with that butcher's boy.

JOEY. I'm sorry because I hoped it wouldn't happen. Now it's a fact and I wish it weren't.

> BEN *laughs, tugs at the cotton wool on his chin and pulls it off. His hand is trembling.*

I'm – I'm sure you could get her back.

BEN. How far back?

JOEY. To live with you. She and Marina.

BEN. That's too far back. Far too far back.

JOEY. Then what will you do?

BEN. Grab my quota of fun, that's all. (*He returns to the telephone.*) I'm working to a very tight schedule. I've given myself a mere

week to get the most boring – and tenacious – man in London
out of his job and home. I'm moving on to his landlady now.

JOEY. Fun?

BEN. Or trouble. I can't remember which I've promised myself.

JOEY. But what's the point of making trouble?

BEN. Fun. (*He dials again.*) Because hounding them from job and
home is no trouble. Local councils, the police, whole govern-
ments do it. Why shouldn't a private citizen be allowed to join
in? (*He waits, then slams down the phone –* JOEY *goes to the door.*)
Where are you going? (*He dials another number.*)

JOEY. The library's open now. I thought I'd go up –

BEN. And hide again? Who from this time?

    JOEY *shrugs.*

From Edna. Yes, it must be Edna.

JOEY. Well, I'm not going to be here when she comes to have it
out with you.

    BEN *laughs.*

I can't help it. *I'm* not going to antagonize her.

BEN. O.K. I'll do it for you. You run along.

    JOEY *looks at him, hesitates, then makes for the door.*

(*Into the telephone.*) Ah, Haylife and Forling, I must say yóu
do drag out your lunch, some of which, by the way, appears
still to be in your mouth, from the sound of you. (*As* JOEY
hurries to him from the door.) This is Joeseph Keyston, Friend to
Reg Nuttall, if you take my meaning, may I speak to him
please? (*He hands the telephone to* JOEY.)

    JOEY *takes the telephone and puts it down.*
    There is a pause.

You see how life repeats itself, with diminishing climaxes.
(*Little pause.*) Well? Is he still out, have you some more
moralizing to do, or are you simply welching on a promise?

JOEY. All right. If you want, I'll cancel Reg. We can go to Bianchi's. Just the two of us.

BEN (*in an American accent*). Cancel Reg? Cancel him? (*Laughs.*) This is a human bean, you're talking about here, kid, not a cheque, or an order of groceries, but a human *bean*! And frankly dear, he's more of an attraction than your shy self, at the moment. All our games together are going a trifle stale, Reg and I may be able to find some new ones.

JOEY. Reg won't be very playful.

BEN. Don't worry. I shall get my fun. Besides, in this bag here, kidneys! Yes, kid, kidneys! (*He waves the carrier bag at* JOEY.)

JOEY (*after a pause*). I'm sorry, Ben. Not tonight.

BEN. Mmm huh. So *you're* not inviting me.

JOEY. I'm not going. We can either eat at the flat or at Bianchi's. It's up to you.

BEN. Well, if you're really not coming then there'll be all the more kidneys for Reginald and myself. What do you think he'll say to that, for an offer?

   A pause.

Don't you care then?

JOEY. No. Not any more.

BEN. You're not breaking off with him, you competitive child you? Is that what you're trying to tell me?

JOEY. No. I'm trying to tell you that it'll be much better if you leave that side of my life alone. (*His voice shaking.*) I can't stop you from phoning him up, you can do it any time, Ben, I'm just advising you, because I don't think you'll get much fun from him, I really don't. I know you've had a bad day already, with Tom and Anne, but you're making it worse.

BEN (*makes as if to dial, hesitates, dials*). You're passing up a chance for a Lawrentian-type wrestle. Can't I interest you?

JOEY. Just remember that I warned you. (*He sits quite still at his desk.*)

BEN. Two warnings in one day.

JOEY *watches tensely.*

Haylife and Forling's? This is Ben Butley, friend to Joeseph Keyston, friend to Reg Nuttall, with whom I'd like to speak, please. (*Little pause.*) Thank you. (*He looks at* JOEY, *grinning, is suddenly stopped by his expression.*) What is it? (*Little pause.*) Joey? (*He starts to put the telephone down, checks himself.*) Hello, is that Reg – (*Little pause.*) Ah, his secretary. (*He hesitates then makes up his mind.*) May I speak to him, please.

Pause, BEN *watches* JOEY, *then offers* JOEY *the telephone. He shakes his head.* BEN *listens again.*

I see. Thank you very much. (*He puts the telephone down, looks at* JOEY.) He's out. (*Smiles.*) Is that a relief?

JOEY. In a sense.

BEN. You'd better tell me about it.

JOEY. What?

BEN. Whatever it is you're warning me about.

JOEY. No. It's nothing.

BEN. Come on, Joey.

JOEY. It doesn't matter. Let it go.

There's a knock on the door. BEN *drops the Scotch bottle. into his pocket.* EDNA *puts her head in.*

EDNA. Are you free now, please? (*She comes in.* BEN *sits down. Very calmly, smiling.*) Now would you kindly tell me what transpired between yourself and this Gardner?

JOEY (*earnestly*). I don't know anything about it, Edna.

EDNA (*still calm*). My teaching, it appears, isn't up to his standard.

BEN. Indeed. Well, I can assure you, Edna, that it's more than up to mine. I know our society has become insolently egalitarian, but I refuse to believe that the gardener's verdict on your teaching will be given too much weight. I didn't know we had a garden – let alone –

EDNA. This is the first time in twenty years teaching that I've been complained about.

JOEY. It's preposterous. You're a very good teacher, Edna.

BEN. All right. Well, let's get this sorted out. To whom did he complain?

EDNA. To James.

BEN. And what did James say?

EDNA. He said you'd promised Gardner he could have tutorials with you. This conversation apparently took place in a pub.

BEN. What? I've had no – well, there was a student, now I come to think of it, but my God I'd completely forgotten – I suppose it might have been Gardner, I scarcely took him in. He wasn't wearing feathers in his cap. (*Little pause.*) Previously you talked of a plumed youth, wasn't it? (*Laughs.*)

EDNA. And you said nothing to him about coming to you for Eliot?

BEN. I have an idea he told me he'd become keen on Eliot. That's all.

EDNA. Keen on Eliot.

BEN. Something of the sort. I suppose I assumed he was after a few tutorials – but really I haven't given him a thought.

EDNA. And did you discuss whether these tutorials are to replace his seminars with me?

BEN. Certainly not.

EDNA. And did you tell him to go to James and explain the circumstances – that he wasn't getting anything out of my seminars.

BEN. Is that what James said?

EDNA. He tried so hard not to tell me what Gardner had said that it was perfectly obvious. He had his diplomatic smile on – the one that makes him look exactly like a rabbit. But I suppose I should be grateful that he didn't encourage that lout to throw my furniture out of the window, or burn my notes. I work very hard for those seminars.

JOEY. We know you do, Edna.

EDNA. I don't expect gratitude, far from it. But I do expect a

minimum of civilized behaviour. And I expect to be backed up
by the Head of the Department and the other members of the
staff when I'm unlucky enough to have a bolshy trouble-maker
in my group.

JOEY. But of course we'll back you up.

EDNA. What happened at the Senate House – it's beginning here.
The Aristotle is just the beginning. (*She sits down, fumbles in her
handbag, closes it.*) But why did they pick on me?

BEN. I don't think anybody would want to pick on you, Edna.

EDNA. Because I'm a woman, that's why. It's always easier to get
at a woman. They think we're more vulnerable. Well, in my
case, they've got another think coming. I haven't finished with
Gardner and like ilk. Not by a long shot. (*Pause.*) How dare he!
How dare he complain!

BEN (*stands up*). Look, perhaps the best thing *is* to let me take him
on.

EDNA. There's not the slightest question of that, Ben. Not the
slightest. He stays in my seminars. That's all there is to it.

BEN. Of course. If that's the way you want it. The only trouble is,
you may not see much of him.

EDNA. In that case, it will be my pleasure to get him suspended.
I've already started a Dean's Report.

BEN. As you wish. It's certainly your privilege. I just don't see
what'll be gained?

EDNA. The satisfaction of causing him trouble.

BEN. Yes, I can see that might be fun.

EDNA. I don't care. (*She opens her handbag, takes out a handkerchief.*) So you two *are* on his side then? (BEN *looks at* JOEY –
they both go over to her.)

JOEY. Certainly not. I think Edna's got every right –

BEN *puts his hand on her shoulder.*

EDNA. Leave me alone. (*She pulls her arm away.*)

BEN. Edna. (*Gently.*) I'm sorry, Edna. It's my fault for not taking
young Gardner seriously.

EDNA. Nobody takes anything seriously any more. But Universities were serious once, yes they were. But now they despise them, yes they do, just as they despise me. Just as you two despise me.

JOEY. Despise you!

BEN. I just didn't want you to be hurt – or worry too much.

EDNA. That's precisely what I mean.

The telephone rings.

BEN. Sorry – (*He answers the telephone.*) Butley, English. Oh, um, hello, actually no this isn't too good a time. I'm in the middle of something –

EDNA (*stands up*). If that's James, please tell him that I'm going home. As education has become optional in this College, I've chosen to cancel my classes for the rest of the day. (*She goes out.*)

BEN. Sorry, James. Could we talk later. (*He puts the telephone down, sits on the edge of the desk, has a swig of Scotch, stares at* JOEY.) Bloody woman!

JOEY. So you did agree to take Gardner in, then.

BEN. One of us took the other in, all right. I shall find out later which way around it is.

JOEY. You'll enjoy that, I'm sure.

BEN. I deserve it, after all this.

JOEY. And what about Edna?

BEN. Bloody woman, that's all about Edna. She's lucky to be rid of him. It's not my fault she's too vain to admit it.

JOEY. And all you had to do just now was to keep quiet, and then tell Gardner it couldn't be managed.

BEN. But I *am* managing it.

JOEY. Oh Christ! But what for? What the hell for?

BEN. Perhaps I had a sense of vacancies opening up in my life. I needed to fill them perhaps.

JOEY. Then why don't you do it from your legitimate students, instead of fobbing them off and refusing to teach them.

BEN (*sitting in armchair*). I haven't got any legitimate students.

They're all bastards. Which is my term of endearment for bores. Gardner's interesting. He actually interests me. At least I think he does, I can't remember him clearly and I'll have to see the hat. You interested me once, dear, and look where it's got you. An Assistant Lectureship. Of course I don't know if my interest can carry you through your board –

JOEY. You mean he'll have a relationship with you, don't you? While all poor Edna can offer him is a relationship with Byron, in a properly conducted seminar.

BEN (*hums 'Christ the Lord has risen today'*). Well, Joeseph, what chance your lectureship now? Edna says you despise her. And she's quite right. Toadying is the sincerest form of contempt.

Pause. They stare at each other.

I remember when you stood in this room, darkly dressed to colour up your melancholy, and I had you read a little Eliot to me. Do you remember? (*Little pause.*) Little did we know that a long time away, far into the future, we would be worrying and fretting together about your promotion. Our beginnings never know our ends. They're always so sad, so sad.

JOEY *turns to go.*

Don't flounce, Dappley. It doesn't suit your mousey hind-quarters.

JOEY. It's not my fault you buggered everything up with Anne. You don't have to bugger everything up for me, too.

BEN. No, I don't. I'm doing it as a favour and for fun.

JOEY. I'm sick to death of your fun! (*He goes to the door.*)

BEN. Bum-twitch, bum-twitch, bum-twitch, bum-twitch!

BEN *laughs and* JOEY *slams the door. He runs after him and shouts down the corridor:*

Teacher's pet!

He comes back – has a swig of Scotch, takes the telephone over

to JOEY's *desk, starts to dial, changes his mind, takes another drink.*
Little pause.

Appley Dappley, little brown mouse
Goes to the cupboard in somebody's house
In somebody's cupboard there's everything nice
Pot, scotch, french letters
For middle-aged mice.

The telephone rings. BEN *answers it.*

Woolly Bear, English. (*Pause.*) What? (*Little pause.*) *Who* would like to see Mr Keyston? (*Little pause.*) Indeed? Yes, yes he's here, just a minute. (*He puts his hand over the receiver, then speaks into it.*) Mr Keyston says kindly send him along to the office. Thank you.

He puts the telephone down, puts the Scotch into a drawer, goes to the desk, sits down, takes out a pen. Feels the cotton wool on his chin. There is a knock. He pores over an essay as there is another knock.

Come.

The door opens.
REG *enters.*

(BEN *goes on working at his essay.*) Minute please. (*Then looks up.*)
REG. Is Joey here?
BEN. Good God, it's Reg, isn't it? Of course it is. (*He gets up, goes over, holds out his hand. As they shake hands.*) I'm terribly sorry, do come in.
REG. Your porter said he was here.
BEN. And so he will be. He just went off to have a brief word with a colleague in distress. How are you?
REG. Very well, thanks. And you?
BEN (*gestures towards his desk*). As you see. (*Laughs.*)

REG. Yes. (*He glances at the desk, appalled.*) Look, you're obviously very busy. If you just tell Joey I'm at the porter's desk –

BEN. Don't be silly. You sit yourself down over there – (*He offers him a chair.*) – and I'll just finish this off, I won't be a minute.

> REG *hesitates, glances at* JOEY's *desk and bookshelves and lights a cigarette.*

(BEN *pretends to go on marking, makes a few exclamations under his breath. Not looking up.*) What brings you down here, anyway?

REG. I just thought I'd look in.

BEN (*writes furiously*). Have to make my script illegible so that they don't find out about my spelling. There. (*He pushes the essay away.*) To check up, eh?

REG. Check up?

BEN. Joey's always saying that if you got your hands on our little room, which is an everywhere, or rather on me, eh? as I'm responsible for the mess we're in – (*Laughs.*) But you should see our flat. Even Joey's room is like a pigsty – naturally, I'm the pig that made it that way. You really must come around and help us out. He says you've done wonders with your little kitchen.

REG. I'm in publishing.

BEN (*puzzled*). Yes?

REG. Not in interior decorating. (*He sits on the hard chair by* JOEY's *desk.*)

BEN. Oh God yes. (*Laughs.*) I'm sorry about that. No, I don't get your job wrong any more. It would be inexcusable. I'm always making Joey tell me about it, in fact.

REG. I know. He's always telling me about having to tell you about it.

BEN. He says you're a marvellous cook.

REG. I'm glad he eats well.

BEN. And keeps his figure, lucky sod. (*Little pause. Gets up and sits on hard chair opposite Reg.*) You know, Reg, I'm very glad to have the chance to speak to you privately – I behaved abomin-

ably the last time we met. I do hope – well, you've forgiven me
for your shoes. I never apologized properly.

REG. It's all right. These things happen.

BEN. But your shoes survived, did they?

REG. They were suede.

BEN. Oh dear. Suede.

Pause.

REG. Look, you must want to get on. I'll go back to the porter –
(*He gets up.*)

BEN. No, you mustn't do that. (*He gets up.*)

REG. I don't mind. In point of fact we were doing a little business
together. He's an Arsenal supporter.

BEN. Good God. Is he really? In point of fact?

There is a pause.

REG. So I can let you get on with –

BEN. Have a drink? (*He goes to his desk, opens the drawer.*)

REG. I don't think I ought to.

BEN (*coming back with the Scotch and two soiled glasses*). You are
lucky. Then you'll really enjoy it. (*He pushes one of the glasses
into* REG*'s hand.*)

REG *peers down into the glass, winces at its condition.* BEN
dashes Scotch into it, then into his own.

I understand you've met my friend Tom. Tom Weatherley, by
the way.

REG. I know Tom, yes.

BEN. You know all my domestic news, too, I gather. I only heard
it myself today.

REG. Yes, I heard something about it. I'm sorry.

BEN. Do you detest warm scotch? I don't know how you drink it
in your part of the world?

REG. This is fine.

BEN. Good. Cheers.

REG. Cheers.

BEN. Thanks. (*He drinks.* REG *goes to* JOEY's *bookshelves.*) It's nice to have some company. These last few hours I've felt quite like Antony at his close – the air is full of the God's departing musics. So do forgive any tendency to babble, eh?

REG. No, that's all right. I understand.

BEN. Cheers. (*He sits on the hard chair by his desk.*) Actually what this whole business has brought home to me is how dependent I am on my past.

REG (*turning to him*). But it was – excuse me – but it was quite a short marriage, wasn't it?

BEN. No, I was talking about Joey.

REG. Oh.

BEN. It's as if my marriage were an intermission, if you see. Now I'm catching up with my past again, which is where I suppose my future is also.

REG. Really?

BEN. Sorry. I'm being literary. But I always think of *you* as a born romantic. From Joey's descriptions of *your* past. A touch of the butterfly, eh?

REG. Really? And what does Joey say to make you think that?

BEN. Oh, I don't know – the way you've pulled up your roots in the North, what I imagine to be your emotional pattern, your love of the bizarre.

REG (*pause*). And how does that express itself?

BEN. Joe's always recounting your experiences – for example with the Gurkhas. You were with them, weren't you?

REG. I was stationed with them, yes. About ten years ago, during my National Service.

BEN. Exactly. And I scarcely knew what a Gurkha was – I still tend to think he's something you get with a cocktail.

REG. Do you?

BEN. They must be tough little towsers.

REG. They are. (*He sits at* JOEY's *desk.*) You didn't do your National Service I take it.

BEN. Oh Christ! Sorry, I mean no.

REG. How come?

BEN. I got took queer.

> *There is a pause.* REG *puts his glass down.*

Oh! You're ready for another one.

REG. No, I – in point of fact, I'd rather not.

BEN. This is an altogether different suburb. (*He refills* REG'*s glass.*)

REG. Sorry? What suburb?

BEN. Oh, it's a little joke of Joey's. Almost impossible to explain out of context. (*He pours himself a drink and leans on the front of his desk.*) But how is the world of fiction?

REG. Can't complain.

BEN. Cheers. What have you got coming out at the moment?

REG. At the moment I'm doing two cookery books, an authoritative guide to bird watching in Lincolnshire, the only intelligent account of the farce of El Alamein – by an N.C.O. needless to say – and a New Testament Commentary.

BEN. That's your *fiction* list?

REG. No, that's our list for next month.

BEN. No novels at all then?

REG. Well, just one of those historical romances where the hero shoves his sword into assorted villains and his cock into assorted ladies. It won't get the reviews but it'll make us money.

BEN. If he did it the other way around you might get both.

REG (*laughs briefly*). But the point is, you see, by putting that one through we can afford to do something worthwhile later. For instance, I've just made a decision about a novel on National Service life.

BEN. Oh, one of those. I thought that vogue was eight years dead.

REG. No, not one of those. This is something special, in my opinion. Of course it mightn't interest you as you didn't do National Service, but personally I found it moving, witty, gracefully organized – genuinely poetic.

BEN. The National Service? Good God! Those qualities are hard enough to come by in art. It's never occurred to me to look for them in life, especially as run by the armed forces. Cheers.

REG. Nevertheless I expect you *will* be curious in this case. Theoretically I can't tell you our author's name as the board doesn't meet until tomorrow, but if I just mention that he's a comprehensive school teacher – (*He raises his glass slowly.*) Cheers.

BEN (*after a pause*). Well well. (*He sits in the armchair.*) The most boring man in London strikes again.

REG. I'm sorry.

BEN. Why?

REG. It must be painful for you.

BEN. Why?

REG. Because of his relationship with you. It was wrong of me to have mentioned it.

BEN. On the contrary. It was the correct move. Has Joey read it?

REG. Not yet. It was offered to me in strict secrecy – at least until I'd made up my mind. But I can tell him about it now. I think he'll like it.

BEN. That's because you don't know him very well, perhaps. He may be something of a dilettante in personal relationships, but he holds fast to standards on important matters. We once drew up a list of the five most tedious literary subjects in the world. National Service came fifth, just behind the Latin poems of Milton.

REG. Really? And what occupied the other three places?

BEN. The English poems of Milton.

REG. When I was at Hull I chose Milton for my special subject.

BEN. That sounds an excellent arrangement. The thing is to confine him to the North. Down here we can dally with Suckling and Lovelace.

REG. And Beatrix Potter? Joey says you've got great admiration for the middle-class nursery poets.

BEN. With reservations. I find some of the novellae a trifle heavy going. (*A pause.*) I call Joey Appley Dappley, did you know?

REG. Do you?

BEN. And he calls me Old Mr Prickle-pin. After
   Old Mr Prickle-pin, with never a coat to
   Put his pins in.
   Sometimes I call him Diggory Diggory Delvet, when he's bur-
   rowing away at his book.

   There is a pause.

REG. What did you mean by being took queer?

BEN (*coyly*). Oh, you know, I'm sure. (*Laughing.*) You do look
   shocked, Reg.

REG. That's surprising, because I'm not surprised even.

BEN. You don't think there's anything shameful in it, then?

REG. In what?

BEN. Dodging the draft.

REG. There are thousands of blokes from working-class homes who
   couldn't. They didn't know the tricks. Besides they'd rather
   have done ten years in uniform than get out of it that way.

BEN. Then you think there's something shameful in being taken
   queer?

REG. I'm talking about people pretending to be what they're
   not.

BEN. Not what?

REG. Not what they are.

BEN. But if people do get taken queer, it's nature we must blame
   or their bodies, mustn't we? Medicine's still got a long way to
   go, Reg.

REG. Why do you use that word?

BEN. What word?

REG. 'Queer.'

BEN. Does it offend you?

REG. It's beginning to.

BEN. Sorry. It's an old nursery habit. One of our chars used to say
   it. Whenever I came down with anything it would be, 'Our
   Ben's took queer again, poor little mite.'

There is a silence.

Although I can see it's a trifle inappropriate for a touch of T.B.–
REG. T.B.?
BEN. They found it just in time. At my board medical, in fact.
Why *do* you object to the phrase though?
REG. No, no, it doesn't matter. A misunderstanding. I'm sorry.
BEN. Oh, I *see. Queer!* – of course. Good God, you didn't think
I'd sink quite so low, did you? (*Laughs.*)
REG. I'm sorry.
BEN. It's all right.
There is a pause.
BEN. Cheers. (*He raises his glass.*)
REG. Cheers.

Another pause.

BEN. Homosexual.

Another pause.

REG. What?
BEN. Homosexual. I was just wondering – should one say that
instead of 'queer' – in your sense of the word. Homosexual.
REG. It doesn't really matter at all. I don't really care –
BEN. Do you feel the same about 'fairies' as you do about 'queers'?
REG. Yes, in point of fact. Since you ask.
BEN. Right, I've got that. (*He gets up and moves towards* REG.)
Of course they've almost vanished anyway, the old-style queens
and queers, the poofs, the fairies. The very words seem to
conjure up a magical world of naughty thrills, forbidden fruits –
sorry – you know, I always used to enjoy them enjoying themselves. Their varied performances contributed to my life's
varieties. But now the law, in making them safe, has made them
drab. Just like the heterosexual rest of us. Poor sods. (*Little
pause.*) Don't you think?
REG (*stands up and puts his glass on the desk*). Oh, there's enough

affectation and bitchiness in heterosexuals to be getting on with. (*He glances at his watch.*) Don't you think?

BEN. Oh don't worry. He'll be here in a minute (*Pause.*) How are things between you two, by the way?

REG. What things?

BEN. No complications?

REG. What kind of complications would there be?

BEN. In that our routine doesn't interfere with your – plural meaning – routine.

REG. Plural meaning? Meaning what?

BEN. Yours and his. Your routines together.

REG. Ah. Well, it has done, frankly, yes. Now you ask. But I don't think it will from now on.

BEN (*sits on the hard chair opposite* REG). Then you're beginning to get the hang of it? Good. Because sometimes I've suspected that our friendship – going back so far and including so much – so much of his history and so much of my history which has really become *our* history – singular meaning this time – must make it difficult for any new people we pick up on the side.

REG. Like your wife, do you mean?

BEN. Well done. Yes, like poor old Anne. She must have felt her share amounted to a minor infidelity, really. I speak metaphorically, of course but then I suppose marriage is the best metaphor for all our intense relationships. Except those we have with our husbands and wives. (*Laughs.*) Naturally.

REG. So you think of yourself as married to Joey, do you?

BEN. Metaphorically.

A pause the telephone rings. BEN *picks it up.*

Butley, English. Oh, hello James – no, I'm afraid I still can't talk properly. I'm in the middle of a tutorial. (*He winks at* REG.) O.K. Yes. Goodbye.

REG. What metaphor would you use when you learned that Joey was going to move in with someone else? Would that be divorce, metaphorically?

BEN (*after a long pause*). What?

REG (*laughs*). Sorry. I shouldn't do that. But I was thinking that it must be odd getting news of two divorces in the same day.

BEN (*pause*). Joey hasn't said anything.

REG. No. I'm giving the news. You might say that when he comes to me our Joey will be moving out of figures of speech into matters of fact. Ours will be too much like a marriage to be a metaphor.

BEN (*little pause*). I thought you didn't admit to being – what? different?

REG. There are moments when frankness is necessary. No, our Joey's just been waiting for the right queen, fruit, fairy, poof or homosexual to come along. He's come.

BEN (*after a pause*). Well, isn't he lucky.

REG. Time will tell. I hope so. But I'm tired of waiting to make a proper start with him. I'm tired of waiting for him to tell you. You know our Joey – a bit gutless. No, the truth of the matter is I've been trying to get Joey to bring you around to dinner one evening and tell you straight, so we could get it over with. I knew he'd never find the nerve to do it on his lonesome. But he's kept dodging about, pretending you were busy, one excuse after another. It's worked out quite well though, hasn't it?

The door opens. JOEY *comes in. Sees* REG.

Hello. We've just been sorting things out. Ben and I.

BEN (*to* JOEY). Cheers.

JOEY *stands staring from one to the other.*

BEN. Yes, our Reg has just been giving me the second instalment of the day's news. But then traditionally, because metaphoric-ally, I should be the last to hear.

JOEY (*after a pause*). I wanted to tell you myself.

BEN. Wanted to, did you? And were you looking forward to a sub-sequent scene?

JOEY. No.

BEN. How unlike each other we are. I would have enjoyed it.

REG (*after a pause*). How did your lecture go?

JOEY. All right.

REG. Grand. Any more teaching today?

JOEY. No.

REG. Come on then. (*He moves over to* JOEY.) Let's go move your things.

JOEY. No, I can't, until later.

REG. Why not?

JOEY. Because there's something I've got to do. (*He glances at* BEN.)

BEN. Oh, don't stay on my account.

JOEY. No. It's something I promised Edna I'd –

REG. Oh. Well, have you got time for a cup of tea?

JOEY. Yes.

They move towards the door.

BEN. Reg.

REG *turns.*

Are you coming back after tea?

REG (*looks at* JOEY). I don't see any reason too. Why?

BEN. I think you're pretty bloody good Reg. In your way. It's not my way, but it seems to get you what you want.

REG. So far. But thanks.

BEN *goes across to the carrier bag, scrambles in it, comes back with a package, hands it to* REG.

(REG *takes it.*) What's this? (*Opening the package.*)

BEN. My kidneys. Best English lamb.

REG. You've been done. They're New Zealand, thawed.

BEN. The small, dapper irony is that I've been trying to join you for supper all day – not to say for the last month. May I anyway?

JOEY. Of course.

REG. I'm sorry. We can't.

JOEY. Why not?

REG. Because I've just bought two tickets for the match tonight. From one of your porters. (*To* BEN.) I'm sorry. Perhaps some other time. (*He passes the bag of kidneys to* JOEY *who passes them to* BEN.)

BEN. Thank you. (*He drops the kidneys on his desk.*)

JOEY. Do we have to go to the match?

REG. Yes. It's an important one. (*To* BEN.) But some other time. Now I'd like that tea please.

JOEY *looks at him and leads the way to the door.*

BEN (*watches them*). Reg!

REG *turns.*

I didn't know you supported a London club too, Reg? (*He picks up the whisky bottle.*)

REG. Leeds are away to Arsenal.

BEN. Ah. Well, enjoy it.

REG. Thanks. (*He turns to the door.*)

BEN. Reg!

REG *turns again.*

Will you wear it all then?

REG. Sorry? What? Wear what?

BEN. Your gear and tackle and trim. Have you got it with you?

REG. What? (*Puzzled, he looks at* JOEY.)

BEN. Your scarf and cloth cap and rattle. Your rosettes and hob-nail boots. Isn't that your road, any road, up your road?

REG. I'm parched. Can we compare customs some other time? (*He turns.*)

BEN. Reg! (*As* REG *seems to go on.*) Reg!

REG *steps back in.*

No, it's not customs, Reg, it's you old cheese. Personally I don't give a fuck that moom and dud live oop Leeds and all, or that the whole tribe of you go to football matches looking like the back page of the *Daily Mirror* and bellow 'Ooop ta Rovers' and 'Clobber busturds' or own a butcher's shop with cush on ta side from parking tickets. (JOEY *laughs* – REG *sees him*.) I really don't, old cheese. No, what's culturally entertaining is yourself. I'm talking about your hypocrisy, old darling.

REG. Is that what you're talking about?

BEN (*making a circle round* JOEY's *desk through the speech*). Because you're only good at getting what you want because you're a fraction of a fake, old potato, you really are. You don't show yourself north except twice a year with your latest boy or sommat in tow, do you? And I bet you get all your football out of ta *Guardian* and television except when you flash a couple of tickets at some soft Southern bugger – do you object to that word, old fruit? – like me, to show some softer Southern bugger like him – (*Gestures at* JOEY.) – how tough you are. Did you cling consciously onto funny vowels, or did you learn them all afresh? I ask, because you're not Yorkshire, you're not working class, you're just a lucky parvenu fairy old fig, and to tell you the truth you make me want to throw up. Pardon, oooop! All over your characteristically suede shoes.

JOEY (*shuts the door*). Shut up, Ben!

BEN (*walking round* REG). Why, have I upset him? What's the matter, Reg? I thought you liked plain talk and straightforward blokes, brass tacks, hard dos and no bloody metaphors. *I* don't blame you for being ashamed of ta folks, except when you want to come the simple sod – sorry, homo – sorry, bloke. I'd feel ta same in thy clogs.

JOEY. Ben!

REG. Anything else?

BEN. Yes, tell me. (*Comes back to confront him*.) Have you had plain talk and brass tacks about thyself with moom, when she's back from pasting tickets on cars, lud, eh, or with dud while he's flogging offal, lud? Thou'd get fair dos all right then, wouldn't thee? From our dud with his strup? Or would he take thee down to local and introduce thee round to all t'oother cloth caps?

'This is our Reg. He's punsy. Ooop, pardon Reg lud, Omo-
sexual. Noo, coom as right surprise to moother und me, thut it
did, moother joost frying oop best tripe and garbuge and me
settling down with gnomes to a good read of Mazo de la
Roche' (*He laughs in* REG's *face.*)

> *There is a pause. Then* JOEY *makes a spluttering sound, as with
> laughter.*

REG (*turns, looks at* JOEY). Oh, I see. The information for all this
drollery comes from you. Perhaps you'd better sort him out.
(*He walks back to the door.*)

BEN. Reg! Coom 'ere lad! You coom and sort me out. Coom on,
lud, it's mun's work!

> REG *stops, walks slowly towards* BEN.

Cloomp, cloomp, cloomp, aye, tha's they moother's feet, Reg!

> JOEY *lets out another gasp.*
> *There is a silence,* REG *standing in front of* BEN.

REG. I don't like these games, Joey. You know that.

JOEY (*spluttering*). I'm sorry, I didn't mean . . .

BEN. Going to cook my kidneys after all then?

REG. Is that what you want?

BEN. Ah coom on –

REG. No, I'm not playing with you. So don't say one more word,
eh? Not a word. (*He turns to go.*)

BEN (*steels himself*). Ah Reg lud –

> REG *turns around.*

Coom on then.

JOEY. Ben!

BEN. Owd sod, feery, punsy –

> REG *hits* BEN *in the stomach, not very hard – he falls to the
> ground.*

JOEY. Don't!

There is a silence, then a shape at the door.

REG. There. Is that what you wanted?

EDNA *knocks, puts her head in.*

EDNA. Oh sorry.

BEN. Living theatre. Next time around in Polish.

EDNA. Oh. (*To* REG.) I'll come back later. (*She goes out.*)

BEN. For a kick at my balls. Why should she be left out?

REG (*calmly*). But you're pitiful, pitiful. This man you've given me all the talk about. That you made me jealous of. (*He turns, goes to the door.*)

BEN. Still, couldn't take it, could you, butcher's boy!

REG (*to* JOEY). It was silly. You'll have to outgrow that kind of thing Joey.

REG *smiles at* BEN, *and goes out closing the door quietly. There is a long moment. Then* BEN *goes and leans on the edge of the desk, smiles at* JOEY.

BEN (*touches his chin*). Your bugger's made me bleed again. (*Laughs.*) You're beginning to get little wrinkles around your eyes. Are they laughter wrinkles, or is it age, creeping up you on little crow's feet? (*Pause.*) You'll be one of those with a crepe neck, I'll be one of the fat ones with a purple face, Reg will be . . . (*Pause.*) I was watching you while you were shaving the morning you were going to Leeds. If you'd moved your eyes half an inch you'd have seen me in the mirror. I was standing behind you studying your neck and my jowels.

JOEY. I saw you.

BEN. Ah! Well, what did you think of all that, with our Reg, eh?

JOEY. I thought it was creepy.

BEN. I wonder what your next will be like? Don't be afraid to bring him home, dear, will you? (*Genteel.*) I do worry so.

JOEY. There isn't going to be a next one. At least, not for some time.

BEN. Ho, reely? I think that's a good plan, h'abstinence makes the 'eart grow fonder. (*He sits on desk.*)

JOEY. I'm moving in with Reg.

BEN (*after a pause*). I don't think he'll have you, dear, after your indiscretions and sauciness.

JOEY. Yes he will.

BEN. You'll go running after him, will you? How demeaning!

JOEY. Possibly. But it's better than having him run after me. I've been through that once, I couldn't face it again.

BEN. You love him then, your butcher's boy?

JOEY. Actually, he's not a butcher's boy, in point of fact. (*He picks up his briefcase and returns to his desk. Little pause.*) His father teaches maths at the university. His mother's a social worker. They live in an ugly Edwardian house . . .

BEN (*after a pause, nods*). Of course. Quite nice and creepy. Creepy, creepy, creepy, creepy!

JOEY. I'm sorry.

BEN. Well, thank you anyway for the fiction. (*He sits on hard chair by his desk. There is a pause.*) So you love him then?

JOEY. No. But I've got to get away from you, haven't I?

BEN. Really? Why?

JOEY (*sits at desk*). For one thing, I'd like to get some work done. During your married year I did quite a bit. I'd like to finish it.

BEN. What?

JOEY. My edition of Herrick.

BEN. If the consequence of your sexual appetites is another edition of unwanted verse then you have an academic duty to control yourself. Could I also mention, in a spirit of unbecoming humility, that if I hadn't taken over your studies when you were an averagely dim undergraduate, you'd never have got a First. Your nature is to settle for decent seconds, indecent seconds, in Reg's case.

JOEY. I know. But those were in the days when you still taught. Now you spread futility, Ben. It creeps in, like your dirty socks do, into my drawers. Or my clean ones, onto your feet. Or your cigarette butts everywhere. Or your stubble and shaving cream into our razor. Or your voice, booming out nursery rhymes into every corner of this department, it seems to me. Or your –

BEN. Shut up! That's rehearsed.

JOEY. Thousands of times.

*[BEN (*after a pause*). He's going to get it published for you, isn't he?

JOEY (*shrugs, after a pause*). Yes. He said he'd help.

BEN (*laughs*). And Appley Dappley has sharp little eyes. And Appley Dappley's so fond of pies.

JOEY. I can't help it. It's the only way I'll get ahead.

BEN. Into what? There's nothing left for you to get ahead in, it's all in the past, and that thins out as the years go by. You'll end up like Edna, sending out Dean's reports on any student you haven't killed off, and extinguishing a poet or two in the library. While it all rots away around you.

JOEY. Perhaps it won't rot away if – (*pauses*) I'd rather end up like Edna than like you. Once you talked to me of literature as the voice of civilization, what was it, the dead have living voices –

BEN. I hope not. I may have quoted . . . 'the communication/ Of the dead is tongued with fire beyond the language of the living/.' I can still quote it when the moment's right.

JOEY. And when will it be right again? It hasn't been with me since your marriage – since before it, really. It's been Beatrix Potter and passages and pastiches from Eliot . . .

BEN. I adjust my selection to the context. Why did you move back into the flat with me then?

JOEY. Habit, I suppose. I'm fairly feeble as both you and Reg point out to me. I don't like being alone, and I couldn't resist – I was actually quite pleased when your marriage broke down.

BEN. That's called friendship. (*Laughs*.)

JOEY. You should have stuck it out. With Anne.

BEN. Should I?

JOEY. But at least you slept with her. You sleep with women –

*The passage in brackets was cut from the production the night before we opened. I am re-instating it because it now seems to me a passage that, whether it should be played in performance or not, conveys a great deal of useful information about Butley's relationship with Joey and about his sexual nature. In the first performance and all subsequent productions, this passage was replaced by the following stage direction:

A long pause – during which BEN *goes to his desk chair and sits – the whisky bottle in his hand.*

BEN. Not when I can help it. Mankind cannot stand too much reality. I prefer friendship.

JOEY.But it's the sort of friendship people used to have with me at school. Abuse, jokes, games . . .

BEN. It's only a language, as good as any other and better than some, for affection.

JOEY. But I've got these wrinkles around my eyes, and my neck will crepe, just as you said. And you're fattening and thirty-five, just as you said, and we don't belong in a school or nursery any more. Reg is right. We're pitiful. We're pitiful together.

BEN. We're all pitiful, together or apart. The thing is to be pitiful with the right person, keep it from everybody else. And from yourselves whenever you can.

JOEY. Well then – well then – I can't keep it from myself any longer. I've been trying to keep you and Reg apart because I knew this would happen. But I've been longing for it, all the same. (*Pause.*)] I'm sorry it had to be today, what with Anne and Tom. I would have waited . . .

BEN (*in senile professional tones*). Which shows you have no sense of classical form. We're preserving the unities. The use of messengers has been quite skilful. (*Pause.*) All right. All right. It doesn't really matter very much.

JOEY. What will you do?

BEN (*after a pause*). Could you, do you think, staunch the flow of blood? (*He lifts his chin back.*)

JOEY (*comes over reluctantly, takes the piece of cotton wool* BEN *holds out to him*). It's just a bubble. (*He hesitates, then bends forward with the cotton wool.*)

BEN. The trouble with – all these confessions, revelations, clean breaks, and epiphanies, shouldn't we call them these days? – is that – cluttered contact goes on. For instance, we still share this room. (*As* JOEY *steps away.*) You're going to have to live with your past, day after day and as messily as ever. I'll see to that.

EDNA (*knocks, opens the door, smiles*). May I?

BEN. Of course. (*Laughs.*) Of course you may, Edna. It's your turn.

EDNA. Now you'll really be able to spread yourself. It's much more sensible. (*To* JOEY.) I've moved out all my files. What can I do now? (*A pause* – BEN *sinks into the chair in realization of the news.*)

JOEY. I can manage down here. (*He moves away, goes to the shelves, takes down his books.*)

EDNA. I'm glad I made one of you take advantage.

JOEY *goes out with a load of books.*

I've quietened down, Ben, you'll be glad to hear. But I'd like to say I'm sorry about my – my little outburst just now. I must learn not to be so sensitive. I suspect it's the only way, with this new generation.

BEN. They are rather frightening.

EDNA. Oh, I don't imagine you're frightened of them.

BEN. I haven't enough pride. I shall continue to throw myself on their mercy. (*He goes to* JOEY'S *shelves* – *takes down a pile of books and puts them on the desk.*)

EDNA. They weren't very merciful to Aristotle in the Senate House.

BEN. He had too many advantages. They couldn't be expected to tolerate that.

EDNA (*laughs*). Well . . .

BEN (*watches her*). I haven't congratulated you on your book.

EDNA. Wouldn't it have been awful if someone had got in ahead of me. Twenty years – I'm really rather ashamed.

BEN. Will you go on to someone else now?

EDNA. I don't know. (*She sits on the hard chair by* BEN'S *desk.*) You know, last night I played a little game – I closed my eyes and turned over groups of pages at a time – and then I looked at a page. It was in the commentary on a letter from his sad wife. And I remembered immediately when I started working on it. It was in Ursula's cottage in Ockham, Surrey. I was still working on it when the summer term of the following year was over. I finished it during my first week back at Ursula's. I can even remember the weather – how's the book on Eliot, by the way?

BEN. It has a good twenty years to go.

EDNA. I'm sure that's not true. James is always saying that you
get through things so quickly. I'm sure you'll be finished with
Eliot in no time. Anyway, don't dally with him. Let me be a
lesson to you –

BEN (*watching her*). Do you still go to Ursula's cottage?

EDNA. Oh, not in the same way. Ursula got married during
chapter Six. (*She laughs and goes to the door, stops.*) Oh hello.
No, don't run away. (*She puts her head back in.*) Mr Gardner's
here.

BEN. Oh! Right.

EDNA. Will you go in, Mr Gardner? (*She goes out.*)

> GARDNER *comes in. He is wearing a hat with feathers in it, a
> white Indian shirt, sandals, no socks.*

BEN (*stares blankly ahead, then looks at him*). Well Mr Gardner –
you're here for your Eliot.

GARDNER. Yes please.

BEN. Tell me, what *did* I say in the pub?

GARDNER. Well, I told you I couldn't stand Miss Shaft's seminars and you told me I was interesting enough to do Eliot, and
that I ought to go and see James. You said he'd pass the buck
back to you because whenever he had a problem he converted it
straight into a buck and passed it. Actually, you called him
Cottontail.

BEN. Did I? (*After a pause, he smiles.*) And here we both wonderfully are.

GARDNER. Yes. (*Smiles.*) Thank God.

BEN. Well let's get going. (*He goes to the shelf, gets a copy of Eliot,
brings it back.*) Can you start by reading me a passage, please.
Don't worry if you can't understand it yet. (*He hands him the
book, open.*) There. Do you mind?

GARDNER. No, I'd like that. (*He sits on the hard chair by* BEN's
desk.)

JOEY (*comes in*). Oh sorry. (*He goes to his desk and begins to pack
the contents of the drawers.*)

BEN. This is Mr Gardner, celebrated so far for his hat. Do you
like it?

JOEY. Of its style.

BEN. Once – some years ago – I taught Mr Keyston. During our
first tutorial we spent a few minutes discussing his clothes.
Then he read me some Eliot. Today I'm actually wearing his
socks. Those are the key points in a relationship that now goes
mainly back.

JOEY (*opening drawers*). So you see, Mr Gardner, you'd better be
careful. If you value your socks.

GARDNER (*looks at his feet: he is not wearing socks*).

> BEN *and* JOEY *look at* GARDNER's *feet, then* JOEY *goes on
> putting papers into his briefcase.*

BEN. Please begin.

GARDNER (*reads*). 'In that open field
If you do not come too close, if you do not come too close,
On a summer midnight, you can hear the music
Of the weak pipe and the little drum
And see them dancing around the bonfire
The association of man and woman
In daunsinge, signifying matrimonie –
A dignified and commodious sacrament.

> JOEY *finished clearing, looks at* GARDNER.

Two and two, necessarye coniunction,
Holding eche other by the hand or the arm
Whiche betokeneth concorde. Round and round the fire.

> JOEY *looks towards* BEN, *they exchange glances, then* BEN
> *looks away,* JOEY *goes out, closing the door gently.*

Leaping through the flames, or joined in circles,
Rustically solemn or in rustic laughter
Lifting heavy feet in clumsy shoes,
Earth feet, loam feet, lifted in country mirth
Mirth of those long since – '

BEN. So you're Gardner, are you?

GARDNER (*stops, looks at him in surprise. Smiles*). Yes.

BEN. Ninny Nanny Netticoat,
>In a white petticoat,
>With a red nose, –
>The longer he stands,
>The shorter he grows.

GARDNER. What?

BEN. I'm moving on, Mr Gardner. I'm breaking new ground.

GARDNER. Oh. (*He laughs.*)

BEN. Furthermore, I hate your hat.

GARDNER. I'm sorry.

BEN. Did you wear it when you bombed the Velium Aristotle? And are you going to wear it for your raids on *Dappley* and *Parsley* eh?

GARDNER. What?

BEN. It won't do you any good. Aristotle in his Velium stood alone, vulnerable, unreadable and so unread. But *Dappley* and *Parsley* are scattered in nursery consciousnesses throughout the land. They can still be tongued with fire.

GARDNER. What are you talking about? – I wasn't anywhere near the Senate House when that happened. I don't even know what it was about, properly.

BEN. No, you're a personal relationships type of chappie, I can sense that. Please go away. Go back to Miss Shaft.

GARDNER. What? But I can't – after all that trouble –

BEN. Trouble for you, fun for me. Go away, Gardner, and take your plumage with you, I don't want to start again. It's all been a ghastly mistake. I don't find you interesting, any more. You're not what I mean at all, not what I mean at all. I'm too old to play with the likes of you.

GARDNER *puts the Eliot down, goes out.* BEN *puts the book back, sits at the desk, turns off the desk lamp and tries feebly three times to turn it on again.*

Curtain.

Otherwise Engaged

For Harold
Two summers 1971 and 1975

OTHERWISE ENGAGED was first presented on 30th July 1975,
at the Queen's Theatre by Michael Codron with the following
cast:

SIMON   Alan Bates
DAVE   Ian Charleson
STEPHEN   Nigel Hawthorne
JEFF   Julian Glover
DAVINA   Jacqueline Pearce
WOOD   Benjamin Whitrow
BETH   Mary Miller

Directed by Harold Pinter

Act One

The living-room of the HENCH's *house in London. It is both elegant and comfortable, but not large. Two sofas, two arm-chairs, a coffee table, a telephone with an answering machine, an extremely expensive and elaborate hi-fi set, and around the walls shelves to accommodate a great range of books (which are evidently cherished) and an extensive collection of records, in which Wagner and other opera sets can be distinguished.*

Stage left is a door that leads onto a small hall, at one end of which is the front door, and at the other a door which, in its turn, when opened, reveals a passage that goes onto stairs going down to the basement. More stairs lead up from the hall to another section of the house. The house has, in fact, recently been divided into two, so that there is a top flat.

Stage right has a door that leads to the kitchen, and as becomes evident, there is a door that opens from the kitchen into the garden.

When the curtain goes up, SIMON *is unwrapping a new record. He takes it out with the air of a man who is deeply looking forward to listening to it - there are several records, in fact - the complete Parsifal. He goes to the hi-fi, puts the first record on, listens, adjusts the level, then goes to the sofa and settles himself in it. The opening chords of Parsifal fill the theatre.*

The door opens, left. DAVE *enters.* SIMON *turns, looks at him, concealing his irritation as* DAVE *wanders into the kitchen, returns, and sits restlessly in the armchair. A pause in the music.*

DAVE. What's that then?

SIMON *gets up and switches off the record.*

SIMON. Wagner. Do you like him?

DAVE (*standing up*). No, well I mean he was anti-semitic, wasn't he. Sort of early fascist, ego-manic type.

SIMON. What about his music, do you like that?

DAVE. Well, I mean, I'm not likely to like his music if I don't like his type, am I?

SIMON (*concealing his impatience*). Everything all right? In the flat, that is. No complaints or other urgencies?

DAVE. No, no, that's all right. Oh, you mean about the rent?

SIMON. Good God no, I wasn't thinking about the rent.

DAVE. It's all right if it waits a bit then, is it?

SIMON. Good God yes, pay us this week's when you pay us last week's - next week, or whenever.

DAVE. OK. I'm a bit short, you know how it is. Your wife out again then?

SIMON. Yes, she's gone to (*thinks*) Salisbury. She left last night.

DAVE. That girl in the first year came round last night for something to eat. I dropped down to borrow a chop or something, fish fingers would have done.

SIMON. Would they really?

DAVE. But she wasn't here, your wife.

SIMON. No, she wouldn't have been, as she was either in, or on her way to, Salisbury.

DAVE. So I had to take her out for a kebab and some wine. Then I had to get her to come back.

SIMON. Ah, she stayed the night then? Good for you!

DAVE. No, she didn't.

SIMON. Oh. You managed to get rid of her, then, instead, well done!

DAVE. She just left by herself.

SIMON. Before you had a chance to get rid of her, oh dear, why?

DAVE. Said she didn't fancy me.

SIMON. Good God, why ever not?

DAVE. I don't know. I mean I asked her if she'd like a screw and she said no. Then I asked her why not, and she said she didn't fancy me, that was why not.

SIMON. Still, she's left the door open for a platonic relationship.

DAVE. Yeah, well, then she went off to see something on television with some friend. I haven't got a television.

SIMON. Well, I'm afraid I can't help you there, nor have we.

DAVE. Anyway she said she might be going to that Marxist bookshop down the road today.

SIMON. What time?

DAVE. About lunch time, she said.

SIMON. But good God, lunch will soon be on you, hadn't you better get going - it would be tragic to miss her.

DAVE. Yeah, well that's it, you see. I'm a bit short, like I said. I mean we can't do anything -

Pause.

SIMON. Can I lend you some?

DAVE. What?

SIMON. Can I lend you some money?

DAVE. Yeah, OK.

SIMON (*giving him a fiver*). Is that enough?

DAVE. Yeah. Right. (*Takes it.*) That's five.

SIMON. Well, I'll get back to my music while you're making your own.

STEPHEN (*enters, through the kitchen door*). Hello. Oh hello.

SIMON (*concealing his dismay*). Oh, Stephen. This is Dave, who's taken over the upstairs flat. Dave, my brother Stephen.

STEPHEN. Oh yes, you're at the Poly, aren't you?

DAVE. That's right.

STEPHEN. What are you studying?

DAVE. Sociology.

STEPHEN. That must be jolly interesting. What aspect?

DAVE. What?

STEPHEN. Of sociology.

DAVE. Oh, the usual stuff.

STEPHEN. Psychology, statistics, politics, philosophy, I suppose.

DAVE. We're sitting in at the moment.

STEPHEN. Really? Why?

DAVE. Oh, usual sort of thing. Well - (*Goes towards the door and out.*)

STEPHEN. What is the usual sort of thing?

SIMON. No idea.

STEPHEN (*after a pause*). Well, I must say!

SIMON. Oh, he's not as thick as he seems.

STEPHEN. Isn't he? He certainly seems quite thick. (*Sits down.*) I'm surprised a student could afford that flat, what do you charge him?

SIMON. Two pounds a week, I think.

STEPHEN. But you could get, good Heavens, even through the rent tribunal, ten times that.

SIMON. Oh, we're not out to make money from it.

STEPHEN. Well, *he* seems rather an odd choice for your charity, with so many others in real need. Beth's not here, then?

SIMON. No, she's taken some of her foreign students to Canterbury.

STEPHEN. Did she go with that teacher she was telling Teresa about?

SIMON. Chap called Ned?

STEPHEN. Yes.

SIMON. Yes.

STEPHEN. What do you think of him?

SIMON. Oh, rather a wry, sad little fellow. Bit of a failure, I'd say, from what I've seen of him.

STEPHEN. A failure? In what way?

SIMON. Oh, you know, teaching English to foreigners.

STEPHEN. So does Beth.

SIMON. True, but Beth isn't a middle-aged man with ginger hair, a pigeon-toed gait, a depressed-looking wife and four children to boot.

STEPHEN. You know, sometimes I can't help wondering how people describe me. A middle-aged public school teacher with five children to boot. A bit of a failure too, eh? Anyhow, that's how I feel today.

SIMON. Why, what's the matter?

STEPHEN. That damned interview.

SIMON. Interview?

STEPHEN. For the Assistant Headmastership. You'd forgotten then!

SIMON. No, no of *course* I hadn't. When is it exactly?

STEPHEN (*looks at him*). Yesterday.

SIMON. Good God! Was it really? Well, what happened?

STEPHEN. I didn't get it.

SIMON. Well, who did?

STEPHEN. A chap called MacGregor. And quite right too, as he's already Assistant Headmaster of a small public school in Edinburgh, very capable, written a couple of text books - in other words he's simply the better man for the job.

SIMON. I don't see what that's got to do with it. I don't know how your Headmaster had the face to tell you.

STEPHEN. Oh, he didn't. Nobody's had the face or the grace. Yet.

SIMON. Then how do you know he's got it.

STEPHEN. It was written all over MacGregor. I've never seen anyone so perky after an interview.

SIMON. Oh good God, is that all? Of course he was perky. He's a Scot isn't he? They're always perky. Except when they're doleful. Usually they're both at once.

STEPHEN. If you'd seen him come bouncing down the library steps.

SIMON. In my experience a bouncing candidate is a rejected candidate. No, no, Steve, my money's on your paddle feet. (*He sits.*)

STEPHEN. Even though my interview lasted a mere half hour

although his lasted fifty-seven minutes? Even though I fluffed my mere half hour, and before a hostile board. Do you know, one of the Governors couldn't get over the fact that I'd taken my degree at Reading. He was unable to grasp that Reading was a university even, he referred to it as if it were some cut-price institution where I'd scraped up some - some diploma on the cheap. MacGregor went to Oxford, needless to say.

SIMON. Did he? Which college?

STEPHEN. And then another Governor harped on the number of our children - he kept saying *five* children, eh? Like that. Five children, eh? As if I'd had - I don't know - five - five -

SIMON. Cheques returned.

STEPHEN. What?

SIMON. That's what you made it sound as if he sounded as if he were saying.

STEPHEN. Anyway, there were the two Governors manifestly hostile.

SIMON. Out of how many?

STEPHEN. Two.

SIMON. Ah, but then your Headmaster was on your side.

STEPHEN. Perhaps. (*Pause.*) At least until I succeeded in putting him off.

SIMON. How?

STEPHEN. By doing something I haven't done since I was twelve years old.

SIMON (*after a pause*). Can you be more specific?

STEPHEN. You will of course laugh, for which I shan't of course blame you, but I'm not sure that I can stand it if you do laugh at the moment. It was something very trivial, but also very embarrassing. (*Pause.*) You see, the Governor who didn't feel Reading was up to snuff had a rather low, husky voice, and towards the end I bent forward, rather sharply, to catch something he said, and this movement caused me to fart.

They stare levelly at each other. SIMON'S *face is completely composed.*

SIMON. You haven't farted since you were twelve?

STEPHEN. In public, I meant.

SIMON. Oh. Loudly?

STEPHEN. It sounded to me like a pistol shot.

SIMON. The question, of course, is what it sounded like to Headmaster.

STEPHEN. Like a fart, I should think.

SIMON. Oh, he probably found it sympathetically human, you've no grounds for believing he'd hold anything so accidental against you, surely?

STEPHEN. I don't know, I simply don't know. (*He gets up.*) But afterwards when he had us around for some of his wife's herbal coffee -

SIMON. Herbal coffee?

STEPHEN. They paid far more attention to MacGregor than they did to me. I had to struggle to keep my end up. Headmaster was distinctly aloof in his manner - and MacGregor, of course, was relaxed and I suppose a fair man would call it charming.

SIMON. What herbs does she use?

STEPHEN. What? What's that got to do with it? How would I know.

SIMON. Sorry, I was just trying to imagine the - the setting, so to speak.

STEPHEN. You know, what really hurts is that I can't complain that it's unfair. MacGregor really is better qualified, quite obviously an admirable bloke. But what I do resent, and can't help resenting, is the edge Oxford gives him - the simple fact that he went there improves his chances - but I suppose that's the way of the world, isn't it? Almost everybody goes along with it, don't they?

SIMON. Oh, I don't know -

STEPHEN. Of course you know. You subscribe to it yourself, don't you?

SIMON. Certainly not. Why should I?

STEPHEN. Because you went to Oxford yourself.

SIMON. Good God, so what?

STEPHEN. Well, how many other members of your editorial board also went there?

SIMON. Only five.

STEPHEN. Out of how many?

SIMON. Eight.

STEPHEN. And where did the other three go, Cambridge?

SIMON. Only two of them.

STEPHEN. And so only *one* of the nine went elsewhere?

SIMON. No, he didn't go anywhere. He's the Chairman's son.

STEPHEN. I think that proves my point.

SIMON. It proves merely that our editorial board is composed of Oxford and Cambridge graduates, and a half-wit. It proves absolutely nothing about your chances of beating MacDonald to the Assistant Headmastership. And it's my view that poor old MacDonald, whether he be Oxford MacDonald or Cambridge MacDonald or Reading MacDonald or plain Edinburgh MacDonald -

STEPHEN. MacGregor.

SIMON. What?

STEPHEN. His name happens to be MacGregor.

SIMON. Absolutely. Has no chance at all. Even if they do believe you have too few qualifications and too many children, even if they suspect that your single fart heralds chronic incontinence, they'll still have to appoint you. And if they've been extra courteous to MacDonald it's only to compensate him for coming all the way from Edinburgh for a London rebuff. (*Stands up.*)

STEPHEN. Actually it would be better, if you don't mind, not to try and jolly me along with reasons and reassurances. I shall have to face the disappointment sooner or later, and I'd rather do it sooner - wouldn't you?

SIMON. No, I have a distinct preference for later, myself. I really do think you'll get it you know.

STEPHEN. Yes, well thanks anyway. I'd better get back. What time's your friend coming?

SIMON. What friend?

STEPHEN. When I phoned and asked whether I could come round, you said it mightn't be worth my while as you were expecting a friend.

SIMON. Good God! Yes. Still, he's one of those people who never turns up when expected. So if I remember to expect him I should be all right.

STEPHEN. You mean you don't want him to turn up? Who is he anyway?

SIMON. Jeff Golding.

STEPHEN. Oh *him*! Yes, well I must say that piece he wrote in one of last week's Sundays, on censorship and children - I've never read anything so posturingly half-baked.

SIMON. Oh, I doubt if he was posturing, he really is half-baked.

STEPHEN. I shall never forget - never - how he ruined the dinner party - the one time I met him - his drunkenness and his appalling behaviour. And I shall particularly never forget his announcing that people - he meant me, of course - only went into public school teaching because they were latent pederasts.

SIMON. Good God, what did you say?

STEPHEN. I told him to take it back.

SIMON. And did he?

STEPHEN. He offered to take back the latent, and congratulated me on my luck. That was his idea of badinage. By God I don't often lose control but I made a point of cornering him in the hall when he was leaving. I got him by the lapels and warned him that I'd a good mind to beat some manners into him. If Teresa hadn't happened to come out of the lavatory just then - she'd rushed in there in tears - I might have done him some damage. I've never told you that bit before, have I?

SIMON. You haven't told me any of it before, it's very amusing. Tell me, who gave this memorable dinner party?

STEPHEN. You did.

SIMON. Did I really? I don't remember it. It must have been a long time ago.

STEPHEN. Yes, but I have a feeling your friend Jeff Golding will remember it all right.

The front door slams and JEFF GOLDING *enters left.*

JEFF. Simon - ah, there you are.

There is a pause.

Weren't you expecting me?

SIMON. I most certainly was. Oh, my brother Stephen - Jeff Golding. I believe you know each other.

STEPHEN. We do indeed.

JEFF. Really? Sorry, 'fraid I don't remember.

STEPHEN. A dinner party Simon gave - some years ago.

JEFF (*clearly not remembering at all*). Nice to see you again. Could I have a scotch please? (*To* SIMON.)

SIMON. Of course. (*Goes to the drinks table.*) Steve?

STEPHEN. No thank you.

JEFF (*collapses into a chair*). Christ! Christ! I've just had a session at the Beeb, taping a piece with Bugger Lampwith. I've got the goods on him at last.

STEPHEN. Lampwith. Isn't he a poet?

JEFF. Not even. He's an Australian. A closet Australian. Went to Oxford instead of Earl's Court. Thinks it makes him one of us. Still, I got him out of his closet with his vowels around his tonsils, once or twice. Thrice, actually. (*Laughs at the recollection.*)

STEPHEN. What exactly have you got against him?

JEFF. Isn't that enough?

STEPHEN. Simply that he's an Australian?

JEFF. They're all right as dentists.

STEPHEN. But could you please explain to me why you have it in for Australians.

JEFF. Once you let them into literature they lower the property values.

STEPHEN. Really? How?

JEFF. They're too fertile, scribble, scribble, scribble like little Gibbons. They breed whole articles out of small reviews, don't

mind what work they do, go from sports journalists to movie
critics to novelists to poets to television pundits, and furthermore they don't mind how little they get paid as long as they
fill our space. So you see if there weren't any Australians
around sods like me wouldn't end up having to flog our crap
to the Radio Times and even the Shiterary Supplement, let
alone spend Saturday morning interviewing buggers like
Bugger Lampwith.

STEPHEN. We've got half a dozen Australian boys in our school
at the moment. They're not only friendly, frank and outgoing,
they're also intelligent and very hard-working.

JEFF. Exactly, the little buggers. Hey! (*To* SIMON.) Roger's
been going around telling people I can't face him since my
review of his turgid little turd of a novel. Have you read it?

SIMON. Which?

JEFF. My review - first things first.

SIMON. Yes, I did.

JEFF. Well?

SIMON. Some good jokes, I thought.

JEFF. Weren't there? And what did you honestly, frankly and
actually think of his turd?

SIMON. I haven't read it.

JEFF. Didn't you publish it?

SIMON. Yes.

JEFF. Well, if you ask me, the blokie you got to write the blurb
hadn't read it either, bloody sloppy piece of crap, who did it
anyway?

SIMON. Actually I did.

JEFF. D'you know what it bloody is - I'll tell you what it bloody
is - I wish I'd come out with it straight when I wrote about
it - it's a piece of - *literature*, that's what it bloody is!

STEPHEN. You don't like literature?

JEFF (*a pause*). I don't like literature, no.

STEPHEN. Why not?

JEFF. Because it's a bloody boring racket.

STEPHEN. You think literature is a *racket*?

JEFF. Are you in it too?

STEPHEN. I happen to teach it, it so happens.

JEFF. Does it, Christ! To whom?

STEPHEN. Sixth formers. At Amplesides.

JEFF. What's Amplesides?

STEPHEN. It happens to be a public school.

JEFF. Does it? Major or minor?

STEPHEN. Let's just say that it's a good one, if you don't mind.

JEFF. I don't mind saying it even if it's not. It's a good one. Christ, I can't remember when I last met a public school teacher.

STEPHEN. Probably when you last met me.

JEFF. But I don't remember that, don't forget.

STEPHEN. Would you like me to remind you? I'm the latent pederast.

JEFF (*after a pause*). Then you're in the right job.

STEPHEN (*to* SIMON). I think I'd better go. Before I do something I regret. (*Turns and goes out through kitchen.*)

SIMON. Oh right. (*Making an attempt to follow* STEPHEN.) Love to Teresa and the kids. (*Calling it out.*)

Sound of door slamming. JEFF *helps himself to another scotch.*

JEFF. Seems a real sweetie, what's he like in real life?

SIMON. Not as stupid as he seems.

JEFF. That still leaves him a lot of room to be stupid in.

SIMON. He *is* my brother.

JEFF. I'm very sorry.

SIMON. Actually, the last time he met you, he offered to fight you.

JEFF. Then he's matured since then. Where's Beth?

SIMON. Gone to Canterbury.

JEFF. With her woggies?

SIMON. Yes.

JEFF. Never seem to see her these days. You two still all right, I take it?

SIMON. Yes, thanks.

JEFF. Christ, you're lucky, don't know how you do it. She's so bloody attractive of course, as well as nice and intelligent. I suppose that helps.

SIMON. Yes, it does really.

JEFF. And she's got that funny little moral streak in her - she doesn't altogether approve of me, I get the feeling. Even after all these years. Christ, women! Listen there's something I want to talk to you about, and I'll just lay down the guide-lines of your response. What I want from you is an attentive face and a cocked ear, the good old-fashioned friendly sympathy and concern for which you're celebrated, O bloody K?

SIMON. Well, I'll do my best.

JEFF. Remember Gwendoline?

SIMON. Gwendoline, no. Have I met her?

JEFF. Hundreds of times.

SIMON. Really, where?

JEFF. With me.

SIMON. Oh. Which one was she - to tell you the truth, Jeff, there've been so many that the only one I still have the slightest recollection of is your ex-wife.

JEFF. Are you sure?

SIMON. Absolutely.

JEFF. Well, that was Gwendoline.

SIMON. Oh, I thought her name was Gwynyth.

JEFF. Why?

SIMON. What?

JEFF. Why should you think her name was Gwynyth?

SIMON. Wasn't she Welsh?

JEFF. No, she bloody was not Welsh.

SIMON. Well, I haven't seen her for years, don't forget, not since the afternoon you threw your drink in her face and walked out on her.

JEFF. And that's all you remember?

SIMON. Well, it *did* happen in my flat, a lunch party you asked me to give so that you could meet the then Arts Editor of the Sunday Times, and you did leave her sobbing on my bed, into my pillow, with the stink of scotch everywhere –

JEFF. Don't you remember anything else about my Gwendoline days, for Christ's sake? What I used to tell you about her?

SIMON (*thinks*). Yes. You used to tell me that she was the stupidest woman I'd ever met.

JEFF. *You'd* ever met.

SIMON. Yes.

JEFF. And was she?

SIMON. Yes.

JEFF. Well, you've met some stupider since, haven't you?

SIMON. Probably, but fortunately I can't remember them either.

JEFF. So you rather despised my poor old Gwendoline, did you?

SIMON. Absolutely. So did you.

JEFF. Then why do you think I married her?

SIMON. Because of the sex.

JEFF. Did I tell you that too?

SIMON. No, you told her that, once or twice, in front of me.

JEFF. Christ, what a bloody swine of a fool I was. (*Pours himself another drink.*) Well, now I'm suffering for it, aren't I? Listen, a few months ago I bumped into her in Oxford Street. I hadn't given her a thought in all that time, and suddenly there we were, face to face, looking at each other. For a full minute just looking. And do you know something, she cried. And I felt as if we were – Christ, you know – still married. But in the very first days of it, when we couldn't keep our hands off each other. In a matter of minutes.

SIMON. Minutes?

JEFF. Minutes. Bloody minutes. All over each other.

SIMON. In *Oxford* Street.

JEFF. I'll tell you - I put my hand out, very slowly, and stroked her cheek. The tears were running down, her mouth was trembling - and she took my hand and pressed it against her cheek. Then I took her to Nick's flat - he's still in hospital by the way.

SIMON. Really? I didn't know he'd gone in.

JEFF. They're trying aversion therapy this time, but it won't do any good. He's so bloody addictive that he'll come out hooked on the cure and still stay hooked on the gin, poor sod. Saline chasers. Anyway, I took her to Nick's, and had her, and had her, and had her. Christ! And when she left what do you think I did?

SIMON. Slept, I should think.

JEFF. I cried, that's what I did. Didn't want her to leave me, you see. I'm in love with her. I think I love her. And since then there have been times when I've thought I even liked her. Well?

SIMON. Well Jeff, that's marvellous. Really marvellous.

JEFF. Oh yes, bloody marvellous to discover that you want to marry your ex-wife.

SIMON. But why ever not? It just confirms that you were right the first time. Why not marry her?

JEFF (taking another drink). Because she's got a new bloody husband, that's why. In fact not so new, five years old. A bloody don in Cambridge called Manfred. Christ knows why he had to go and marry her!

SIMON. Perhaps he likes sex too.

JEFF. According to Gwen he likes TV situation comedies, football matches, wrestling, comic books, horror films and sadistic thrillers, but not sex.

SIMON. What does he teach?

JEFF. Moral sciences.

SIMON. Then there's your answer. Philosophers have a long tradition of marrying stupid women, from Socrates on. They think it clever. Does she love him?

JEFF. Of course she does, she loves everyone. But she loves me most. Except for their bloody child. She bloody dotes on the bloody child.

SIMON. Oh. How old is it?

JEFF. Two - three - four - that sort of age.

SIMON. Boy or girl?

JEFF. Can't really tell. The one time I saw it, through my car window, it was trotting into its nursery school with its arm over its face, like a mobster going to the grand jury.

SIMON. Haven't you asked Gwen which it is?

JEFF. Yes, but only to show interest. Anyway, what does it matter, what matters is she won't leave Manfred because of it. She's *my* wife, not his, I had her first, and she admits as much, she'll always be mine, but all I get of her is two goes a week when I drive up to Cambridge - Tuesdays and Thursdays in the afternoon when Manfred's conducting seminars. In the rooms of some smartie-boots theologian.

SIMON (*pacing up and down*). Do you mean Manfred conducts his seminars in the rooms of some smartie-boots theologian or you have Gwen in the rooms of some smartie-boots theologian?

JEFF. I have Gwen there. He's a friend of Manfred's you see.

SIMON. So Manfred's asked him to let you use his rooms?

JEFF. Oh no, Manfred doesn't know anything about it. Or about me. No, smartie-boots seems to have some idea that it's part of his job to encourage what he calls sin. Oh Christ, you know the type, a squalid little Anglican queen of a pimp the little sod. Turns my stomach. (*Adds more scotch.*) Christ, you know, Simon, you want to know something about me?

SIMON. What? (*Sinks into an armchair.*)

JEFF. I'm English, yes, English to my marrow's marrow. After years of buggering about as a cosmopolitan literateur, going to PEN conferences in Warsaw, hob-nobbing with Frog poets and Eyetye essayists, German novelists and Greek composers, I suddenly realise I hate the lot of them. Furthermore I detest women, love men, loathe queers. D'you know when I'm really at bloody peace with myself? When I'm caught in a traffic jam on an English road, under an English heaven - somewhere between London and Cambridge, on my way to Gwen, on my way back from her, rain sliding down the window, engine humming, dreaming - dreaming of what's past or is to come.

Wrapped in the anticipation or the memory, no, the anticipation *of* the memory. (*Pause.*) Oh Christ - it's my actual bloody
opinion that this sad little, bloody little country of ours is
finished at last. Bloody finished at last. Yes, it truly is bloody
well actually finished at last. I mean that. Had the VAT man
around the other day. That's what we get now instead of the
muffin man. I remember the muffin men, I'm old enough to
remember the muffin men. Their bells and smells and lighting
of the lamps - do you remember? Sometimes I even remember
hansom cabs and crinoline, the music halls and Hobbes and
Sutcliffe . . . (*Smiles.*) Or the memory of the anticipation, I
suppose. Stu Lampwith. Christ, the bugger! (*Pause.*) Well
Christ - I suppose I'd better go and write my piece. (*He gets to
his feet.*) Did I tell you what that cold-hearted bitch said last
night, in bed? Christ!

SIMON. Who?

JEFF. What?

SIMON. What cold-hearted bitch?

JEFF. Davina. (*Takes another scotch.*)

SIMON. Davina?

JEFF. You don't know about Davina?

SIMON (*wearily*). No.

JEFF. You haven't met her?

SIMON. No, no - I don't think -

JEFF. But Christ, I've got to tell you about bitch Davina. (*Sits
down.*)

SIMON. Why?

JEFF. Because she is actually and completely the most utterly
and totally - (*Lifts his hand.*)

There is a ring at the door-bell.

What?

SIMON. Just a minute, Jeff. (*Goes to the door, opens it.*)

DAVINA. Hello, is Jeff here, by any chance? (*JEFF groans in
recognition and sits down on the sofa.*)

SIMON. Yes, yes he is. Come in.

(DAVINA *enters.* JEFF *ignores her.*)

DAVINA. I'm Davina Saunders. (*To* SIMON.)

SIMON. I'm Simon Hench.

DAVINA. I know.

There is a pause.

SIMON. Would you like a drink?

DAVINA. Small gin and bitters, please.

SIMON *goes across to the drinks table.*

JEFF. How did you know I was here?

DAVINA. You said you would be.

JEFF. Why did I tell you?

DAVINA. Because I asked you.

JEFF. But why did I tell you. Because you see, I wanted a quiet conversation with my friend, Simon, you see.

DAVINA. You're all right then, are you?

JEFF. What? (*A pause.* SIMON *brings* DAVINA *her drink.*)

DAVINA. How did the interview go?

JEFF. All right.

DAVINA. What's he like?

JEFF. Who?

DAVINA. Bugger Lampwith.

JEFF. OK.

DAVINA. What's OK about him?

JEFF. He's all right.

DAVINA. Good.

JEFF. What do you mean, good?

DAVINA. That he's all right. (*Sits down.*)

JEFF. Well, what d'you want me to say, you follow me across bloody London, you turn up when I'm having a private bloody conversation with my old friend Simon, you're scarcely in the room before you ask me whether I'm drunk -

DAVINA. As a matter of sober precision, I did not ask you

whether you were drunk. I asked you whether you were all right.

JEFF. Then as a matter of drunken precision, no, I'm not all right, I'm drunk.

DAVINA. That's surprising, as with you being all right and being drunk are usually precisely synonymous.

JEFF. But now you're here, aren't you, and that alters everything, doesn't it?

DAVINA. Does it?

JEFF. I thought you were going to spend the morning at the British Bloody Museum. I thought we'd agreed not to see each other for a day or two, or even a year or two -

There is a pause.

SIMON. What are you doing at the BM, some research?

JEFF. That's what she's doing. On Major Bloody Barttelot. Got the idea from *my* review of that Life of Stanley - naturally.

SIMON. Really, and who is Major Bloody Barttelot?

DAVINA. Major Barttelot went with Stanley to the Congo, was left in a camp to guard the Rear Column, and ended up flogging, shooting, and even, so the story goes, eating the natives.

JEFF. Pleasant work for a woman, eh?

SIMON. Major Barttelot was a *woman*?

DAVINA. He was an English gentleman. Although he did find it pleasant work from what I've discovered, yes.

SIMON. Really? And are you planning a book?

JEFF. Of course she is, cannibalism, sadism, doing down England all at the same time, how can it miss? Why do you think she's on to it?

SIMON. I must say it sounds quite fascinating. Who's your publisher?

DAVINA. I haven't got one yet.

JEFF. Is that what summoned you away from the BM, the chance of drawing up a contract with my old friend, the publisher Simon? (*Refills his glass.*)

DAVINA. Actually, I haven't been to the BM this morning. I've been on the telephone. And what summoned me here was first that I wanted to give you your key back. (*Throws it over to him.*)

JEFF (*makes no attempt to catch it*). Thank you.

DAVINA. And secondly to tell you about the telephone call.

JEFF. What? Who was it?

DAVINA. Your ex-wife's husband. Manfred.

JEFF. What did he want?

DAVINA. You.

JEFF. Why?

DAVINA. He wanted you to know the contents of Gwendoline's suicide letter.

JEFF (*after a pause*). What? Gwendoline - what - Gwen's dead!

SIMON. Good God!

DAVINA. No.

JEFF. But she tried - tried to commit suicide?

DAVINA. Apparently.

JEFF. What do you mean apparently, you mean she failed?

DAVINA. Oh, I'd say she succeeded. At least to the extent that Manfred was hysterical, I had a wastefully boring morning on the telephone, and you look almost sober. What more could she expect from a mere bid, after all?

JEFF. For Christ sake, what happened, what actually happened?

DAVINA. Well, Manfred's narrative was a trifle rhapsodic.

JEFF. But you said there was a letter.

DAVINA. He only read out the opening sentences - he was too embarrassed by them to go on.

JEFF. Embarrassed by what?

DAVINA. Oh, Gwendoline's epistolary style, I should think. It was rather shaming.

JEFF. Look, where is she?

DAVINA. In that hospital in Cambridge probably. And if you're thinking of going up there, you should reflect that Manfred is looking forward to beating you to a pulp. A *bloody* pulp was his phrase, and unlike yourself he seems to use the word literally, rather than for rhetorical effect or as drunken punctuation. I like people who express themselves limpidly (*to* SIMON) under stress, don't you?

JEFF (*throws his drink at her, splashing her blouse, etc.*). Is that limpid enough for you?

DAVINA. No, tritely theatrical, as usual. But if you're absolutely determined to go, and you might as well because what else have you to do? I advise you not to drive. Otherwise you may have to make do with one of the hospitals *en route*.

SIMON. Yes, you really shouldn't drive, Jeff . . .

> JEFF *turns, goes out, left, slamming the door. There is a pause.*

I'll get you something to wipe your shirt -

DAVINA. Don't bother, it's far too wet. But another drink please. (*Hands him her glass.*)

SIMON. Of course.

> *Takes it, goes to the drinks table.*
> DAVINA *takes off her shirt and throws it over a chair. She is bra-less. She goes to the large wall mirror, and dries herself with a handkerchief from her bag.*
> SIMON *turns with the drink, looks at* DAVINA, *falters slightly, then brings her her drink.*

DAVINA. God, what a stupid man, don't you think?

SIMON. Well, a bit excitable at times, perhaps.

DAVINA. No, stupid really, and in an all-round way. You know, when I was at Oxford one used to take his articles quite seriously - not very seriously but quite. But now of course one sees that his facility, though it may pass in the Arts pages as intelligence and originality, was something merely cultivated in late adolescence for the examination halls. He hasn't developed, in fact his Gwendoline syndrome makes it evident that he's regressed. Furthermore his drunken bravado quickly ceases to be amusing, on top of which he's a fourth-rate fuck.

SIMON. Oh well, perhaps he's kind to animals.

DAVINA (*sitting on the sofa*). To think I thought he might be

of some use to me. But of course he's out of the habit, if he
was ever in it, of talking to women who like to think and
therefore talk concisely, for whom intelligence does actually
involve judgement, and for whom judgement concludes in
discrimination. Hence the appeal, I suppose, of a pair of tits
from which he can dangle, with closed eyes and infantile
gurglings. Especially if he has to get to them furtively, with a
sense of not being allowed. Yes, stupid, don't you agree?

SIMON. Did you really go to Oxford?

DAVINA. Came down two years ago, why?

SIMON. From your style you sound more as if you went to
   Cambridge.

DAVINA. Anyway, he's nicely gone, you will admit, and four
   bad weeks have been satisfactorily concluded.

SIMON. Aren't you a little worried about him, though?

DAVINA. Why should I be?

SIMON. Well, Manfred did threaten to beat him to a bloody
   pulp, after all. And it may not be an idle boast. Men whose
   wives attempt suicide because of other men sometimes become
   quite animated, even if they are moral scientists.

DAVINA. Oh, I think the wretched Manfred will be more
   bewildered than belligerent. I composed that fiction between
   Great Russell Street and here. Of course I didn't know until
   I met his glassy gaze and received his boorish welcome
   whether I was actually going to work it through. It was quite
   thrilling, don't you think?

SIMON. You mean, Gwendoline didn't try to commit suicide?

DAVINA. Surely you don't imagine that *that* complacent old
   cow would attempt even an attempted suicide?

SIMON. Why did you do it?

DAVINA. Spite of course. Well, he told me he wanted to bring
   it all to a climax, although he wanted no such thing of course,
   prolonged and squalid messes that lead least of all to climaxes
   being his method, so my revenge has been to provide him
   with one that should be exactly in character - prolonged,
   squalid and utterly messy even by Cambridge standards, don't
   you think? *You're* married, aren't you? To Beth, isn't it?

SIMON. That's right.

DAVINA. I've only just realized she isn't here, is she?

SIMON. Well, I suppose that's better than just realizing she was, isn't it?

DAVINA. I'd like to have met her. I've heard a great deal about you both, you mainly, of course. Are you two as imperturbably, not to say implacably *married* as he and everyone else says?

SIMON. I hope so.

DAVINA. And that you've never been unfaithful to Beth, at least as far as Jeff knows.

SIMON. Certainly never that far.

DAVINA. Don't you even fancy other women?

SIMON (*sits in the armchair*). My not sleeping with other women has absolutely nothing to do with not fancying them. Although I do make a particular point of not sleeping with women I don't fancy.

DAVINA. That's meant for me, is it?

SIMON. Good God, not at all.

DAVINA. You mean you do fancy me?

SIMON. I didn't mean that either.

DAVINA. But do you fancy me?

SIMON. Yes.

DAVINA. But you don't like me?

SIMON. No.

DAVINA. Ah, then do you fancy me *because* you don't like me? Some complicated set of manly mechanisms of that sort, is it?

SIMON. No, very simple ones that Jeff, for instance, would fully appreciate. I fancy you because of your breasts, you see. I'm revolted by your conversation and appalled by your behaviour. I think you're possibly the most egocentrically unpleasant woman I've ever met, but I have a yearning for your breasts. I'd like to dangle from them too, with my eyes closed and doubtless emitting infantile gurglings. Furthermore they look deceptively hospitable.

DAVINA. If they look deceptively hospitable, they're deceiving you. (*Comes over and sits on the arm of his chair.*) You're very welcome to a nuzzle (*Pause.*) Go on then. And then we'll see what *you* can do.

SIMON *sits, hesitating for a moment, then gets up, gets* DAVINA'S *shirt, hands it to her.*

Because of Beth?

SIMON. This is her house, as much as mine. It's *our* house, don't you see?

DAVINA. Fidelity means so much to you?

SIMON. Let's say rather more to me than a suck and a fuck with the likes of you. So, comes to that, does Jeff.

DAVINA. Yes, well I suppose that's to be expected in a friend of his. He doesn't begin to exist and nor do you.

SIMON. That's excellent. Because I haven't the slightest intention of letting you invent me.

DAVINA. And what about my Barttelot book?

SIMON. There I'm sure we shall understand each other. If it's any good, I shall be delighted to publish it. And if you've any sense, and you've got a hideous sight too much, you'll be delighted to let me. I shall give you the best advance available in London, arrange an excellent deal with an American publisher, and I shall see that it's edited to your advantage as well as ours. If it's any good.

DAVINA. That means more to me than being sucked at and fucked by the likes of you.

They smile. DAVINA *turns and goes out.*
SIMON, *with the air of a man celebrating, picks up the keys and glasses, puts them away. Makes to go to the gramophone, stops, goes to the telephone answering machine.*

SIMON (*records*). 348-0720, Simon Hench on an answering machine. I shall be otherwise engaged for the rest of the day. If you have a message for either myself or for Beth could you please wait until after the high-pitched tone, and if that hasn't put you off, speak. Thank you.

Puts the button down, then goes over to the gramophone, bends over to put a record on.

DAVE *enters,* SIMON *freezes, turns.*

DAVE. She didn't show.

SIMON. What?

DAVE. Suzy. My girl. She didn't show. You know what I'd like to do now, I'd like to get really pissed, that's what I'd like to do.

SIMON. I don't blame you, and furthermore, why don't you? You'll still catch the pubs if you hurry -

DAVE. Well, I'm a bit short, you see.

SIMON. But didn't you have a few pounds -

DAVE. Yeah, well I spent those.

SIMON. Oh, what on?

DAVE. Usual sort of stuff.

SIMON. Well then, let me. (*Pause.*) I've got just the thing.

Goes to the drinks table, fishes behind, takes out a bottle of Cyprus sherry.

Here. Go on, one of Beth's students gave it to her - it's yours. (*Hands it to* DAVE.) A Cyprus sherry. Nice and sweet. Now you settle down in some dark corner, with a receptacle by your side, and forget yourself completely. That's what I'd want to do if I were you. (*Points him towards the door.*)

DAVE *goes out.* SIMON *turns back to the hi-fi. Voices in the hall.*

DAVE (*opens the door*). Bloke here for you. (*Withdraws.*)

SIMON. What? (*Turns.*)

WOOD (*enters*). Mr Hench?

SIMON. Yes.

WOOD. Can you spare me a few minutes? My name is Wood. Bernard Wood.

SIMON (*as if recognising the name, then checks it*). Oh?

WOOD. It means something to you, then?

SIMON. No, just an echo. Of Birnam Wood, it must be, coming to Dunsinane. No, I'm very sorry, it doesn't. Should it?

WOOD. You don't recognise me either, I take it?

SIMON. No, I'm afraid not. Should I?

WOOD. We went to school together.

SIMON. Did we really, Wundale?

WOOD. Yes. Wundale. I was all of three years ahead of you, but I recall you. It should be the other way around, shouldn't it? But then *you* were very distinctive.

SIMON. Was I really, in what way?

WOOD (*after a little pause*). Oh, as the sexy little boy that all the glamorous boys of my year slept with.

SIMON (*after a pause*). But you didn't?

WOOD. No.

SIMON. Well, I do hope you haven't come to make good, because it's too late, I'm afraid. The phase is over, by some decades. (*Little pause, then with an effort at courtesy.*) I'm sure I would have remembered you, though, if we had slept together.

WOOD. Well, perhaps your brother Stephen, isn't it? would remember me as we were in the same year, how is he?

SIMON. Oh, very well.

WOOD. Married, with children?

SIMON. Yes.

WOOD. And you're married?

SIMON. Yes.

WOOD. Good. Children?

SIMON. No.

WOOD. Why not?

SIMON. There isn't enough room. What about you?

WOOD. Oh, as you might expect of someone like me. Married with children.

There is a pause.

SIMON. Well . . . um - you said there was something - ?

WOOD. Yes, there is. It's of a rather personal - embarrassing nature.

Pause.

SIMON (*unenthusiastically*). Would a drink help?

WOOD. Oh, that's very kind. Some sherry would be nice, if you have it.

SIMON. Yes, I have it.

WOOD. Then some sherry, if I may.

SIMON. Yes, you may. (*Pours* WOOD *a sherry.*)

WOOD. My many thanks. Your very good health. I thought you might have heard my name the day before yesterday.

SIMON. Oh, in what context?

WOOD. From my girl, Joanna. In your office, at about six in the evening.

SIMON. Joanna?

WOOD. She came to see you about getting work in publishing. She's only just left art school, but you were kind enough to give her an appointment.

SIMON. Oh yes, yes. I do remember a girl - I'm terrible about names, a nice girl, I thought.

WOOD. Thank you. How did your meeting go? Just between us?

SIMON. Well, I thought she was really quite promising.

WOOD. But you didn't make her any promises.

SIMON. Well, no, I'm afraid I couldn't. What work of hers she showed me struck me as a - a trifle over-expressive for our needs. (*Pause.*) Why, is her version of our, um, talk different, in any way?

WOOD. She hasn't said anything about it at all.

SIMON. I see. And you've come to me to find out about her potential?

WOOD. Not really, no. I've come to ask you if you know where she is.

SIMON. Have you lost her then?

WOOD. She hasn't been home since I dropped her off at your office.

SIMON. Well, I'm very sorry, but I haven't seen her since she left my office.

WOOD. I only have one rule with her, that she come home at night. Failing that, that at least she let me know where or with whom she is spending the night. Failing that, that at least she telephone me first thing in the morning. Could I be more unreasonably reasonable? So before doing the rounds among her pals, from Ladbroke Grove to Earls Court, I thought it might be worth finding out from you if she let anything slip about her plans.

SIMON. Nothing that I can remember.

WOOD. She didn't mention any particular friend or boy-friend?

SIMON. Just the usual references to this drip and that drip in the modern manner. Look, from what one makes out of today's youth, isn't it likely that she'll come home when she feels in the mood or wants a good meal, eh?

WOOD. I suppose so.

SIMON. I can quite understand your worry -

WOOD. Can you? No, I don't think you can.

SIMON. No, perhaps not. But I really don't see how I can help you any further.

WOOD. Did you have it off with her?

SIMON. What? *What*?

WOOD. Did you have it off with her?

SIMON. Look, Wood, whatever your anxiety about your daughter, I really don't think, old chap, that you should insinuate your-self into people's homes and put a question like that to them. I mean, good God, you can't possibly expect me to dignify it with an answer, can you?

WOOD. In other words, you did.

SIMON (*after a long pause*). In other words, I'm afraid I did. Yes. Sorry, old chap.

Curtain.

Act Two

Curtain up on exactly same scene, WOOD *and* SIMON *in exactly the same postures. There is a pause.*

WOOD. Tell me, does your wife know you do this sort of thing?

SIMON. Why, are you going to tell her?

WOOD. Oh, I'm not a sneak. Besides, Joanna would never forgive me. She'd have told me herself, you know. She always does. She thinks it's good for me to know what she and her pals get up to. Do you do it often. (*Smiling.*)

SIMON. Reasonably often. Or unreasonably, depending on one's point of view.

WOOD. And always with girls of my Joanna's age?

SIMON. There or thereabouts, yes.

WOOD. Because you don't love your wife?

SIMON. No, because I do. I make a point, you see, of not sleeping with friends, or the wives of friends, or acquaintances even. No one in our circle. Relationships there can be awkward enough -

WOOD. It's a sort of code, is it?

SIMON. No doubt it seems a rather squalid one, to you.

WOOD. So that's why you chose my Joanna, is it?

SIMON. I didn't really choose her, you know. She came into my office, and we looked at her work, and talked -

WOOD. Until everybody else had gone. You decided, in other words, that she was an easy lay. And wouldn't make any fuss, afterwards.

SIMON. I also realized that I couldn't possibly do her any harm.

WOOD. What about the clap? (*Pause.*) I think I have a right to know.

SIMON. I keep some pills at my office.

WOOD. So your post-coital period together was passed gobbling down anti-VD pills.

SIMON. One doesn't exactly gobble them - one swallows them, as one might digestive tablets.

WOOD. What about going back to your wife, reeking of sex?

SIMON. What?

WOOD. What do you do about the stench of your adulteries?

SIMON. I confess I find this enquiry into method rather depressing. I'd willingly settle for a burst of parental outrage -

WOOD. And I'd far rather satisfy my curiosity. Won't you please tell me?

SIMON. Very well. I stop off at my squash club, play a few points with the professional, then have a shower.

WOOD. But you don't suffer from any guilt afterwards? No post-coital distress, no angst or even embarrassment?

SIMON. Not unless this counts as afterwards.

WOOD. So really, only your sexual tastes have changed, your moral organism has survived intact since the days when you were that lucky sod, the Wundale Tart?

SIMON. Look, are you here because I slept around at thirteen, with the attractive boys of your year, or because I sleep around with attractive girls of your daughter's generation, at thirty-nine. Good God Wood, I'm beginning to find something frankly Mediterranean in this obsession with your child's sex-life - and mine - after all, let's face it, in the grand scheme of things, nothing much has happened, and in the Anglo-Saxon scheme of things, your daughter's well over the age of consent. That may sound brutal, but it's also true.

WOOD. Except in one important point. She's not my daughter.

SIMON. What? What is she then?

WOOD. My (*hesitates*) fiancée.

SIMON. Is it worth my saying sorry over again, or will my earlier apologies serve. (*Pause.*) But I thought you said her name was Wood -

WOOD. Yes.

SIMON. And your name is Wood.

WOOD. Yes. I changed my name as she refuses to change hers, and won't marry me.

SIMON. In that case you're not Wood of Wundale.

WOOD. No, I'm Strapley - Strapley of Wundale. Known as Wanker Strapley. Now do you remember me?

SIMON. Strapley - Strapley, Wanker Strapley. No.

WOOD. Well, your brother certainly would. He was known as Armpits Hench. We were two of a kind, in that we were both considered drips - what was the Wundale word for drip?

SIMON. I really can't remember.

WOOD. It was 'plop'.

SIMON. Plop.

WOOD. Those of us who were called it are more likely to remember it than those of you who called us it. Plop. Yes, I'm a plop, Hench. Whom one can now define, after so many years ploppily lived, as a chap who goes straight from mastur- bation to matrimony to monogamy.

SIMON. Oh, now there I think you're underestimating yourself. After all you have a wife, didn't you say, and now Joanna -

WOOD. I haven't got my wife any more. I doubt if I've got Joanna any more. But it's only appropriate that *you* should be the last common factor in our relationship. The first time I set eyes on her she reminded me of you.

SIMON. Where was that?

WOOD. At our local amateur theatricals. Joanna was playing in *The Winslow Boy*. She came on the stage in grey flannel bags, a white shirt and starched collar. She walked with a modest boy's gait, her eyes were wide with innocent knowledge. So did you walk down the Wundale Cloisters, that first year of yours. So I watched you then as I watched her. And there on my one side, were my two poor old sons, who've never reminded me of anyone but myself. And on the other, my poor old wife, the female plop, who from that second on ceased even to remind me that we shared a ploppy past. The years we'd spent together brooding over her mastoids, my haemorrhoids, and the mortgage on our maisonette, watching over our boys' sad little defeats, their failure to get into Wundale, their scrabbling for four O levels and then two A levels, their respective roles as twelfth man and scorer - they haven't even the competitiveness for sibling rivalry, poor old boys - all seemed, it all seemed such a waste, such a waste.

SIMON. But still you did succeed, to some extent at least, in breaking free. And you did succeed, to some extent I take it, with Joanna - so not altogether a case for predestination, when you think of it.

WOOD. Free meals, lots of gifts, little loans by the usual ploppy techniques of obligation and dependence - not that she felt dependent or obliged. She took what I offered and then asked for more. A generous nature. Did she get anything from you?

SIMON. She didn't ask for anything.

WOOD. Just as you never asked for anything from those boys - Higgens, Hornby, Darcy.

SIMON. It's true that Darcy was very kind with his tuck, but I hope I never took it as payment, nor did he offer it as such.

WOOD (*pause*). What was it like with Joanna?

SIMON. Well, it was, um, I'm sure you know - she's a very uninhibited um -

WOOD. It was, then, satisfactory?

SIMON. Well, as these things go.

WOOD. They don't for me. I'm incapacitated by devotion.

SIMON. But you live together?

WOOD. She allows me to share the flat I've leased for her. We have different rooms - I sometimes sit on the side of her bed when she's in it. More often when she's not.

SIMON. You're obviously in the grip of a passion almost Dante-esque in the purity of its hopelessness. You know, I really feel quite envious - for you every moment has its significance, however tortured, I just have to get by on my small pleasures and easy accommodations, my daily contentments -

WOOD. So she actually talks of me as a drip, does she?

SIMON. The ignorance of youth. Drips have neither your capacity for ironic self-castigation, nor more importantly your gift for the futile grand gesture.

WOOD. If she comes back, do you know what she'll do? She'll tell me about the boys she's slept with, the adults she's conned, the pot she's smoked. She'll tell me what a good time she had with you on your office floor -

SIMON. Sofa, actually.

WOOD. If she comes back. And I'll sit listening and yearning and just occasionally I'll soothe myself with the thought that one day she'll be dead, or even better old and unwanted and desperate - what I resent most about you, little Hench, is the way you seem to have gone on exactly as you promised you would at Wundale. If life catches up with everybody at the end, why hasn't it with you?

SIMON. But I haven't got to the end yet, thank God. I'm sure it will eventually.

WOOD. Sweet little Hench from Wundale, who picks off my Jo in an hour at his office, munches down a few pills, and then returns, without a worry in his head, the whole experience simply showered off, to his wife, who is doubtless quite attractive enough - is she?

SIMON. I find her quite attractive enough for me. Though taste in these matters -

WOOD. I'd like to kill you, Hench. Yes - kill you!

STEPHEN (*enters through the kitchen*). Si — (*sees* WOOD) Oh sorry, I didn't realise . . . Good God, it is, isn't it? Old Strapley, from Wundale?

WOOD. The name's Wood.

STEPHEN. Oh, sorry. You look rather like a chap who used to be at school with us, or rather me, in my year, Strapley.

WOOD. Really? What sort of chap was he?

STEPHEN. Oh actually, a bit of what we used to call a plop, wasn't he, Simon? So you're quite lucky not to be Strapley who almost certainly had a pretty rotten future before him. (*Laughs.*)

WOOD. Thank you for the sherry. (*Turns quickly, goes out.*)

SIMON. Not at all.

STEPHEN. I hope I haven't driven him off.

SIMON. Mmmm. Oh no, it's not you that's driven him off.

STEPHEN. What did he want?

SIMON. He was looking for somebody I once resembled. A case
of mistaken identity, that's all.

STEPHEN. Well, if he had been Strapley, he'd hardly have
changed at all, except that he's a quarter of a century older.
Poor old Wanker Strapley. (*Sits down.*)

There is a pause.

Well Si, you were quite right, of course.

SIMON. Mmmm?

STEPHEN. I got it.

SIMON. Got what?

STEPHEN. The Assistant Headmastership.

SIMON. Oh. Oh good! (*Pause.*) Goody.

STEPHEN. You can imagine how stunned I was. I was so
depressed when I got home, not only because I thought I'd
lost the appointment, but because of that friend of yours -

SIMON. What friend?

STEPHEN. Golding. Jeff Golding. That he didn't even remember
me, let alone what I'd threatened to do to him - and I could
hear the children quarrelling in the garden, the baby crying
in her cot, and when I sat down in the sitting-room there was
a piece in *The Times* on the phasing out of public schools and
private health, lumped together, and it all seemed - well!
Then Teresa called out. I couldn't face her, you know how
lowering her optimism can be - but I managed to drag myself
into the kitchen - she had her back to me, at the oven, cooking
up some nut cutlets for the childrens' lunch - and she said:
'Greetings, Assistant Headmaster of Amplesides.' Yes, Headmaster's wife had phoned while I was here, isn't that ironic?
I could hardly believe it. So. I crammed down a nut cutlet -

SIMON. What was it like?

STEPHEN. What?

SIMON. The nut cutlet.

STEPHEN. Oh, it was from one of Headmaster's wife's recipes. They're semi-vegetarian, you know.

SIMON. What did it *taste* like?

STEPHEN. Rather disgusting. But she's going to give us some more recipes if we like this one. Perhaps they'll be better.

SIMON. But you didn't like this one.

STEPHEN (*pause*). Aren't you pleased or even interested in my news?

SIMON. Of course I am.

STEPHEN. In spite of thinking MacDonald the better man? Well, you needn't worry about him, he's been offered a job too. As head of sixth form English.

SIMON. But you're head of sixth form English.

STEPHEN. Not any more. Headmaster reckons that with my new responsibilities I should step down from some of my teaching. I shall be head of fifth form English.

SIMON. Ah, fewer hours then.

STEPHEN. Actuallv more hours, but at fifth form level.

SIMON. Ah, less cerebration. That's even better. So - (*loses thread, picks it up*) so justice has been done to two excellent candidates.

STEPHEN. I shall still be senior to MacDonald, you know.

SIMON. Isn't his name MacGregor?

STEPHEN. Yes. (*Little pause.*) Thanks, Si. (*Ironically.*)

SIMON. What for?

STEPHEN. Sharing my triumph with me.

SIMON. Why don't you - have a drink.

STEPHEN. No, thank you. Headmaster's asked Teresa to ask me to look in after lunch for a celebration glass.

SIMON. Oh. Of what?

STEPHEN. Pansy wine, I expect, as that's their favourite tipple.

SIMON (*after a pause*). Do they make it themselves?

STEPHEN. Headmaster's wife's aunt's husband does.

SIMON. Does he? (*Little pause.*) What's it like?

STEPHEN. You know what it's like.

SIMON. No, I don't. What's it like?

STEPHEN. Why do you want to know what it's like?

SIMON. Because I can't imagine what it's like, I suppose.

STEPHEN. Oh yes you can. Oh yes you can.

> *Turns, goes out through the kitchen.* DAVE *enters left. He's slightly drunk. There is a pause.*

DAVE (*swaying slightly*). She's come. She's upstairs. She came all by herself.

SIMON. Who?

DAVE. That girl. Suzy. She dropped in for a cup of nescafe.

SIMON. That's very good news, Dave. But should you, now you've got her, leave her to have it all by herself. She sounds a highly-strung creature -

DAVE. Yeah, well the only thing is, I'm out of nescafe.

SIMON. Oh.

DAVE. Well, have you got any, man?

SIMON. No, I'm sorry, we don't drink it.

DAVE. Anything else?

SIMON. Nothing at all like nescafe, I'm afraid.

DAVE. What, no coffee at all?

SIMON. Oh yes, we've got coffee. But we use beans, a grinder, and a rather complicated filter process. Metal holders, paper cones -

DAVE. That'll do. Is it in the kitchen? (*He moves towards kitchen.*)

SIMON. Actually, it's rather a precious set.

DAVE. What? (*Returning.*)

SIMON. It's one of those few things I feel rather specially about.

DAVE. You mean you've got something against lending it to me?

SIMON. Not at all. The beans are in a sealed bag in an airtight tin -

DAVE. Oh yes you have. I can tell by your - your tone.

SIMON. My tone? Oh come now, Dave, that's only one possible gloss of my tone. No, you take the grinder, take the filters, the jug, the paper cones and the metal holders, and the coffee beans which come from a small shop in Holborn that keeps uncertain hours and can therefore be easily replaced with a great deal of difficulty, and don't addle your head with questions about my tone, good God! (*Pause.*) Go ahead. Please. (*Wearily.*)

DAVE. No thanks. No thank you! Because you do mind all right, you bloody mind all right.

SIMON. No, I don't.

DAVE. No, you don't, no, you don't bloody mind, do you - why should you, you've got it all already, haven't you? Machines for making coffee, a table covered with booze, crates of wine in your cellar, all the nosh you want, all the books you want, all the discs, the best hi-fi on the bloody market, taxis to work every morning, taxis home in the evening, a whole bloody house just for you and your sexy little wife - oh, you don't bloody mind anything you don't, what's there for you to mind, you shit you!

SIMON. Now that's not quite fair, Dave. It's not really a whole house, you know, since we converted the top floor at considerable expense and turned it over to you at an inconsiderable rent which you don't pay anyway. But then I don't mind that either.

DAVE. 'Course you bloody don't, why should you, you bloody like to run a pet, don't you, your very own special deserving case.

SIMON. I swear to you, Dave, I've never once thought of you as my pet or as a deserving case. If we'd wanted the former to occupy our upstairs flat we'd have got a monkey, and if we'd wanted the latter we'd have selected from among the unmarried mothers or the dispossessed old age pensioners. We thought quite hard about doing that, in fact.

DAVE. Then why didn't you?

SIMON. Because unmarried mothers mean babies, and babies mean nappies, and crying. While old age pensioners mean senility and eventual death.

DAVE. So I salve your bloody conscience without being a nuisance, eh? Right?

SIMON. Wrong. You salve my conscience by being a bloody nuisance. Your manners irritate me, your smell is unusually offensive, you're extremely boring, your sex-life is both depressing and disgusting, and you're a uniquely ungrateful cadge. But you really mustn't mind, because the point is that I don't, either. You have your one great value, that you run a poor third to recent births and imminent deaths.

DAVE. I'm not staying - I'm not staying - I'm not staying in the fucking top of your fucking house another fucking minute. You - you - (*Makes as if to hit* SIMON.)

SIMON *remains impassive.* DAVE *turns, goes out left. Noise of door slamming.* SIMON *closes door left. As he does so* STEPHEN *enters right.*

STEPHEN. It's sugary and tastes of onions. And it's quite revolting, just as you imagine.

SIMON. Well, I did imagine it would be revolting and probably sugary, but it never occurred to me it would taste of onions. But you can't have come back to report on its flavour already, you've only just left.

STEPHEN. I've been sitting in the car, thinking.

SIMON. What about?

STEPHEN. You, and your sneers. Oh, I don't altogether blame you, but I wish - (*sits down, looks at* SIMON) you'd had the guts to say it outright.

SIMON. Say what?

STEPHEN. That it's taken me twenty-four years to advance from Second Prefect of Wundale to Assistant Headmaster of Amplesides.

SIMON (*sitting down*). But that seems very respectable progress to me. At that rate you should make it to Eton, if it still exists, by your mid-fifties. And as that's what you want, why should I have a word to say against it?

STEPHEN. Nor against the way I'm doing it? My stuffing down nut cutlets, and herbal coffee and pansy wine. And then coming back for seconds.

SIMON. But you do rather more than eat the inedible and drink the undrinkable. You're among the best Junior Colts football managers in the country.

STEPHEN. You despise my job.

SIMON. You've a family to support.

STEPHEN. So you do despise my job, and despise me for doing it. Why don't you say it. That's all I'm asking you to do.

SIMON. But I don't want to say it! I can't remember when you were last as you've been today, or what I said then to make you feel any better. I wish I could, because that's what I'd like to say now.

STEPHEN. The last time I felt like this was eleven years ago, after Teresa had broken off our engagement, and you didn't say anything to make me feel any better. What you did say was that I was well out of it.

SIMON. Well, as you've been back in it for eleven years, you'll agree that it has little relevance now.

STEPHEN. It had little relevance then, either. As I was desperately in love with her.

SIMON. Good God, all I probably meant, and I don't even remember saying it, was that if she didn't want to marry you then it was better to be out of it before the wedding.

STEPHEN. Oh no, oh no, all you meant was that *you* were relieved to be out of it.

SIMON. Out of what?

STEPHEN. Out of having for your sister-in-law a girl you thought tedious and unattractive. And still do. And still do.

SIMON. Look Stephen, this is really rather eccentric, even in the English fratricidal tradition. First you hold it against me that I won't join you in abusing yourself, and then you hold it against me that not only did I fail to abuse your intended wife eleven years ago, but won't join you in abusing her now that she is your wife and has borne you seven children -

STEPHEN. Six children.

SIMON. Nearly seven.

STEPHEN. Nearly six.

SIMON. Well, straight after the sixth, it'll be nearly seven. (*He gets up.*)

STEPHEN. Teresa's absolutely right about you. She always has been. You're just indifferent. Absolutely indifferent!

SIMON. In what sense? As a wine is indifferent, or prepositionally, as in, say, indifferent to -

STEPHEN. Imbeciles like Teresa. Go on, say it!

SIMON. But I don't want to say it.

STEPHEN. Not to me, no. But that's what you tell your clever-clever metropolitan Jeff Goldings, isn't it? That Teresa and I are imbeciles.

SIMON. I swear to you, Stephen, I've never told a soul.

STEPHEN. Answer me one question, Simon. *One* question! What have you got against having children?

SIMON. Well Steve, in the first place there isn't enough room. In the second place they seem to start by mucking up their parents' lives, and then go on in the third place to muck up their own. In the fourth place it doesn't seem right to bring them into a world like this in the fifth place and in the sixth place I don't like them very much in the first place. OK.

STEPHEN. And Beth? What about her?

SIMON (*after a little pause*). Beth and I have always known what we're doing, thank you Stephen.

STEPHEN. You think she's happy, do you?

SIMON. Yes, I do. And let's not let you say another word about her, because I don't want to hear it. Have you got that, Steve, *I don't want to hear it. (With low emphasis.)*

STEPHEN. No, I'm sure you don't. I'm sure you don't. The last thing you want to hear is how unhappy she is.

SIMON. Steve!

STEPHEN. Well, she is! So unhappy that last week she came around to Teresa and sobbed her heart out!

SIMON. Steve!

STEPHEN. She's having an affair, Simon. An affair with that Ned whom you so much despise. *That's* how unhappy your happy Beth is.

There is a long pause.

SIMON. With Ned. (*Pause.*) Beth's having an affair with Ned? (*Pause.*) Really? With Ned? Good God! (*Sits down.*)

STEPHEN. It's time you knew.

SIMON. No it isn't.

There is a pause.

STEPHEN. I had to tell you.

SIMON. Now that's a different matter.

There is the sound of a door opening left. BETH *enters.*

BETH. Hello. Hello, Stephen.

STEPHEN. Hello, Beth.

SIMON (*goes over, gives* BETH *a kiss*). You're back nice and early, aren't you?

BETH. Yes, I got an earlier train.

SIMON. Ah, that explains it. How was it, then, old Salisbury?

BETH. Old *Canterbury*, actually. Much as it ever was, except for the parts they've turned into new Canterbury.

SIMON. But the Cathedral's still there?

BETH. Although the French students were more interested in the new Marks and Spencers.

SIMON. And Ned?

BETH. Oh, he preferred the Cathedral.

STEPHEN. I really must be getting along. Headmaster will be wondering what's happening to me.

SIMON. Oh,. but first you must tell Beth your news.

There is a slight pause.

The Assistant Headmastership, Steve.

STEPHEN. Oh. Oh yes. I got it.

BETH. Steve - how marvellous! (*Comes over, gives him a kiss.*) Congratulations - Teresa must be thrilled!

STEPHEN. Yes, she is. I've had some black moments since the interview, but she was absolutely sure - and old Si jollied me along a bit this morning. It's all a great relief, more than anything. Well, I really must dash - see you both very soon - (*goes towards the kitchen door*) Oh, by the way, Si - I was a bit carried away just now, spoke a lot of nonsense, don't know why I said it.

SIMON. Don't you?

STEPHEN. Yes, well I suppose I meant to hurt, but I didn't mean harm, if you see.

SIMON. Well then that's fine, because no harm's been done. I didn't take it seriously.

STEPHEN. Good. (*Hesitates, turns, goes out.*)

BETH. What did he say? (*Sits and lights a cigarette.*)

SIMON. Actually I could hardly make out - he was in a post-success depression, I think, suddenly realising that what he's got can therefore no longer be striven for. He'll be all right the moment he sets his sights on a full Headmastership. Or Amplesides is abolished. Triumph or disaster - you know, like a drug. What about tea or coffee?

BETH. No, I've had some, thanks.

SIMON. Where?

BETH. On the train.

SIMON. Oh, then you're probably still trying to work out which it was.

BETH. Did you enjoy your Wagner?

SIMON. I enjoyed some things about it, very much. The picture on its cover for example, its glossy and circular blackness when unsheathed, its light balance - and if the sound is any good it'll be quite perfect.

BETH. You haven't managed to play it then?

SIMON. Very nearly, very nearly. But what with Dave and Stephen, Jeff and Davina, the odd bod and sod, you know -

BETH. Oh, you poor thing, and you'd been looking forward to it all week.

SIMON. Still, one mustn't snatch at one's pleasures, nor over-plan them it seems. (*He puts the record away in its box.*)

BETH (*pause*). How was Jeff?

SIMON. Oh, in excellent form, really. He got drunk, threw his scotch in his girl's face, dashed off to Cambridge where he's been having it off with his ex-wife, Gwynyth. Did you know Gwynyth, or was she a little before your time?

BETH. Isn't it Gwendoline?

SIMON. Yes, yes, Gwendoline. Anyway, usual sort of Jeff saga, quite droll in its way.

BETH. And what's his girl like?

SIMON. She's got good tits and a nasty sense of humour.

BETH. And did she try to get you to bed?

SIMON. She did.

BETH. And how did you get out of it?

SIMON. Rudely, I'm afraid, as she's on to rather a good book, from the sound of it. Ah well -

BETH. Ah well, you can play your records now, can't you?

SIMON. Oh no. Wouldn't dream of it.

BETH. Why not?

SIMON. Well, for one thing, you hate Wagner.

BETH. Well, I'm going to have a bath.

SIMON. A four-hour bath?

BETH. Afterwards I've got to go along to the school - sort out the fares and docket them, that sort of thing.

SIMON. Ah! Well, in that case -

   SIMON *moves to hi-fi and takes out record.* BETH *rises, hesitates, and moves towards him.*

BETH (*stops, looks at* SIMON). Stephen told you, didn't he?

SIMON. Mmmm? Told me what?

BETH. About me. At least I hope he has.

SIMON. Why?

BETH. So I shan't have to tell you myself.

SIMON. You don't have to.

BETH. What?

SIMON. Tell me.

BETH. What?

SIMON. Tell me anything you don't want to tell me. Stephen said nothing of significance about anything.

BETH. But you see, I may not want to tell you, but I do want you to know.

SIMON. Why?

BETH. Because there's an important problem we shall have to discuss. And I want you to understand. (*Sits on sofa.*)

SIMON. In my experience, the worst thing you can do to an important problem is discuss it. You know - (*sitting down*) - I really do think this whole business of non-communication is one of the more poignant fallacies of our zestfully over-explanatory age. Most of us understand as much as we need to without having to be told - except old Dave, of course, now I thought he had quite an effective system, a tribute really to the way in which even the lowest amongst us can put our education (or lack of it, in Dave's case) and intelligence (or lack of it, in Dave's case) to serving our needs. He's done really remarkably well out of taking the metaphors of courtesy literally, as for example when he asks for a loan that is in fact a gift, and one replies, 'Of course, Dave, no trouble, pay it back when you can.' *But* this system completely collapses when he's faced with a plainly literal reply, as for example when he asks to borrow our coffee set, and he's told that it'll be lent with reluctance and one would like him to be careful with it. Weird, isn't it, he can take one's courteous metaphors literally, but he can't take one's literals literally, he translates them into metaphors for insults, and plans, I'm reasonably happy to inform you, to move out at once. So I've managed one useful thing today, after all. When we come to think of his replacement, let's narrow our moral vision slightly, and settle for a pair of respectably married and out of date homosexuals who still think they've something to hide. They'll leave us entirely alone, and we can congratulate ourselves on doing them a good turn. We'll have to raise the rent to just this side of exorbitant of course, or they'll smell something fishy, but we'll pass the money straight on to charities for the aged, unmarried mothers, that sort of thing and no one need be the wiser, what do you think?

BETH. In other words, you do know.

SIMON. In other words, can't we confine ourselves to the other words.

BETH. What did Stephen tell you? Please Simon.

SIMON. Nothing. Nothing, except for the odd detail, that I haven't known for a long time. So you see it's all right. Nothing's changed for the worst, though it might if we assume we have to talk about it.

BETH (*long pause*). How long have you known for?

SIMON. Oh - (*sighs*) about ten months it would be roughly. (*Pause.*) How long has it been going on for?

BETH. For about ten months, it would be. (*Pause.*) How did you know?

SIMON. There's no point, Beth -

BETH. Yes, there is. Yes, there is. How did you know?

SIMON. Well, frankly, your sudden habit, after years of admirable conversational economy on such day-to-day matters as what you'd done today, of becoming a trifle prolix.

BETH. You mean you knew I was having an affair because I became boring?

SIMON. No, no, over-detailed, that's all, darling. And quite naturally, as you were anxious to account for stretches of time in which you assumed I *would* be interested if I knew how you'd *actually* filled them, if you see, so you sweetly devoted considerable effort and paradoxically imaginative skill to rendering them - for my sake I know - totally uninteresting. My eyes may have been glazed but my heart was touched.

BETH. Thank you. And is that all you had to go on?

SIMON. Well, you have doubled your bath routine. Time was, you took one immediately before going out for the day. These last ten months you've taken one immediately on return too. (*Pause.*) And once or twice you've addressed me, when in the twilight zone, with an unfamiliar endearment.

BETH. What was it?

SIMON. Foxy. (*Little pause.*) At least, I took it to be an endearment. Is it?

BETH. Yes. I'm sorry.

SIMON. No, no, it's quite all right.

BETH. You haven't felt it's interfered with your sex-life then?

SIMON. On the contrary. *Quite* the contrary. In fact there seems to have been an increased intensity in your - (*gestures*) which I suppose in itself was something of a sign.

BETH. In what way?

SIMON. Well, guilt, would it be? A desire to make up -

BETH (*after a pause*). And did you know it was Ned, too?

SIMON. Ned *too*? Oh, did I also know it was Ned? No, that was the little detail I mentioned Stephen did provide. Ned. There I *was* surprised.

BETH. Why?

SIMON. Oh, I don't know. Perhaps because - well, no offence to Ned, whom I've *always* as you know thought of as a very engaging chap, in his way, no offence to *you* either, come to think of it, I'd just imagined when you did have an affair it would be with someone of more - more -

BETH. What?

SIMON. Consequence. *Overt* consequence.

BETH. He's of consequence to me.

SIMON. And *that's* what matters, quite.

BETH. What did you mean, when?

SIMON. Mmmm?

BETH. *When* I had an affair, you said.

SIMON. A grammatical slip, that's all. And since the hypothesis is now a fact -

BETH. But you used the emphatic form - when I *did* have an affair - which implies that you positively assumed I'd have an affair. Didn't you?

SIMON. Well, given your nature, darling, and the fact that so many people do have them these days, I can't see any reason for being bouleversé now that you're having one, even with Ned, can I put it that way?

BETH. Given what about my nature?

SIMON. It's marvellously responsive - warm, a warm, responsive nature. And then I realized once we'd taken the decision not to have children, - and the fact that you work every day and therefore meet chaps - and pretty exotic ones too, from lithe young Spanish counts to experienced Japanese businessmen - not forgetting old Ned himself - it was only realistic -

BETH. From boredom, you mean. You know I'm having an affair because I'm boring, and you assumed I'd have one from boredom. That's why I'm in love with Ned, is it?

SIMON. I'm absolutely prepared to think of Ned as a very, very lovable fellow. I'm sure *his* wife loves him, why shouldn't mine.

BETH. You are being astonishingly hurtful.

SIMON. I don't want to be, I don't want to be! That's why I tried to avoid this conversation, darling.

BETH. You'd like to go back, would you, to where I came in, and pretend that I'd simply caught the early train from Salisbury, and here I was, old unfaithful Beth, back home and about to take her bath, as usual?

SIMON. Yes, I'd love to. (*Little pause.*) I thought it was Canterbury.

BETH. It was neither. We spent the night in a hotel in Euston, and the morning in Ned's poky little office at the school, agonizing.

SIMON. Agonizing? Good God, did you really?

BETH. About whether we should give up everything to live together properly.

SIMON. Properly?

BETH. We want, you see, to be husband and wife to each other.

SIMON. Husband *and* wife to each other? Is Ned up to such double duty? And what did you decide?

BETH. Do you care?

SIMON. Yes.

BETH. His wife isn't well. She's been under psychiatric treatment for years. And his daughter is autistic.

SIMON. Oh. I'm sorry. I can quite see why he wants to leave them.

BETH. But I could still leave you.

SIMON. Yes.

BETH. But you don't think I will. Do you?

SIMON. No.

BETH. And why not?

SIMON. Because I hope you'd rather live with me than anybody else, except Ned of course. And I know you'd rather live with almost anyone than live alone.

BETH. You think I am that pathetic?

SIMON. I don't think it's pathetic. I'd rather live with you than anyone else, including Ned. And I don't want to live alone either.

BETH. But do you want to live at all?

SIMON. What?

BETH. As you hold such a deeply contemptuous view of human life. That's Ned's diagnosis of you.

SIMON. But the description of my symptoms came from you, did it?

BETH. He says you're one of those men who only give permission to little bits of life to get through to you. He says that while we may envy you your serenity, we should be revolted by the rot from which it stems. Your sanity is of the kind that causes people to go quietly mad around you.

SIMON. What an elegant paraphrase. Tell me, did you take notes?

BETH. I didn't have to. Every word rang true.

SIMON. But if it's all true, why do you need to keep referring it back to Ned?

BETH. It's a way of keeping in touch with him. If I forgot in the middle of a sentence that he's there and mine, I might begin to scream at you and claw at you and punch at you.

SIMON. But why should you want to do that?

BETH. Because I hate you.

The telephone rings. SIMON *makes a move towards it. After the fourth ring, it stops.*

SIMON. Oh, of course. I've put on the machine. (*Pause.*)

BETH (*quietly*). You know the most insulting thing, that you let me go on and on being unfaithful without altering your manner or your behaviour one - one - you don't care about me, or my being in love with somebody else, or my betraying you, good God! least of all that! But you do wish I hadn't actually *mentioned* it, because then we could have gone on, at least *you* could, pretending that everything was all right, no, not even pretending, as far as *you* were concerned, every-thing was all right, you probably still think it *is* all right - and - and - you've - you've - all those times we've made love, sometimes the very same evening as Ned and I - and yet you took me - in your usual considerate fashion, just as you take your third of a bottle of wine with dinner and your carefully measured brandy and your cigar after it, *and* enjoyed it all the more because I felt guilty, God help me *guilty* and so tried harder for your sake - and you *admit* that, no, not admit it, simply state it as if on the difference made by an extra voice or something in your bloody Wagner - don't you see, don't you see that that makes you a freak! You're - you're - oh, damn! Damn. Damn you. (*Pause.*) Oh, damn.

There is a silence.

So you might as well listen to your Wagner.

SIMON. I must say you've quite warmed me up for it. And what are *you* going to do, have your cleansing bath?

BETH. No, go to Ned for a couple of hours.

SIMON. Oh dear, more agonizing in his poky little office. Or is that a euphemism for Ned's brand of love-play? Excuse me, but what precisely has all this been about? You complain of my reticence over the last ten months, but what good has all this exposition served, what's it been for Beth? Ned's not going to leave his wife, I don't want you to leave me, you don't even think you're going to leave me - we have a perfectly sensible arrangement, we are happy enough together you and I, insultingly so if you like but still happy. We could go on and on, with Ned, until you've gone off him, why, why did you have to muck it up between you with your infantile agonizings.

BETH. Because there's a problem.

SIMON. What problem?

BETH. I'm going to have a baby.

SIMON (*stares at her for a long moment*). What? (*Another moment.*) Whose?

BETH. *That* is the problem. (*Goes out.*)

SIMON *sits in a state of shock.* DAVE *enters left.*

DAVE (*stands grinning at* SIMON). Well, I worked it out, you'll be unhappy to hear. Suzy put me onto you. She just laughed when I told her the stuff you'd said, she and her bloke had dealings with your type in their last place. You were trying to get me out, that's all. Well, it hasn't worked, see. I'm staying. See. And another thing, Suzy and her bloke are looking for a new place. I said they could move in upstairs with me. Got that? Got that? You won't like tangling with them either. (*Stares at* SIMON.) Having a bit of trouble sinking in, is it? (*Turns, goes out, leaving the door open.*)

SIMON *remains sitting, dazed. Then he goes to the drinks table, pours himself a small scotch. Looks at it. Frowns. Adds some more. Stands uncertainly, looks at the telephone, goes over to it. Remembers something vaguely, presses the play-back machine.*

WOOD (*his voice*). Hello, Hench, Bernard Wood, né Strapley here. I expect by now my little visit has passed entirely out of your consciousness, it was all of an hour ago that I left, and you've no doubt had any number of amusing little things to engage your attention. Your life goes on its self-appointed way, as I sit in my empty flat, my home. I've taken off my jacket, and I've lowered my braces so that they dangle around me - a picture, you might say, of old Wood, né Strapley, quite abandoned at the last. Imagine it, the jacket off, the braces down, thinking of you as I speak into the telephone, clasped tightly in my left hand as my right brings up, not trembling too much - Hench - sweet little Hench - and point the gun at my forehead - no, through the - no, I can't do the mouth, the metal tastes too intimate - it'll have to be

- picture it - picture it - and as I - as I - Hench, as I squeeze
- squee . . .

SIMON *switches off the machine, interrupting the message.*
He sits motionless.
JEFF *appears in the doorway left.*

SIMON (*sees him. Gets up slowly*). Ah yes. Jeff. Yes. All right,
are we then? Get back to - (*thinks*) Oxford, did you?

JEFF. I didn't get to the bloody corner.

SIMON. Oh really. Why not?

JEFF. There was a police car, Simon, right behind me, then
right beside me, then right on bloody top of me with the cops
all bloody over me, breathalysing me, shaking me about, and
then down at the station for the rest of it. That's why bloody
not. And you tipped the buggers off, friend, Christ!

SIMON. What? (*Vaguely.*) What?

JEFF. No, don't deny it, don't deny it, please Christ don't deny
it. Davina told me when I phoned her. She told me - you
tipped them off. Christ!

SIMON. Oh. (*Thinks.*) That's what you believe, is it?

JEFF. That's what I bloody know, Simon.

SIMON (*calmly*). What sort of man do you think I am? (*He
throws his scotch in* JEFF's *face.*) What sort of man do you
think I am?

JEFF (*sputtering, gasping*). Christ, Christ! My eyes! My eyes!

SIMON *watches him a moment, then takes out his handker-*
chief, gives it to JEFF.

Christ - (*Takes the handkerchief.*) Thanks. (*Little pause.*)
Thanks. (*Little pause.*) Sorry. Sorry, Simon. (*Pause, goes and
sits down.*) Can I have a drink? (*Pause.*) The bitch.

SIMON *hesitates, then goes and gets him a scotch, brings it to*
him.

Thanks.

There is a pause.

Don't throw me out, eh? I've got nowhere to bloody go, and
I don't want to go there yet.

SIMON. I'm going to play Parsifal. Do you mind?

JEFF. No, lovely. Lovely.

SIMON. You sure?

JEFF. Christ yes. You know I adore Wagner.

SIMON. No, I didn't know that.

JEFF. Christ, I introduced you. At Oxford. I bloody introduced you.

SIMON. Did you really? (*Looks at him.*) Such a long time ago. Then I owe you more than I can say. Thank you, Jeff. (*Goes over to the hi-fi, puts on the record.*)

> *The opening bars of* Parsifal *fill the theatre. They sit listening as the music swells.*
> *The light fades.*

Curtain.

The Rear Column

Author's Note

I had a purple patch between March 1969 and February 1971 when I managed three flops in a row.

I seem in retrospect to have spent most of this period with my head down, to conceal as I went about my daily business cheeks that flamed easily and eyes that watered over trifles. The only glimmer of compensation came from my old friend and sticker-by Tony Gould, who over a long lunch in a Chinese restaurant (probably) told me the story of Stanley's march to the relief of Emin Pasha, and more particularly the fate of his rear column, left behind in the encampment of Yambuya, by the banks of the Arruwimi River, in the Year of Grace 1887. There were times during the working years that followed when, stuck in some Yambuya of my own making, with five characters I could neither completely abandon nor conduct to their final destinies, I regretted the lunch more than the flops from which it had promised redemption. In the worst patches I turned away to write other stage plays – *Butley*, *Otherwise Engaged*, *Dog Days* and *Molly*; and two television plays – *Plaintiffs and Defendants* and *Two Sundays* – but in between I always, for shorter or longer periods, returned to Yambuya: and a few months ago, some seven years after I first heard the story, got Mr Stanley to come back at last, and bring a painful relief to us all.

7th December, 1977

Dedicated to the memory of Clive Goodwin, to whom I owe more than I can say!

THE REAR COLUMN was presented by Michael Codron at the Globe Theatre, London, on 22 February 1978 with the following cast:

BONNY	Donald Gee
JAMESON	Jeremy Irons
WARD	Simon Ward
TROUP	Clive Francis
BARTTELOT	Barry Foster
STANLEY	Michael Forrest
JOHN HENRY	Riba Ackabusi
NATIVE WOMAN	Dorrett Thompson

Directed by Harold Pinter
Designed by Eileen Diss
Lighting by Nick Chelton

Act One

Scene One

A large store room in the Yambuya Camp, on the banks of
the Arruwimi River, the Congo. It is June, 1887. Late afternoon.
There are boxes back left and back right of stage. Between
them, back stage centre, large double doors. A canvas flap, stage
right. A large table, centre stage. Some travelling chests which
also serve as chairs. Stage left, a travelling desk and a chair, a
settee.
The double doors are partly open, to let in light. There are two
turtles, attached by lengths of string to the table legs.
BONNY is studying the room, clearly having just entered it for
the first time. He goes to the work desk, gives something on it a
cursory, rather contemptuous glance, goes over to the table, lets
out an exclamation, picks up a turtle, then the other one. Puts
them on the table.

JAMESON (*enters through flap*). Oh, Mr Bonny — you've met
  Herman and King, I see.

BONNY. Oh. I was hoping I'd met some soup.

JAMESON (*laughs*). One evening, no doubt. But one needs time
  to prepare.

BONNY. It doesn't take long to boil up a pair of turtles, does it?

JAMESON. I meant for the loss.

BONNY. What, they're pets, are they?

JAMESON. Well, they've kept the Major and myself company
  through some pretty lonely times. When he was ill, they were
  all I had to talk to, and when I was ill I used to imagine the
  three of them passing riotous evenings together. I got them
  from one of the village chiefs on my first trip out after
  Stanley's departure. He assumed I was a slaver, come to steal

his wife and ransom her for food. He offered me these before I
could put him straight — I couldn't speak much of the lingo
then.

BONNY. What was the wife like?

JAMESON. I didn't see her, but I'm sure she wouldn't have
made into soup.

BONNY. No, but she might have done for a pet. Then when you'd
finished with her, you could have traded her in for the soup.

JAMESON (*laughs politely*). This one's Herman because he reminds
me of a German Professor of Zoology under whom I once
studied, and this is King because he reminded the Major of the
horse on which he was taught to ride, as a child in Sussex. Two
patient, comforting, slow-witted fellows from our past, whose
own pasts go far further back than ours. If you look at Herman's
markings, you'll see he must be nearly a hundred.

BONNY. Oh. (*He looks quickly, without interest.*)

JAMESON. While King is a mere stripling of some six decades. I'm
sorry to ramble on. One's got out of the habit of succinctness
these last two months. Where are your two companions, by
the way?

BONNY. Troup's dealing with his Soudanese, and Ward with his
Zanzibaris.

JAMESON. You've got your men down already have you, good.

BONNY. Oh, I didn't have charge of any men — as I'm the one with
medical training Mr Stanley made me responsible for the mules.

JAMESON. Did they give you a bad time?

BONNY. Let's say we only understood each other when I was
having them fed.

JAMESON. In that respect, they don't seem too unlike the
men.

BONNY. A bit unlike your men, in that they were at least fed. I
took a stroll around the compound after I'd done with the
brutes. You're in a bad way here, aren't you? A very bad way.
(*Pause.*) How many have you lost?

JAMESON. Nineteen Zanzibaris, twelve Soudanese.

BONNY. Well, you'll lose a few more tonight. Fever, ulcers on
the back and legs — malnutrition, in other words. What have
the poor devils been eating?

JAMESON. Much the same as the Major and myself. The odd
   fish they buy from the natives, or a goat, sometimes a fowl.
   But the staple diet is the manioc root. For the Soudanese,
   that is. The Zanzibaris won't eat meat, so for them it's
   manioc and more manioc. Of course they won't cook it
   properly. The manioc has to be boiled slowly and then drained.
   They toss it into the pot then swallow it straight down. It
   frequently swells in their stomachs . . .

   WARD *enters.*

   The Major and I have given at least twenty cooking
   demonstrations between us. But they pay no attention.

BONNY. Was it like this when Mr Stanley was here?

JAMESON. Perhaps the Soudanese had a little more meat, and
   the Zanzibaris a little more fish, as Mr Stanley is famously
   clever at trading with the natives. But some of the
   Zanzibaris had begun to die before he left.

WARD. In other words, you've been having a rather grim time.

JAMESON. It's not particularly pleasant to watch men dying.
   They seem, the Zanzibaris especially, to settle into death
   before they become properly ill — as if death itself were the
   disease. They lie in their own dung waiting — the flies come
   up — well, you've seen and smelt for yourselves. At first we
   tried to keep them on the move, our policy was work and
   more work, but once we'd built the palisades and fenced
   ourselves in there was no work, to speak of. We can't let
   them out except in small details to gather wood, and even
   then they try to quarrel with the natives or what's worse
   trade them their guns for food. And as we'd rather be
   surrounded by natives who are reasonably friendly and
   unarmed . . . So we're left with the camp routine, and that's
   not adequate. These men are porters by nature, used to
   marching for long periods and to camping for short ones.

WARD. So the fact of it is, they're dying of hunger and
   boredom.

JAMESON. In a sense, Mr Ward. Though it doesn't quite
   catch the feeling of the two months they've spent doing it in.

WARD. And how many have died of a flogging?

JAMESON (*after a pause*). One.

WARD. But there's been more than one flogging, I take it? I
   saw a creature out there whose back was in ribbons.

JAMESON. There have been several floggings, Mr Ward. Once
they'd realized they could get a chicken or some fish or
even a goat for their rifles, and once they'd started thieving —
the Major began by issuing warnings, and when they didn't
take was forced to back them up with floggings.

WARD. Which doubtless haven't taken either.

JAMESON. An old debate, Mr Ward. We have no way of knowing,
have we? how many we've deterred. We only know how many
haven't been. You blame us for it, then?

WARD. Good God, no. Once you start, you have to go on, and
nobody's yet discovered an alternative to starting. I can't really
see that there's anything here to surprise. Constant sickness
punctuated by regular floggings — the inevitable conditions of
a large, stationary camp in the Congo. The only solution is to get
moving as quickly as possible.

JAMESON. Amen to that!

TROUP (*enters*). It appears I'm not to get one after all, can you
believe it? It's not enough that we find Stanley gone in spite of
his reassurances that he'd wait on us, it's not enough that we
were misled on that, but it turns out that after weeks of hard
travelling by day and the utmost misery and discomfort at
night, I'm still to be deprived — what the devil am I to do?

WARD. Mr Troup is talking of a bed, Mr Jameson.

JAMESON. A bed? But weren't you issued with a bed in London?

TROUP. Oh yes, Mr Jameson, I was issued with one, and here's my
chit to prove it — you see, it entitles me to one bed at the
expedition's expense. When I met with Mr Stanley at the Falls,
I presented him with this chit, signed by Mr MacKinnon of the
Committee, and he said that as all the beds were packed in the
steamer, I'd have to wait until we met up here. Well, here I
am, and here's my chit, but as there's no Stanley, there's no
bed. (*He laughs bitterly*.) Anyway, that'll teach me a little
savvy. I saw a bed lying free on the wharf at the Falls, but I
refrained from taking it. And what happened? Old Ward here took
it instead. He was quite right, by God, if I'd known the plight
my scruples were to land me in, I'd have fought him for it, I
would you know, Ward!

WARD. Yes, old chap, I know, but look, there must be a spare bed
somewhere in the Camp, there always is.

TROUP. Oh yes, three. Three spare beds. But according to the

Major, they belong to Mr Stanley, and are on no account to be touched. According to the Major. Though why the devil he thinks Stanley would object —

JAMESON. Mr Troup, I think I can help you. Mr Parke brought up an extra bed for Jephson, who fortunately brought his own. Parke asked me to add it to the loads for him, but he and I are good friends, I'm sure he wouldn't mind my letting you have the use of it.

TROUP. What? You mean there is a bed — I shall have a bed — tonight, you mean?

JAMESON. This very minute, if you like.

TROUP. No, no, it's just that — (*laughs*) after sleeping on wet grass between damp blankets — or propped against trees — I can hardly grasp — it's uncommonly kind of you, Mr Jameson, thank you.

BARTTELOT (*enters, through the flap, carrying a wooden stick with a metal tip*). Ah, Mr Troup, Mr Ward, here you are, I've been looking for you, and Mr Bonny. We must be careful that your Soudanese, Mr Troup, and your Zanzibaris, Mr Ward, are kept separate from those already in the camp. We've had a bout of sickness, as you've probably noticed, and there's no point the fresh men being contaminated. We'll have to put guards on them or they'll drift — they'll drift — and Mr Bonny, your mules, a guard on those too, if you please. Mule meat is something of a delicacy with the Soudanese — with Mr Jameson and myself, come to think of it, eh Jamie? (*He laughs.*) Well gentlemen, by this time you'll have some idea of our situation. I've no doubt you're as disappointed to find Mr Stanley gone as Mr Jameson and I were when we were left behind to wait for you. But he was anxious to make all possible speed to Emin Pasha, and pull him out before the Mahdi gets to him and with luck we'll either catch him up or not be too far behind him.

BONNY. As I understand it, we have to wait on for more porters.

BARTTELOT. Yes, Mr Bonny, another six hundred. We have nine hundred loads, each one of which Mr Stanley believes essential — food, quinine, rifles — and including the ones you've brought up just over three hundred porters. So we can't move until we have the other six hundred.

TROUP. Where are they going to come from? As Bonny, Ward and I were the only officers left behind —

BARTTELOT. They're being brought up by Tippu-Tib.

WARD. Tippu-Tib!

BARTTELOT. That's right, Mr Ward. Tippu-Tib. He and Mr Stanley came to an arrangement here before Stanley set out.

BONNY. Who is Tippu-Tib?

WARD. He's an Arab slave trader. Half Arab that is, and half Manyema. Which makes him wholly abominable.

BARTTELOT. But a particular friend of Mr Stanley's. You know him then?

WARD. By reputation, of course. No one who's spent any time in this part of the Congo could fail to. And I've come across his auxiliaries, who usually turn out to be his relatives as well. I've also come across his victims. I met poor Deane at Stanley Falls a year ago, just after the Arabs had burnt him out.

JAMESON. But on that occasion Tippu-Tib wasn't the Arab responsible.

WARD. Oh, Tippu is always the Arab responsible. This country is really his bazaar, you see, and the people in it his merchandise, and every Arab a relative, and every relative an agent.

BARTTELOT. Nevertheless, as I said, he and Mr Stanley are the greatest of friends.

WARD. They both choose their friends wisely.

JAMESON. And they have an agreement for the porters.

BONNY. When is he expected then, Major, with the porters?

BARTTELOT. Mr Stanley couldn't be precise. But he was hoping they'd arrive shortly after you.

BONNY. Any day now then.

WARD. Did you yourselves take part in these arrangements with Tippu-Tib?

BARTTELOT. No, Mr Stanley and Tippu-Tib kept themselves to themselves during the time the Arabs were in the Camp. None of the other officers had the pleasure of being introduced to him either, he has an aversion to any shows of white strength, apparently, we scarcely got a glimpse of him.

TROUP. And this is the man we're to wait for! An Arab slaver who distrusts white men —

JAMESON. He doesn't distrust Mr Stanley.

BONNY. Have you heard anything of him since he left?

JAMESON. Oh, just rumours. A few weeks ago the natives were full of talk of Arabs, I went over to explore but couldn't find any trace — the natives have a particular interest in Arabs, of course, they fear them as slavers but desire them as food.

TROUP. Food!

JAMESON. They believe they can take their cunning into their own systems, by eating them.

TROUP. But look here — do you mean to say — I thought cannibalism had been wiped out in these parts, by Stanley himself when he was here before. There was a long report in *The Times*, only last year —

WARD. The local chiefs probably haven't received their copies yet.

JAMESON (*laughs*). The problem is, Mr Troup, that it's hard to wipe out an appetite. Mr Stanley made the chiefs promise to stop gobbling each other up —

WARD. As he made the slavers promise to give up slaving. A promise in the jungle may become a fact in London, but you don't believe that Tippu-Tib is going to hire our six hundred men, do you? Or that Stanley believes he is.

TROUP. But good God — good God — Stanley told us nothing of this sort of thing in London. We signed on to march direct to the relief of Emin Pasha — and instead here we are hanging about waiting for some brigand of an Arab to enslave some porters —

BARTTELOT. While outside there are cannibals and inside three hundred hungry and contagious niggers. Exactly, Mr Troup. That is our situation, and will remain our situation until Tippu-Tib arrives to release us from it.

WARD. What is Mr Stanley's alternative proposal?

BARTTELOT. Alternative to what?

WARD. In the event of Tippu's not turning up shortly. He's notorious for a number of things, but not for his punctuality. At least I've never heard of it.

BARTTELOT. There is no alternative.

WARD. But in the event of his not turning up at all.

BARTTELOT. There is still no alternative. Mr Stanley will accept no alternative to the safety of his loads. He is clear that he expects·them and must have them. There is no alternative, Mr Ward. Tippu-Tib must turn up. And until he does we shall have to make the best of it.

WARD. But surely — (*He stops.*)

JAMESON. You'll be wanting to settle into your quarters — there's a shower behind my tent. The water comes up from the Arruwimi, it's dirty, warm and it smells, I'm afraid, but it's wet.

BARTTELOT. We've been in the habit of eating at sun-down, if that suits you. We've kept a goat specially for this occasion — though we've been tempted by it often enough, haven't we, Jamie? — so at least this first night you'll have meat rather than manioc. By the way, an unnecessary warning, I'm sure, but anything you have in the way of provisions should be kept locked in your trunks — they're not above trying to slip into the tents, we caught one just the other day — and your rifles, goes without saying.

WARD. Actually, Major, I've no provisions whatsoever. So I'd be very glad to have what's coming to me as soon as you can manage it.

BONNY. Yes, I'm right out of tea.

BARTTELOT. I'm sorry, Mr Ward. There's nothing coming to you that I know of.

TROUP. Six months provisions, guaranteed by the Committee.

WARD. To be provided when we got our men up here.

BARTTELOT. I know nothing about it.

TROUP. But they must surely have been left behind by Mr Stanley.

BARTTELOT. Very possibly. But as Mr Stanley left no instructions on the matter, there's no way of knowing.

TROUP. But what about you and Jameson? Have you had yours?

BARTTELOT. Mr Stanley did give some out before he left, yes. But he left me no authorisation to give you any.

TROUP. My authorisation comes from the Committee in London.

BARTTELOT. Then perhaps you should take it up with the Committee in London.

WARD. Personally I shan't be needing jungle provisions in London, at least as long as there are still shops and restaurants there. Anyway, my chit is signed personally by Mr Stanley.

BARTTELOT. Then it's to Mr Stanley you must apply, when we catch up with him.

TROUP. We need our provisions now, sir.

BARTTELOT. I can't help you, sir.

TROUP. But you can, sir. They must be here, among the loads Mr Stanley left behind.

BARTTELOT. As Mr Stanley didn't say, how can you know that?

WARD. Ratiocination, possibly. In that if Mr Stanley owes us some provisions, which he does; and has left behind a large number of loads, which he has; and arranged for us to wait here with you, to help bring up those loads, which he did; then he's scarcely likely to have taken our provisions on with him; which one can therefore conclude he hasn't.

BARTTELOT. Are you making fun of me, sir!

WARD. No, Major. I was simply helping you to a conclusion.

BARTTELOT. Well, one may conclude anything with Mr Stanley, as a sure way of ending up in the wrong for it. But one thing one can be sure about, in the matter of Mr Stanley's intentions, is that his instructions are to be carried out to the very letter, and only to the very letter, however inconvenient that may be to the rest of the world. Mr Jameson will confirm that as Commanding Officer of this Rear Column, I must do as Mr Stanley said, but I may on no account do what I think he might have said, had he been here to say it. Isn't that so, Mr Jameson? I sympathise with you, of course, and if my Commanding Officer weren't Mr Stanley, you'd find your Commanding Officer a very much more obliging fellow, believe me.

TROUP. Do you mean to say that we're not to have our provisions simply because Stanley forgot to include them in his instructions?

BARTTELOT. But we cannot say that he forgot. He may well have remembered not to include them.

TROUP. And why should he do that?

BARTTELOT. Because — because — I don't know, how should I?

TROUP. This is nonsense, nonsense! You tell us we're not to
  have provisions which we were guaranteed as members of this
  expedition, provisions that do not belong personally to Mr
  Stanley, because in your view Mr Stanley is some sort of —
  some sort of — punctilious lunatic. Well sir, let me remind
  you that I have had dealings with Mr Stanley, and a saner and
  more practical man I've never met. Sir, I believe you're making
  us the victims of some private misunderstanding between Mr
  Stanley and yourself.

BARTTELOT. Have no fear of that, sir, there's no misunderstanding
  at all between Mr Stanley and myself. I understand him only
  too well. Certainly too well to allow myself to be the victim of
  your misfortune. He wouldn't hesitate to use this opportunity
  to ruin my career, my reputation at home —

WARD (*after a pause*). Stanley will ruin your career and your
  reputation if you furnish us with provisions that are rightly
  ours?

BARTTELOT. Ask Mr Jameson if I'm over-stating the case?

JAMESON. The Major has reason to be careful, where Mr
  Stanley's orders are in question. Mr Stanley on an
  expedition is a very different man from Mr Stanley on the Falls
  or sitting with Mr MacKinnon on the Committee in London.
  Jephson, Parke, Stairs — all the officers who've gone on with
  him would concur.

BARTTELOT. And it is through his orders, some of them
  impossible to perform, that he gets at us. He's as savage with
  initiative as he is with inefficiency. Well, he'll not get at me,
  sir, not any more. And I'm sorry if others must suffer for it.

TROUP. Can we see these orders, Major? As we're to be so
  strictly governed by them?

BARTTELOT (*after a pause, during which he stares at*
  TROUP). You would have seen them in due course, Mr
  Troup, whether you'd requested to or not.

TROUP (*reads them through quickly*). There's very little to them,
  and what there is can scarcely be said to have been written in a
  spirit of animosity. (*Passing them to* WARD.) Rather the
  reverse.

BARTTELOT. He knew that I would not be the only one to read
  them.

TROUP. I see he expressly requests you to take Mr Ward's, Mr Bonny's and my advice — along with Mr Jameson's.

BARTTELOT. No, Mr Troup, he tells me to ask you for your advice, not take it. The responsibility remains entirely mine. It's in the same sentence — heed their advice while being solely answerable for the decisions. At a first reading you will fail to detect, as Mr Jameson and I failed to detect, the real subtlety of what he's written. Or notice a major anomaly.

WARD. I certainly can't find an anomaly — or even much in the way of subtlety. It's all most emphatic, down to the number of brass-rods we're to pay to the porters per day.

BARTTELOT. The brass-rods — oh yes — he'd be emphatic about the brass-rods. He knows the value of a brass-rod in the Congo as a Jew knows a sovereign in Kensington.

JAMESON. But apart from the brass-rods he is emphatic. But without being precise.

BARTTELOT. Exactly. Exactly. And look — see what he says about the palisade.

WARD (*looks*). Merely that you're to build one. Which you have — an admirable one. What could be more sensible?

BARTTELOT. Ah, but what follows the order — (*He recites.*) For remember, it is not the natives alone who may wish to assail you, but the Arabs and their followers may, through some cause or other, quarrel with you and assail the camp.

WARD. Well?

BARTTELOT. Well, Mr Ward, you yourself have confirmed our worst suspicions. By Arabs whom can he mean but Tippu-Tib. So Stanley has gone out of his way to warn us against a man he claims as his friend, on whom he has made us depend, without whose arrival we cannot move!

WARD. But good God, of course he'd warn you! He knows better than anyone — friend or not, Tippu-Tib is a very dangerous man. But he also knows that Tippu is the only man in the Congo who could raise six hundred porters, by whatever means. Tippu is both totally indispensable and completely untrustworthy. That is the nature of the beast!

JAMESON. But as you've pointed out, he leaves us with no alternative.

WARD. And as Major Barttelot pointed out — with considerable force — there is no alternative. If the loads are essential, then the porters are essential. If the porters are essential —

TROUP. So is this Tippu-Tib. Exactly! I must say (*laughs*) if this is all!

BARTTELOT. It isn't all! Or rather it is all — and that's the damned subtlety of it. Not what he's put in, but what he's left out!

TROUP. Oh this is the sheerest — the sheerest — how could he cover every contingency — look, you tell us that Stanley always gets at you through his orders — well, surely you examined him on every sentence when he took you through them.

BARTTELOT. I did not.

TROUP. Why not?

BARTTELOT. Perhaps, Mr Troup, because he didn't take me through them.

TROUP. That's irregular, I admit — but then he's not a military man — but you could have gone to him yourself, I suppose you read them before he left?

BARTTELOT. You suppose incorrectly. Mr Stanley made it impossible — quite impossible — for me to read them until he'd marched out of the Camp.

TROUP. But the fact remains there is nothing there to prevent you giving us our provisions. Good God, man, can you not see — I have two ounces of sugar, an ounce of tea — Mr Ward tells you he has nothing — Mr Bonny is out of —

BONNY. Tea.

TROUP. And the only reason you offer for denying us is that Stanley hasn't actually written it down that you should give us them. As if he didn't have enough on his mind —

BARTTELOT. Mr Stanley's last verbal orders to me, delivered before Jephson and Stairs as witnesses, was that I was on no account to exceed his written orders. On no account!

TROUP. You were on no account to exceed written orders that he prevented you from reading until he'd gone?

BARTTELOT. This is a trivial subject, trivial! There are more important matters — look outside, sir, at the state of the niggers Stanley's left us with — he made sure to take only the healthy with him — don't doubt that — there's sickness, pilfering — and you fret at me with your tea and sugar — by God, I've said my last word on the subject. The subject is closed! (*He exits through the flap.*)

TROUP. Well, it's not closed as far as I'm concerned — I've no intention —

JAMESON. Mr Troup, your bed. Shall we go and find it?

TROUP. What? Yes, yes, the bed! At least I have a bed! (*He laughs bitterly.*) I'm much obliged to you, Mr Jameson. (*He follows* JAMESON *through the flap.*)

WARD. I remember a governess rather similar to the Major. Her most infuriating prohibitions always depended upon some illogically spiteful but unuttered edict of my father's. It's no good blaming me, it's your papa says no. But he hasn't said no. But he would if you asked him. In fact our papa hadn't the slightest interest in us, and would have said yes to anything. Did you have a governess like that, Bonny?

BONNY. No. But this governess'll say yes, don't you worry.

WARD. What makes you think that?

BONNY. Mr Jameson's face.

WARD. Ah, I see. That's why you kept the peace, was it? Because you'd read Mr Jameson's face?

BONNY. Well, there was no good going on at him, was there, it just made him more determined.

WARD. And did you like him for that?

BONNY. I didn't like him or dislike him. I recognised him for what he is.

WARD. And what's that?

BONNY. Our Commanding Officer. (*He exits.*)

WARD *stares after him, then walks around the store-room, stops to look at the turtles, then walks casually on to Jameson's desk, picks up a sketch, studies it.*

JAMESON *enters, as if expecting to find the room empty. Stops on seeing* WARD.

WARD. You've bedded old Troup, then?

JAMESON. He couldn't get off with it fast enough. He was probably afraid I'd change my mind and wrestle it back from him.

WARD. I was just admiring your work — it is yours, I take it?

JAMESON. Yes. A plover, he rested ten minutes on a branch right outside my tent this morning. I shall have to wait until I get home to do full justice to his colouring — the forehead's light brown — reddish brown, really — and the crest here (*coming over, pointing*) is blacker than I've managed with charcoal — so is the top of the head. And the cheeks are a delicate grey, as is the lower half of the throat. The whiteness of the paper is about right for the whiteness of the rest of the throat, but the wing crests are a wonderful ash-green — and no paper would serve for the white bar across the centre of the wing — and the eye — imagine an ochre iris around the black pupil.

WARD. That collection in one of the small huts — it's entirely yours then?

JAMESON. Why yes. Yes it is.

WARD. Good God, I thought it had been done by four men at least. A lepidopterist, an ornithologist, an entymologist and an ethnologist. What unified them must be the artist.

JAMESON. Or perhaps a dilettante, who separates them. Do you sketch, Mr Ward?

WARD. A little. Which is how I do most things. So I'm the dillettante, Mr Jameson, and now you've come face to face with the real article, you'll have to drop your pose. Unless, of course, it's assumed for the Major's sake.

JAMESON. Major Barttelot and I have been together in rather difficult circumstances recently. We've had to depend on each other too much, in sickness, and in health, to assume poses with each other.

WARD. Good Heavens, that sounds rather like a marriage!

JAMESON. I already have a marriage.

WARD. Really? And children?

JAMESON (*after a pause*). Two. At least I trust and pray two. The second was due last month.

WARD. May I congratulate you. Not least on your wife, who must be very understanding.

JAMESON. She is, Mr Ward. Thank you.

WARD. Did Mr Stanley choose you to stay behind with the Major, or did the Major choose you, or did you choose yourself?

JAMESON. It was understood that Stairs was to be left behind, but at the last moment Mr Stanley changed his mind, and appointed me. Mr Stanley being Mr Stanley, he offered no explanation. Have you any further questions?

WARD. I'm sorry, I've been impertinent. It's just that — look — I know from my own experience of this continent how quickly one can come to brood on a subject when cut off — isn't it possible that you and the Major —

JAMESON. Went a trifle mad together? Yes, quite possible. Nevertheless Stanley did threaten to destroy the Major's reputation.

WARD. Why?

JAMESON. Perhaps the Major wasn't used to being spoken to as Mr Stanley is used to speaking to gentlemen who accompany him on his expeditions. And Mr Stanley was even less used to being answered as the Major answered him.

WARD. And because of this — this clash of temperaments, Stanley would go to the length of ruining a man —

JAMESON. At the moment, Stanley is almost as powerful in London as he is in Africa. He'd only have to speak a few words — and Stanley is too jealous of his own fame to care much about another man's honour. The Major is a military man from a military family. His honour means a great deal to him.

WARD. Yet Stanley did make him Commanding Officer of his Rear Column. That could be construed as an honour.

JAMESON. It could also be construed as one of his insults. The Major was appointed Senior Officer to the Relief of Emin Pasha, and has been left behind to guard the supplies. He is a brave and active man, rendered temporarily inactive.

WARD. A sort of Samson, blinded and chained. And yet you were left with him — so Stanley showed some compassion to the Major. And to the rest of us, I suspect. Bonny has already singled you out as the peacemaker.

JAMESON. We had all of us better keep the peace, Mr Ward.

WARD. Oh, I shan't give you any more trouble, my word on it. And old Troup is really a decent enough fellow who's never been to the Congo before and has been out of bed too long — one good night'll probably settle him.

JAMESON (laughs). Well, you've only to settle Mr Bonny, and we shall be all right.

WARD. Mr Bonny has already informed me that he's quite settled.
It seems that he likes his Commanding Officers to be
commanding, which the Major evidently is. Did you know, by
the way, that he's the only white man on the whole expedition
who's being paid for his services? Can that be because he's the
only one among us whose services are worth hiring? Whatever
you say about Stanley, his recruitment drive in London was a
spectacular success — why, they said at the Falls he'd
actually got some rich nincompoop to pay for the privilege of
marching with him, God knows how much! (*He laughs.*)

JAMESON. One thousand pounds, Mr Ward, and in view of
what I've learnt so far, I count it a bargain as well as a
privilege. So the Major is for honour, and Troup, I presume, is
for honour, and Bonny for money, and I for study — what
about you, Mr Ward, what are you here for?

WARD. I'm a patriotic Englishman, Mr Jameson.

JAMESON. I see.

WARD. And as Emin Pasha is an eccentric German employed by
the Egyptians to maintain their interest in South Equatorial
Africa, it is surely the duty of all patriotic Englishmen to
sign up with a Welsh adoptive American to rescue him from
a rampaging Muslim. While at the same time helping the Welsh
adoptive American to extend a little more Belgian influence
along the Arruwimi River. Isn't it?

JAMESON. You believe the rumours then? That Stanley is really
doing all this for Leopold of Brussels?

WARD. Certainly not. He's using Leopold of Brussels so that he
can do it all for Stanley.

JAMESON. But if you don't believe the cause is noble —

WARD. Noble! (*He laughs.*) There are no noble causes in the
Congo, and never have been. In the Congo there are only
cannibals and other natives, Arab slavers, European interests
and magnificent opportunists. Along with birds, butterflies and
snakes, of course, for artists and naturalists like yourself.

JAMESON. Then what are you doing here?

WARD. I haven't the slightest idea. All I know is that after three
years travelling around the continent, I was suddenly
desperate for the sight of England. Nothing could have
persuaded me to stay on another month except, it seems, the
very first opportunity to do so. Stanley's expedition was the

first opportunity. Perhaps it's simply the fickleness of the dilettante who decides to put up with something he's tired of, for a change, eh?

JAMESON. Or the impulse of a serious man who's not yet discovered what it is he came here to find out.

WARD. Unless, finally, I'm an unwitting agent of one of history's more grandiose schemes.

JAMESON. What would that be?

WARD. Why, to ruin the reputation of a certain Major — from Norfolk, is it?

JAMESON. Sussex, it is.

WARD. In his Sussex family, with his Sussex hunt, and in his London clubs. Think, if only Gordon hadn't fallen at Khartoum the Mahdi wouldn't be driving on to destroy Emin Pasha, Stanley wouldn't be in the Congo, and ergö: I wouldn't be quarrelling with the Sussex Major for my flour, coffee, sugar, tea and gentleman's relish, at Yambuya, on the banks of the Arruwimi River, in June, this year of Grace, 1887.

JAMESON (*laughs*). Well, whatever the whirligigs of history or fate, Mr Ward, I believe I'm glad they've brought you to us.

BARTTELOT (*enters through the flap*). Ah, you're still here then. (*To* JAMESON.) I was looking for Bonny, as a matter of fact. Thought I'd better find out whether he brought up any quinine. He's not in his tent.

JAMESON. Well, he hasn't come in. He went off some time ago.

BARTTELOT. Oh.

JAMESON. He may be having a shower.

BARTTELOT. Looked there. No one in the shower.

Pause.

WARD. In that case, I'll be able to have one. (*He goes towards the flap.*)

BARTTELOT. Don't forget, Mr Ward. Roast goat. Roast goat and palm wine at sun-down, eh?

WARD *exits*.

BARTTELOT. You've been having a chat with him, then?

JAMESON. Yes.

BARTTELOT. Ah. And what's he like — when he's not drawling out his sarcasms?

JAMESON. Oh, rather sympathetic. Certainly intelligent.

BARTTELOT. You like him, then?

JAMESON. I found him rather a relief. (*Hurriedly*.) I mean, from what I'd feared earlier.

BARTTELOT. God Jamie, I wish I had your knack — but by God, what a business, eh! Hardly arrived and they're set against me. Even Stanley couldn't have hoped for such a swift success — grown men at each other's throats — over what! Fortnum and Mason's! That's the joke of it! And that Troup — (*pacing about*) dead set, dead set against me —

JAMESON. Ward assures me that now he's got a bed he'll calm down.

BARTTELOT. What, a bed, how?

JAMESON. I remembered Parke's — the one for Jephson —

BARTTELOT. There you are, you see! And I didn't think of it — not at all, all I could think was that he was after me for one of Stanley's beds — and now the bad feeling's there!

JAMESON. We'll find a way to win them around.

BARTTELOT. Hah! You'd find a way all right, Jamie. (*Pause*.) If I weren't here.

JAMESON. Oh now come, old man, you mustn't give in —

BONNY *enters through the flap.*

BARTTELOT. Ah, Bonny! Here you are — I've been looking for you.

BONNY. One of the nigger boys only just told me, sir. I was talking to Troup in his tent.

BARTTELOT. What? Talking to Troup?

BONNY. Yes, sir.

BARTTELOT. Well Bonny, we'd better have a think about our medical supplies, eh?

JAMESON. I'll see you at mess. (*He exits*.)

BARTTELOT. Right, Jamie, at mess. Yes, first thing is to make sure we keep our supplies separate from Stanley's — Oh, that reminds me — here's a (*takes a little package from his pocket*) as you're desperate, not much I'm afraid, almost at the end myself, but enough to make you a pot at least.

BONNY. That's — that's very kind of you, sir.

BARTTELOT. Not at all. Not at all. (*Pause.*) Now there's one other matter. I need your advice on. I've been ill.

BONNY. Yes. Mr Jameson mentioned that you and he —

BARTTELOT. This is something different. Something a medic can't detect — (*Pause.*) I don't sleep at nights, not for months, not since Stanley left, get the shakes, the fever, nightmares, that sort of thing and I can't — I find my temper, well, scarcely seems to be mine any more as if — how to explain it — as if I were being — being poisoned, do you see?

BONNY. Well, you probably are, Major, from what Mr Jameson was telling me of your diet here.

BARTTELOT. No it's not the diet, Jameson sleeps like a top most nights. He has the same diet. These nightmares, I tell you — and headaches — I can't go on with them. (*Pause.*) Well? What do you — ?

BONNY. Morphine, sir.

BARTTELOT. Morphine! Certainly not. Morphine's not the answer. (*He looks at him.*)

BONNY. No, Major, it isn't. The answer is obvious enough. A return to a different life, different food, a different country. In other words, the answer for you is England.

BARTTELOT *looks at him, waits.*

But as the answer's out of the question —

BARTTELOT. Why?

BONNY. I beg your pardon, sir?

BARTTELOT Why is it out of the question?

BONNY. Well — because you're in command here, sir.

BARTTELOT. It might be better for everybody if I weren't. (*Pause.*) Jameson — is more — more fit.

BONNY. Mr Jameson isn't an army man, though, is he, sir? He's a gentleman of leisure, from what I can make out.

BARTTELOT. Mr Jameson happens to be the finest man I've ever met.

BONNY. But Mr Stanley appointed you the Commanding Officer.

BARTTELOT. But between you, you and Troup and Ward and Mr Jameson — you could — (*pause*) do you understand what I'm asking?

BONNY. Yes, I do.

BARTTELOT. Well then, man!

BONNY. I'm not sure my recommendation would carry much weight.

BARTTELOT. But you would write one for me?

BONNY. Naturally, sir. If you ordered me to.

BARTTELOT. Ordered you to?

BONNY. I could hardly write a letter recommending that you be invalided home, without your asking me to, first. Which you have done. And I agree.

BARTTELOT. With the recommendation?

BONNY. To write the letter. It is an order, isn't it?

BARTTELOT. Of course it isn't an order! What value would a letter have that I'd ordered you to write — good God man, you have qualifications, you can judge a situation and act accordingly. Nobody would challenge a doctor's findings.

BONNY. That's true, sir, yes. But then I'm not a doctor.

BARTTELOT. Not a doctor?

BONNY. I'm a medical orderly. And that's less than third class in the medical profession. Did you take me for a doctor?

BARTTELOT. I didn't think about it one way or another. I assumed you had medical experience, I assumed — as they signed you up — you'd be, yes, properly qualified —

BONNY. I'm properly qualified as a medical orderly. And a medical orderly's services come considerably cheaper than a properly qualified doctor's. I expect Mr Stanley took that into account when he appointed me.

BARTTELOT. In that case, we've been at cross-purposes, haven't we?

BONNY. No, sir. (*Little pause.*) Well, at least I understood.

BARTTELOT. What? What did you understand? (*He moves towards him threateningly.*)

BONNY. Well, that you wanted my assurance, in as much as I could give it, that you're fit to carry on.

BARTTELOT. You want me to stay, do you?

BONNY. Yes, I do.

BARTTELOT. Why?

BONNY. Because you're the Commanding Officer. And if we're to be here a while yet, then Mr Stanley will be getting further and further away from us. The country is dangerous, there are cannibals around, there could be fighting. And this Tippu-Tib, who sounds as likely to attack us as give us our nigger porters. We'd need you then, very badly, however nicely Mr Jameson were to run things in the meanwhile.

BARTTELOT. You'll do for me, Bonny. You'll do for me very well.

BONNY. Thank you, Major. (*Little pause.*) You'll do for me too, if I may say so. (*He turns, makes to go out, stops.*) Oh sir, I shan't —

BARTTELOT. What?

BONNY. Needless to say, it shall never be mentioned by me that this conversation took place. The others might misconstrue —

BARTTELOT *stares at him.*

BONNY. And thank you again for the tea, sir. Much appreciated. (*He goes out.*)

BARTTELOT (*stands, for a moment, then lets out an exclamation, loud, of despair. He begins to stride up and down*). Damn — damn — damned insolence!

He drives the point of his stick into the ground, plucks it out, strides up and down.

(*Bellowing.*) John Henry! John Henry! (*He continues to stride, and as lights fade to black, still striding and jabbing his stick into the ground, at the very top of his lungs.*) John Henry!

Scene Two

*About an hour later. The stage is in darkness. JAMESON enters.
through the flap. He strikes a match, puts it to the lamp.*

BARTTELOT is sitting at the table, his hands to his face.

*JOHN HENRY is sitting at the end of the table staring
straight ahead.*

*JAMESON takes in the scene, quickly lights the other two
lamps, goes over to BARTTELOT, puts a hand on his shoulder.*

BARTTELOT (*jumps, removes his hands*). Oh — oh Jamie — there
you are! Well, supper, eh? Manioc soup, prime cuts of manioc,
pudding of manioc —

JAMESON. Not tonight, old man. Can't you smell the goat?

BARTTELOT. What, by God, yes — goat, eh, how did you —
oh, oh yes, those others, they've arrived, it's for them. (*He
looks, sees JOHN HENRY.*) What? (*Stares at him.*) Ah, that's
right, there's a good boy, John Henry, told him to sit down,
not on the floor like a monkey, but at the table, like a human
being, eh John Henry — and then when I — I — you just sat on,
eh? Yes, that's a good lad, now go and get the palm wine,
John Henry. Palm wine. Fancy that. (*He gets up.*) Falling
asleep — and a nice sleep, a dream not a nightmare, I've got a
feeling the old pater was in it, we were walking across the
paddocks, a spring morning — smelt something good — perhaps
it was the goat, eh? Well, now I'm back, they'll be here in a
minute —

JAMESON. Look, something's occurred to me that may help —
What do you say to giving them half their six months'
provision now, and leave it to Stanley to give them their other
half when we get up with him? That way, you'll be recognizing
their claim, while still respecting Stanley's ultimate authority.
Do you see?

BARTTELOT. But it would still be a breach.

JAMESON. Yes, but if you don't give them anything then they
could complain to Stanley and it might suit him to take their
side. There was nothing in my orders, he could say, and no
reason that you shouldn't have obliged these men.

BARTTELOT. And so he gets me either way! For being in breach
of his orders if I do, or failing to exercise my command if I
don't!

JAMESON. Ah, but if he says you shouldn't have given them even half their provisions, then Ward, Troup and Bonny would have to come to your defence, you see. And Stanley wouldn't like that.

BARTTELOT. I don't know, Jamie. I don't know. All I know is that I'm well and truly in Stanley's web and whatever I do — I'll have to think — make a decision — but you believe that would be all right, do you?

There is a pause.

Look, old man, I must tell you. I — the fact is, I've just done something rather shameful. I asked Bonny if he could have me invalided home. (*He looks at* JAMESON, *distressed.*) It suddenly seemed a solution, you see, that as a medical man he could get me out of all this — a letter would do it, that was my thought. Then you and the others could do as you like, wouldn't have me to contend with. I'd be out of his trap honourably and the rest of you'd be out of his trap too, d'you see? But it's not to be. He's not a doctor, it turns out. Just a medical orderly. I'd have to order him to recommend me to leave — you can imagine what Stanley would have made of that — how he could get at me as far worse than a coward — a cunning coward. Eh? (*He laughs.*)

JAMESON. Poor old boy. I don't blame you, not at all, I'm only sorry —

BARTTELOT. No, don't be soft on me. I did wrong. I shouldn't have tried. But you know, there's something I want you to understand. I couldn't have done it. Couldn't have left, I'm sure of that. All I wanted was the letter in my pocket, that meant I could if I wanted to, you see? Something I could — could touch as — to confirm I'd made a choice — a choice not to go back even though I'd been let off. I'd never desert. Not desert you, old man, after the two months we've been through. I count you my closest — my closest —

TROUP *comes through the flap.*

Ah, Mr Troup — well, I hear you have a bed, thank God for that, eh?

JOHN HENRY *enters with a jug.*

And here's the palm wine — on the table — there's a boy — now the glasses —

WARD *enters.*

BARTTELOT. Ah, here you are then, Ward — showered and — and
— and one for Mr Ward too, John Henry — now the jug — be
careful not to spill, we've only about a quart of the-stuff left,
old Jameson bought it from the cannibals, so you see they have
their uses, Troup, eh? (*He laughs*.) Not brandy, I know, but not
as fierce as you'd expect from a cannibal brew —

As JOHN HENRY, *having filled* WARD's *and* TROUP's
and JAMESON's *glass comes to fill his,* BONNY *enters.*

Ah, Bonny — Mr Bonny first, John Henry — that's right, there's
a boy, and now mine — John Henry's quite a little find of
mine, used to be one of Mr Stanley's boys, eh, John Henry? He
was in the tent the morning Stanley was leaving — Stanley's
tent — all the hullabaloo and John Henry crying, weren't
you, John Henry, because Stanley had chosen to take one of
his other boys instead, heartbroken because of it, eh, John
Henry? And when Stanley marched out — by God, what a
business he makes of it, struts yards ahead of his officers —
poor old Jephson in a terrible state of indecision, whether to
keep him company or maintain a respectful ten yards behind,
Parke and Stairs trying to look unconcerned, at the back, but
getting caught up in the Zanzibaris who wouldn't move fast
enough for all the damned fuss, drums rolling, pipes blowing,
and all the time Stanley not seeing the farce of it all, strutting
along eyes focussed on posterity by way of the London *Times*
and his publishers, old Jameson did a marvellous sketch, one of
the Soudanese he left for us to bury managed to die just as
Stanley passed him, old Jameson got him in the sketch, eyes
rolling, what was it you called it, A Faithful Zanzibari says his
Farewell to H. M. Stanley, Esq. H. M. standing for His
Majesty, hah, hah, not Henry Morton by God, and above it
Jameson's put, what was it, homage to a great man. (*He
laughs*.) And there was little John Henry trailing behind,
blubbering away, right out of the Camp, hoping right to the
end His Majesty would pardon him and take him along after all,
but I knew he wouldn't, knew he'd send him back and next
morning — next morning I kept a look out for him, found him
skulking with the Soudanese, and took him on. After a
shower, of course. Now John Henry showers once a day, don't
you, John Henry, and is my personal boy, sleeps outside my
tent — tell them how Mr Stanley came by you, John Henry.

JOHN HENRY. Tippu-Tib, he give me Mr Stanley.

BARTTELOT. That's right, our old friend Tippu-Tib. He

captured John Henry from one of the villages, and made a present of him to Stanley the last time Stanley was in these parts. Stanley made him his chief boy, then when he went back to England, stuck him in a missionary school at the Pool. Collected him when he got back three months ago. And leaves him behind all over again. Jameson and I've spent hours grilling him about Tippu-Tib, haven't we, Jamie, but he only knows three things about him, Tell us, John Henry, is Tippu-Tib a good man, good man?

JOHN HENRY. Tippu-Tib good man.

BARTTELOT. And is Tippu-Tib a bad man.

JOHN HENRY. Bad man, bad man.

BARTTELOT. Now tell us why he's called Tippu-Tib? Why name Tippu-Tib?

JOHN HENRY (*lifts his arm, points it about*). Tippu-tippu-tippu, tib, tib, tippu tib, tippu tib.

JAMESON. Onomatopoeic, you see.

BONNY. What?

JAMESON. The noise of the rifle, when Tippu and his men come firing on the villages. Far more exact than bang, really.

WARD. Tippu's real name is Hamed bin Mahamed el Marjebi. But I never thought to ask why he was known as Tippu-Tib —

BARTTELOT. No, but Jameson did, eh Jamie? Anyway, those are the three things that John Henry knows about Tippu-Tib, that he's good, that he's bad, and how he got his name.

WARD. Which is one thing more than we know about most people.

BARTTELOT (*laughs with false enthusiasm*). Very neat, Mr Ward. Very neat.

JAMESON. Gentlemen, before you finish your glasses, may I propose a toast. To the Rear Column.

BARTTELOT. To the Rear Column.

TROUP.)
WARD.) To the Rear Column!
BONNY.)

BARTTELOT (*catches Jameson's eye*). I've been thinking — rather Jameson and I've been putting our heads together — and what do you say to this? Three months provision now, three months when we catch up with Stanley. Eh? What do you say? Troup?

TROUP. Well, sir, given your — your uneasiness with Mr Stanley's orders, that seems fair enough.

WARD. I think it's a marvellously sensible compromise. (*Glancing at* JAMESON.)

BONNY. Certainly do' for me.

BARTTELOT. Very well, gentlemen. Now I've something to show you.

He looks to JAMESON, *winks, goes to a crate, brings it over, swings it up, jabs the point of his stick in, prises up the lid, and begins to plonk down items.*

One and a half pounds of coffee. One pound of tea. One and a half tins of salt. One and a half tins of jam and of chocolate milk. One tin of cocoa and milk. One tin of sardines. One of sausages. One pound of fancy biscuits. One third of a tin of red herring. Half a pound of flour. One pot of Liebig. One quarter of a pound of tapioca. Times three, of course.

During this drums have begun to pound.

TROUP. Oh, I see, This is a *month's* rations.

BARTTELOT. No, this is three months.

WARD. Three months' — that!

BARTTELOT. It is.

TROUP. But good God, who made up these provisions?

JAMESON. Fortnum and Mason's. They'd have done us quite nicely for an afternoon at Lord's Cricket Ground, don't you think?

TROUP. Good God, good God!

BARTTELOT. So there you, gentlemen! One half of what we were quarrelling about. And now perhaps you'll understand something about Mr Stanley, the greatest African explorer of our age! He has his expedition provisions made up by Fortnum and Mason's. (*He laughs.*)

The drums increase in volume.

Now if you excuse me while I put a stop to the accompaniment — (*He goes to the doors, unlatches them, throws them open.*)

From outside, fires flaming; low keening sounds; the drums louder; dim shapes everywhere. BARTTELOT *strides into their midst, with his stick.*

JAMESON. The Zanzibaris — the Major has a running battle with them every night —

BARTTELOT (*off*). That's enough of the drums — damn you, enough I say —

The drums diminish, without stopping.

JAMESON. There's a particular couple I call the Minchips because it's a Dickens-sounding name, and they're both out of Dickens — he'd have set them in the Mile End Road. The husband's as lazy a vagabond as you could expect to meet — lies on his side all day while the wife collects wood, bargains for food, gathers manioc — then at night after he's eaten he retires to his tent and cleans his rifle while the wife plays for him on the drums, I think she starts all the others off, and she's always the last to stop —

BARTTELOT (*still shouting, off*). Quiet I say — quiet —

WARD *goes towards the door, watches.*

TROUP *joins him.*

BONNY *pours himself some more palm-wine.*

There is now only one drum beating.

JAMESON *goes over to his desk, picks up the picture, looks at it.*

Drum plays a few seconds longer, then stops.

On this tableau:

Lights.

Curtain.

Act Two

Scene One

The Same. Six months later. Morning.

The doors are open. Outside, blazing sun-light and intense heat. Off, the sound of a voice, faint and unidentifiable, although it is WARD's. *A thudding sound, also faint, follows each count.*

WARD (*off*). Forty-five, forty-six, forty-seven, forty-eight, forty-nine, fifty, fifty-one, fifty-two, fifty-three, fifty-four, fifty-five, fifty — (*Stops, pause.*) Take him down, will you? Down! Take him down!

Movements, voices off. There is a pause.

TROUP *enters through the main doors, goes to the water bucket, pours himself a mug of water, sits down, wipes his forehead, drinks.*

BONNY *enters. He is carrying salt and bandages. He puts them in a box. Goes to the water bucket, pours himself a mug of water.*

BONNY. Jameson's due back this morning, isn't he?

TROUP. Is he? (*Pause, sips. Laughs.*)

BONNY (*looks at him*). What?

TROUP. Well, you're not setting any store by that, are you?

BONNY. Not setting store by it, no. Just wanting to find out.

TROUP. Well, you don't have to wait for him — I can tell you. There're rumours. As he knew before he left.

BONNY. There're rumours in the villages here. They may turn out to be facts further down.

TROUP. They're always rumours, never facts.

BONNY. But he thought these were worth following up.

TROUP. Of course he did. As they coincided with a distasteful duty.

BONNY. Oh well, can't say I blame him. He's a gentleman, after all.

TROUP. And the rest of us aren't?

BONNY. Oh, I only meant he's not an officer.

TROUP. Some of us try to be both. Not that I blame him either, if he can get away with it. But I wonder that Barttelot lets him, he wouldn't let me, or Ward, it's a collective responsibility, we take votes on it, we should all stand by the decision.

BONNY. But Jameson voted against, didn't he? This time.

TROUP. This time, last time and the time before.

BONNY. Still, what would be the point of a vote, if we all had to vote one way.

TROUP. That's not my complaint.

BONNY. But what is your complaint?

TROUP. Only that Jameson doesn't take any of the —

BARTTELOT (off). Here you nigger — move that nigger out of the way —

BONNY. What?

TROUP. It doesn't matter.

BARTTELOT (enters, followed by JOHN HENRY). Water.

JOHN HENRY goes to the cask, pours a mug of water.

BARTTELOT. Ward went over. Over by five. We entered fifty on the log, damn nuisance!

JOHN HENRY brings the mug over to BARTTELOT, who swills it down, hands the mug to JOHN HENRY, who goes over, pours more.

BARTTELOT. Jameson should be back by now, he likes to get in before the heat — God what a business, Ward going on, thought he'd never stop. (He takes the mug from JOHN HENRY again, drinks.)

BONNY. No, but I don't understand what your complaint is.

TROUP. It doesn't matter.

BARTTELOT. What complaint?

There is a pause.

BONNY. About Mr Jameson's absence, wasn't it?

BARTTELOT. What about his absence?

TROUP. I was just saying that it was unfortunate that Jameson missed the flogging.

BARTTELOT. Why? Do you think he would have enjoyed it?

TROUP. They're meant to be a joint responsibility. We're all supposed to stand by the majority decision.

BARTTELOT. And when has Jameson rejected the majority decision?

TROUP. My point is simply that he should see it through with the rest of us.

BARTTELOT. He's seen enough of them to know how they go.

TROUP. But he voted against, and then stayed away.

BARTTELOT. And so?

TROUP. It's a way of keeping in the clear, isn't it?

BARTTELOT. Clear of what?

TROUP. The responsibility, of course.

BARTTELOT. Oh, what are you talking about, Troup? Somebody had to go up river to check the rumours —

TROUP. And does that someone always have to be Jameson? And always when there's a flogging?

BARTTELOT. Jameson goes because he's learned the lingo and is good with the natives. All right. (*Pause.*) All right?

TROUP (*grunts*). He'll bring back some sketches.

BARTTELOT. What?

TROUP. I said he'll bring back some nice sketches, of birds and leaves and toads and butterflies, and whatnot, I expect.

BARTTELOT. Let's hope he brings back some news of Tippu-Tib, eh?

TROUP. Whether he does or not, he'll bring back some sketches.

BARTTELOT (*after a pause*). Well?

TROUP. Well, he's down in the log as dissenting, *and* down in the log as absent from proceedings. In the six months I've been here he's not supervised the floggings once.

BARTTELOT. And in the six months you've been here you haven't stopped complaining, to one of us about the rest of us, to the rest of us about one of us, if it's not the flogging it's wood patrol, if it's not wood patrol it's — it's something else.

BONNY. I'm sorry if I've given you cause for complaint.

TROUP. You still haven't answered the facts, have you?

BARTTELOT. What facts?

TROUP. I've done my turn on the floggings, Bonny's done his, you've done yours and so's Ward.

WARD (*entering wearily*). Done what?

TROUP. Your turn on the floggings.

WARD. Over-done it, I think, didn't I? This time.

BARTTELOT. By five strokes, what came over you, anyway?

WARD. Sorry. I didn't keep count of my counting. Let's just hope he didn't, either.

BONNY. He couldn't. Anyway not after the first twenty. He wasn't conscious.

WARD. How very fortunate. After all, what would one do if he asked for the last five strokes to be taken back. (*He laughs weakly.*) Anyway, I gave orders for two days remission in chains, hope that's all right?

BARTTELOT. What! No, it's not all right! You should have spoken to me first.

WARD. Yes, well, sorry again. I felt as it was my mistake I must make up in some way —

BARTTELOT. You made the mistake, it wasn't for you to make it up.

WARD. Well, what do you suggest we do? Eh? Eh? (*Fiercely.*) Anway, what difference does it make whether it's three or five, he won't last the night, will he Bonny?

BONNY. I shouldn't think so.

WARD. There! You see! (*Puts his face in his arms.*)

TROUP. You all right, old man?

WARD. Yes, yes, thank you.

TROUP (*to* BONNY). You'd better give him some quinine.

BONNY. Is that all right, Major?

BARTTELOT. How are the stocks?

BONNY. Beginning to run low.

TROUP. Still, if a man's ill, he must have medicine.

BARTTELOT. He can only have medicine if there's medicine to give him.

TROUP. But it's no good making sure there's medicine to give him by not giving him any.

WARD (*laughs*). Very neat, Troup, very neat.

TROUP. It wasn't meant to be. Because it's not funny when you think about it. If Barttelot starts refusing us medicine —

BARTTELOT. I've never refused when Bonny's said it's absolutely necessary. Nevertheless the fact remains there soon won't be any medicine.

WARD. Oh, don't squabble over my health, I'm all right, I tell you, short on sleep, that's all, my tent isn't conducive to it, the glow from their fires throws up peculiar images and their voices go on very shrill and the whole effect — you know it occurs to me, at least it did occur to me, when I'd counted to twenty-three strokes or twenty-four, somewhere in that passage anyway, the twenties it did occur to me that old Jameson was quite right, he usually is, you know, when he put forward the argument that we should abandon flogging for a while, we really are losing them fast enough at what's the current rate, one and an eighth a day Bonny worked it out at, from starvation, sickness etc, for us not to need to flog them to death too.

BARTTELOT. It's the one matter on which Jameson is not right. We have no choice. If a nigger thieves or deserts or trades his rifle for food or sleeps on sentry duty, he is to be flogged.

TROUP. But we do have a choice, that's what I was saying. If Jameson votes against, and now Ward votes against, it only needs one more vote — then what would you do?

BARTTELOT. I see. You intend to vote against, do you, in future?

TROUP. Or Bonny might.

BARTTELOT *turns, looks at* BONNY.

BONNY. What, me? Of course I wouldn't.

BARTTELOT (*to* TROUP). Well?

WARD. If Troup votes against, I shall have to vote for. I agree
with the Major. But I'll tell you what, Troup, shall we make a
deal, take it in turns, that way we honour the law and
satisfy conscience, how many judges manage that? With the
Major's permission of course.

BARTTELOT. I don't give a damn what you do between you as
long as discipline is maintained. If you all voted against I'd
enter it in the log and still have them flogged. And by God!
order whichever of you I wanted to supervise it. And now
that we've cleared that up, I've work to do — (*He exits.*)

WARD. Work, what work?

BONNY. He's counting the brass-rods. He started last night, in
here. I was just going to bed, he came bursting in, didn't even
notice me, started pulling the cases out — then at dawn he was
into the tents —

WARD. Well, it put him in a good humour for the flogging, didn't
it? I saw him joking with a couple of Zanzibaris just before I
began the count, you were at his side Bonny, as you usually are,
was it a good joke?

BONNY. It wasn't a joke. He was grinning at them.

WARD. Grinning at them?

BONNY. He's discovered that they're more frightened of him
when he grins at them.

WARD. Really? Well he's got an excellent set of teeth. Why,
that might solve our problem, instead of lashing a man to the
post and having him flogged, we can lash him to a post and
have Barttelot grin at him. Fifty, fifty-five times, it wouldn't
make any difference . . .

BONNY. Yes, it would. They'd go off from fright even quicker.

TROUP. They hate him.

WARD. They hate us all.

TROUP. But they hate him most. He goes out amongst them
looking for trouble, poking at them with his damned stick, as if
trying to stir them up.

BONNY. Perhaps that's what he's trying to do. Stir them up to
life. Hate might sustain them a day or two longer —

TROUP. That's not why he does it. He does it because he hates them back.

WARD. So do I.

TROUP. What?

WARD. When I see them lying about in the compound, in their sickness, as if they were the image of sickness itself. Or while they stand there, heads lolling, while I supervise one of them flogging another of them to death. That makes me hate them.

TROUP. We can't go on week after week — something must be done, and soon.

BONNY. But what do you propose, Troup?

TROUP. Simply that we do something, anything, to get on the move. Look here, Bonny, this is confidential.

WARD (*laughs*). Yes, do be discreet old man. By the way, that woman I saw you with last night —

BONNY. What? What woman?

WARD. I saw you in silhouette, tip-toeing past my tent —

BONNY. Then you were seeing things.

WARD. Yes, lots of things, you and the woman among them. But you've got a way with the ladies, haven't you? Old Troup here was telling me the other day how you managed coming out on the boat, you had to travel tourist as you were on the expedition's expense, isn't that right, old man, but before you were three days out — you did say three days, didn't you, Troup? You'd insinuated yourself among the ladies in First Class, by making free with little remedies for *mal de mer*, and ended up dining between two absolute beauties, Troup called them, didn't you, Troup, at the Captain's table. Two absolute beauties?

TROUP. Look here, Ward, I didn't mean — I didn't intend any slight —

WARD. Of course you didn't, he was most complimentary about your gifts, Bonny, he didn't end up at the Captain's table between two absolute beauties, did you, Troup, even though you went first at your own expense, he was envious, you see, so there's nothing to be ashamed of in taking a Zanzibari or Soudanese or native lady by the neck, eh, as long as there's no outraged husband —

BONNY (*gets up, comes over*). Lift your arms.

WARD. What?

BONNY. Lift your arms.

WARD *does so*.

BONNY (*feels in Ward's arm-pits*). Swollen. (*He puts his hand to Ward's brow*). You'd do better lying down.

WARD. No, I wouldn't.

BONNY. Well, if you don't lie down soon, you'll fall down later.

WARD. Right. I'll wait until then.

BONNY. Then you're a fool. And that wasn't me or a woman you saw last night, it was your delirium.

TROUP. Look here, let's get back to what's important. Can I speak plainly?

WARD (*laughs*). Plainly, Troup. Good God! You certainly can.

TROUP. What, look, I'm not advocating going behind Barttelot's back, but simply that we all have a reasoned and proper discussion —

WARD (*gets to his feet, as sudden noises off*). He's here!

TROUP. What?

JAMESON *enters through the flap. He is carrying a shoulder-bag.*

WARD. Welcome back, old man. (*He shakes his hand.*)

JAMESON. Thank you. Troup — Bonny — how are you —

TROUP. Any news?

JAMESON. Oh, nothing very definite, I'm afraid, although —

BARTTELOT (*comes striding in*). Ah, here you are then, Jamie, thank God, I was getting worried, well, what news, what news?

JAMESON. None really, I'm afraid. Lots of rumours, but I didn't actually find a native who'd seen an Arab. Mark you, there was a great deal of excitement, more than usual, but the only significant thing was that in the village by the second river bend — where the Chief wears those boots Stanley gave him — a more preposterous figure — (*He laughs.*)

BARTTELOT. Well, what about him?

JAMESON. I know it doesn't sound much, but you see, he claimed he hadn't heard anything at all, not even a rumour.

TROUP. It certainly doesn't sound much, other than that there might be one honest nigger in the Congo after all.

JAMESON. No, my impression was the opposite. I couldn't be sure the other chiefs were telling the truth, but I was quite sure he wasn't. He knew something —

BARTTELOT. By God, you mean you believe he's seen Tippu-Tib?

JAMESON. Not quite that. But perhaps an Arab or two.

BARTTELOT. But by God, that's something. That's something more than we've had this last six months!

TROUP. But you're only guessing. It doesn't seem much to me, to go on.

JAMESON. There was one small piece of evidence. Just outside his village I came across the remains of a feast, a few bones —

BARTTELOT. An Arab feast?

JAMESON. Oh no, quite distinctly a native feast. But an exceptional one. An Arab might have furnished it.

TROUP. Furnished what? A goat?

JAMESON. No, no. Himself. He might have been caught and eaten. But really there was no way of knowing, because if it was an Arab, he was presumably in the belly of the Chief who said there wasn't.

WARD. That's what's called digesting the evidence.

JAMESON. There were only a few digitals sucked clean and a couple of shin bones to go on. It could equally well have been a nigger from one of the other villages who'd come up too far, and the chief might well have been emphatic about there being no Arabs because he didn't want a fuss over his meal. I can't say.

BARTTELOT. And nothing else?

JAMESON. No.

BARTTELOT (after a pause). So we're no further ahead?

JAMESON. Not really. I'm sorry.

BARTTELOT. Not your fault, old man.

JAMESON. Still, the bearer of no news — I say, (*to* WARD) you don't look at all well, your fever still running?

WARD (*gestures*). Oh, I'm much better. Much.

JAMESON. That's good. By the way, I caught the most beautiful parakeet, I shall have to stuff him this evening — and look — (*He takes a sketch out, shows it to* WARD.)

BARTTELOT (*to* BONNY). You'd better come and have a look at a Soudanese lying on the bank, some sort of green bile coming out of his mouth —

WARD. Ah, and here's our Stanley-booted Chief. Yes, I see what you mean, embarrassed but replete — certainly a large, illicit meal not far from his memory —

TROUP. No! no! (*Suddenly loud.*) What are we going to do? Are we going to look at Jameson's sketches, or study sick Soudanese we can't do anything for anyway, or are we going to talk, to talk for once about what we're going to do? This situation can't go on, don't you see, Barttelot, you Jameson, surely you see — all we have to show for six months' waiting, for some sixty dead men, is a loathsome story of shin bones and cannibalism. It's the last straw. (*Pause.*) Don't you see! We must act! We must act!

BARTTELOT. And what action do you suggest we take?

TROUP. Stanley can't possibly want us to linger on here —

BARTTELOT. I assure you he does.

TROUP. Well, for how long? Another month? Another two months? What use will we be to him then? He might already have reached Emin Pasha, for all we know. He might even be dead, they might all of them have been massacred by the Mahdi —

BARTTELOT. Yes.

TROUP. And meanwhile we're to go on waiting?

BARTTELOT. Yes.

TROUP. Rot among rotting niggers for no reason? Or wait for them to turn on us when we're in the middle of one of our floggings and tear us to pieces, do you really think that's what Stanley would want? Tippu-Tib's not coming. We all know it. There will be no six hundred porters. There's nothing to wait here for —

BARTTELOT. Except one's honour.

TROUP. Your honour, you mean, with Stanley. Oh, come man, your silly feud with Stanley is eight months past, he's long forgotten it, if he's even alive. Don't you see —

BARTTELOT. I see what you're proposing. It's desertion.

TROUP. I'm proposing that we act with common sense. I tell you, Barttelot, whatever you may claim, Stanley is not a murdering maniac.

BARTTELOT. I never said he was.

TROUP The other night you accused him of attempting to poison —

WARD. A figure of speech, old chap. A figure of —

TROUP. Well, his attitude to Stanley is poisoning us, that's the point. Good God man, those orders of his you're so frightened of contravening, they were written on the supposition that Tippu would be here months ago — Stanley didn't even deal with the contingency that's arisen, he never expected it.

BARTTELOT. You've forgotten the brass-rods.

TROUP. What? You mean we're running out of those, too? Then we'll certainly have a rebellion to deal with, the only thing the niggers look forward to is their brass-rods —

BARTTELOT. We're not running out. Stanley's left us enough to pay the men for another six months. Another six months, Troup.

There is a pause.

JAMESON (*suddenly laughs*). No, just a minute old man, you've forgotten that we also have to pay Tippu's men on the march. He'd take that into account.

BARTTELOT. I did. If Tippu's men had been paid from the day Stanley left, we'd still have enough for another six months. As Tippu's men haven't arrived we've enough for another year and a half. This from Mr Stanley, who knows the value of a brass-rod in the Congo as a — a Jew does of a sovereign in Kensington. So there you are, Troup, there's your evidence, Stanley acknowledges through the brass-rods that we might have to wait, and wait, and wait.

There is silence.

TROUP. Then what about the quinine, how do you explain that?

WARD. Perhaps he got Fortnum and Mason's to package the quinine.

BONNY. In my experience of medical supplies, there are never enough of them. Specially quinine.

TROUP (*goes to sit down*). Oh this is all — all speculation. The fact of the matter is, we don't know what Stanley intended — if only you'd found some way of getting him to take you through those damned orders. I still don't understand how it is you didn't get the chance, did he refuse to let you read them before he left, what?

JAMESON. I really don't see the value of going back —

BARTTELOT. No, I'll tell you what happened, Troup. I wasn't going to give him the satisfaction. That's what happened.

TROUP. What satisfaction?

BARTTELOT. Of watching me read them. When I went to his tent to get them he wasn't even dressed, that's how much — how much — he was just getting into those damned ridiculous togs he puts on specially for his marches, I had to stand there, to stand there while he crammed himself into those knicker-bockers he wears for showing off his calves and then his Norfolk jacket, which he thinks turns him into an English gentleman, and his German officer's cap, which he thinks turns him into a — a — German officer, and all the time strutting about gobble-de-gooking John Henry here who was blubbering away, and gobble-de-gooking the Soudanese in Soudanese and Zanzibaris in Zanzibari or the other way around for all I knew, to let me see the niggers were more important than his own senior officer, and sending messages to Jephson and Parke and Stairs — and in the middle of it all he shoved the orders into my hands and went on gobble-de-gooking, and when he saw I'd just shoved them into my pocket, that I was just going to go on standing there watching him with a smile he was forced to come back to me, and by God how he hates that, standing eye to eye with another white man. Well, Major (*He does a poor imitation of a high voice with a nasal twang.*) not interested in your orders? I take it, I said, I take it they don't apply until you've left the camp, Mr Stanley. Besides there's really no need, sir, as they shall be carried out to the letter, whatever they are. But not beyond the letter . . . or to your own letter . . . something like that, because I turned on my heel, and walked over here, leaving him to get on with his circus — so Troup, now you know why it was impossible, and why I wasn't going to give him the satisfaction, I hope it's given you some, eh?

TROUP. I can't believe it! You mean he actually invited you, — I can't believe it!

WARD. If you'll excuse the observation, old chap, one of your small weaknesses is that you can't believe what you clearly know to be true, it's far too human to be anything else, surely. You can believe it, can't you? If you try?

TROUP. Do you really find all this *amusing*, Ward?

WARD. Well yes, it's odd, I admit, but I put it down to my temperature or temperament —

TROUP. Well, because you didn't want Stanley to have the satisfaction, what it comes to is this. We have no idea what to do next —

BARTTELOT. We wait.

TROUP. For death?

JAMESON. Oh, I don't really think it'll come to that —

BARTTELOT. In view of the brass-rods anything else would be desertion. And that's what Stanley hopes for.

WARD. Well, actually Major, the brass-rods have nothing to do with anything at all. The perfectly simple and reasonable explanation for them came to me while you were describing — with great vivacity may I say — your last meeting with Stanley and then I became so engrossed with the — sorry — sorry — the delightful interchanges between yourself and our good Troup that I forgot to mention — and then you've such an assertive manner, do you see?

BARTTELOT. What are you talking about?

WARD. What?

JAMESON. It's his fever — (*goes to him*) old man, do lie down.

BONNY. I warned him.

WARD. Nonsense, no old boy, I'm quite — if you don't mind — the brass-rods, yes, the reason Stanley left them behind, yes, well it's because they're damned heavy, you see. Took as many as he calculated he'd need, and left us to bring up the rest with the porters, which porters and what porters being an entirely different question, but what would be the use of them if they weren't to bring up the brass-rods among the other things, eh?

There is a pause.

JAMESON. He's perfectly right, of course.

TROUP. Of course! My dear old Ward — well — so there we are, the rods mean nothing. Surely you agree?

BARTTELOT. It's a — possible — explanation.

TROUP. Well now can we — can we discuss it in a different atmosphere, I've been partly to blame, I admit, we bring out the worst in each other at times, eh, Major?

BARTTELOT. We wait. That's what we must do. For Tippu-Tib, or for a message from Stanley, or for news that Stanley is dead. We wait.

TROUP. No. No, I'm not going to wait. I'm going home. Who's coming with me? Ward, Jameson — you must see this is madness — come with me —

JAMESON. Excuse me, may I? (*Gently, takes* BARTTELOT's *stick.*) Stanley appointed me to stay with the Major, my place has been with him from the beginning — (*Moving gently towards* TROUP.)

WARD. There's no doubt honour's involved somewhere, you know, Troup, even if one can't — can't quite —

BONNY. I'm staying too. If you're interested, that is.

TROUP. Honour, there's no honour —

JAMESON *springs forward, with stick upraised, as if to strike* TROUP, *knocks him out of the way, and brings it down again and again, violently.*
TROUP *has lurched back with a cry of terror.*

JAMESON (*fishes up a dead snake with the tip of the stick*). Probably the mate of that one I got a few days ago — or were you simply after a spot of shade and a drop of water, can't blame you for that. (*He loops it over the rafters.*) You all right?

TROUP. What? All right? Yes, yes — what does another snake or two matter in all this madness.

BARTTELOT. When will you be leaving, Mr Troup?

TROUP. I can't go on my own, you know that.

BARTTELOT. One of us would accompany you, with the soundest of the Soudanese. We won't let you end up in the belly of an Arruwimi, don't worry.

TROUP. That's not what I meant. I stand by the majority decision.

BARTTELOT. We've each decided for ourselves, what our duty is. If you think yours is to leave —

TROUP. I'm staying.

BARTTELOT. In that case, Mr Troup, perhaps you will allow me to get on with my duties. Mr Bonny, shall we go and look at the Soudanese — (*He goes towards the flap, turns, looks at* TROUP.) But by God, Troup, by God I shall put it in the log! (*He goes out.*)

TROUP. The log? What does he mean? We had a discussion, I stand by the majority decision — does he mean I was proposing to desert, to abandon you and Stanley — he can't put that in the log! I shall — I shall write a letter to the Committee in London, to Mr William MacKinnon himself, stating my position. I shall get it on record that there was never any question — never — (*He goes out.*)

WARD. I wonder who he thinks is going to deliver his letter, or perhaps he'll ask for a majority decision to pop over with it himself to, what's the address, somewhere in Cutter's Lane, Holborn, isn't it? I say Jameson, that's a fine specimen you slaughtered there, much better than its wife or husband, was it? Are you going to add it to your collection or have you got one already, how you sense these things! The way you moved I thought — I thought you were going to strike down old Troup or even the rest of us, all of us, a single blow, while you were away I've taken up sculpting again, but fretfully, fretfully, tried to model Herman and King, but they would keep their heads in, because of Bonny's remarks about cooking them, you know, I was looking forward to showing you, but it's rotten work, rotten work I'm afraid, I (*swaying as he speaks, and collapses just as*):

JAMESON (*gets to him quickly, to support him*). My poor old fellow — here — let me — better get you to bed —

WARD. No, not to my tent. Not to my tent, if you please.

JAMESON. Well then, come — (*He helps* WARD *over to settee.*) There, lie down.

WARD. Sorry, sorry, Jameson — did you know I went on to fifty (*very brightly*) five and a fraction, didn't matter though, Bonny says he'll die anyway, it became a bit hypnotic, you see, telling off the strokes, and he got into a rhythm you know, his arm sweeping back and then forward, and then the scream, and then my voice, and his arm sweeping back and the screams stopped, and my voice, and his arm, and my voice —

JAMESON. It must have been quite horrible for you.

WARD. No, no, it was quite pleasant, (*fretfully*) quite pleasant, don't you see, could really have gone on and on, why don't you do it, Jameson, don't you enjoy it, Troup says Barttelot lets you off, is that true?

JAMESON. I supervised it once or twice, before you other chaps came up.

WARD. And didn't you find it pleasant?

JAMESON. No. But I didn't have a fever when I did it, perhaps that helps.

WARD (*sitting up, very brightly*). What about your wife and child, children you pray and trust, it must be awful for them having you away, when people count on you so much, if we need you here she must need you there, do you ever think about them, do you, Jameson, do you worry if they're all right?

JAMESON. Yes.

WARD. And I worry about you, you know, when you're away, so does Barttelot tramping about at top speed ordering floggings and kicking niggers and grinning, have you heard about his grinning? And worrying about you, he misses you, doesn't he?

JAMESON. You're really rather ill, you know. You must try and sleep.

WARD. No, but Jameson —

JAMESON. You must sleep. You must.

WARD. But you'll look in on me later, won't you?

JAMESON. Of course. (*He goes to the doors, makes to shut them.*)

WARD. Oh, don't shut them, if you please.

JAMESON. Oh, I think so. They'll light their fires, and the din —

WARD. Oh, I don't mind, truly I want the light please.

JAMESON (*hesitates*). All right, I'll leave them half and half — (*He half closes the doors, then turns, looks at WARD, goes out through the flap.*)

The stage dims slowly to night. WARD *is tossing and turning on his bed, in a troubled and feverish sleep.*
Suddenly a blaze off, and cries. The light of a large bonfire getting brighter and brighter. Voices chattering.
The drums begin, as at the end of Act One.
WARD *lets out a cry. Sits upright. The drums continue.*
WARD *stares wildly about, then fixes his gaze on the snake which appears, in the changing light from the blaze, to be writhing.*
WARD *stares transfixed, then begins to babble, shaking his head and clasping himself tightly. He is shivering. He moans, lets out shrill cries.*
TROUP *enters, through the flap, carrying a lamp. He goes to* WARD's *bed.*

WARD. The worm, the worm — (*Pointing.*)

TROUP. What worm? (*He turns.*) Good God! (*Laughs.*) It's only Jameson's snake — (*He goes to the rafter, pulls it down.*)

WARD. Be careful — be careful — Jameson will want it.

TROUP *puts the snake on the table, then goes to the doors.*

BARTTELOT (*off*). Stop it, damn you! Stop it, I say!

TROUP. There's old Barttelot on his rounds again, eh? Having a go at Mrs What-d'you call her, Minchip —

BARTTELOT (*off*). Damn you, will you stop it!

The drums begin to quiet, as at the end of the previous scene.

TROUP (*closes the doors, comes over*). I say, old boy, you've got it badly, eh?

WARD (*is sitting up, shaking hideously*). You mustn't go away again, you mustn't leave me again.

TROUP. No, no, of course not, old man, I'll sit by you. (*He gently pushes* WARD *back.*) There now, old man, that's better, isn't it? I'll be here, you'll be all right, eh?

JAMESON *enters through the flap, also carrying a lamp and some blankets, comes over, looks down at* WARD.

Not too good, eh?

JAMESON. No. (*He begins to put blankets over* WARD, *assisted by* TROUP.)

WARD. Jameson, Jameson — you there. (*Teeth chattering.*)

JAMESON. Yes. Right here.

WARD. You will stay, won't you?

JAMESON. Yes. Yes, I'll stay.

BONNY (*enters through flap*). Here we are, some quinine, compliments of the Major.

TROUP. Thank God for that.

BONNY (*goes to WARD, lifts his head*). Now get this down you — (*He administers it.*) There we are.

WARD. Thank you, Jameson.

BONNY. He's very bad. Very bad. If he'd lain down at the beginning — somebody'd better stay with him.

JAMESON. Yes, I'm going to.

BONNY. Then the rest of us better leave him in peace.

TROUP. Right. If you're sure —

JAMESON. Quite sure.

TROUP. Well then — (*He puts his hand on WARD's shoulder.*) Good night, old man.

BONNY. Good night.

JAMESON. Good night.

TROUP *and* BONNY *go towards the flap.*

BARTTELOT. Ah, you're all here are you, how is he?

BONNY. At the crisis. Jameson's going to sit with him.

BARTTELOT. Ah. (*He comes over to the bed.*)

TROUP *and* BONNY *exit.*

BONNY. Good night, Major. (*As he goes.*)

There is a pause.

BARTTELOT. He's had the quinine then?

JAMESON. Yes.

BARTTELOT. Ah. Well, be careful, Jamie, don't want you going out on us, we can take turns.

JAMESON. No, I'll be all right.

BARTTELOT. Ah. (*Pause.*) Well — (*He puts his hand on JAMESON's shoulder.*) Good night, old Jamie.

JAMESON. Good night.

> BARTTELOT *hesitates, turns, goes out through the flap.*
>
> *There is a silence.*

WARD. Jameson!

JAMESON. Yes.

WARD. Jameson, are you there?

JAMESON. Yes, I'm here.

> *There is a silence.* JAMESON *sees the snake, goes over, picks it up, then draws a chair to the bed, arranges the lamp so that the light falls on him. He takes a knife from his pocket, and begins to skin the snake.*
>
> *On this, lights.*

Scene Two

Some days later. Night.
> *A brazier is the first glow, followed by the other lights.*
> WARD's *make-shift bed has been disestablished.* JOHN HENRY *is moving around the table, clearing away the remnants of a meal.* BARTTELOT, BONNY *and* TROUP *are seated around the brazier.* BARTTELOT *is smoking a pipe. After a pause,* JAMESON *gets up, goes to the brazier, stokes it up.*
> *Off, a single drum starts, very low, almost a murmur.*

BARTTELOT. There she goes.

TROUP. I can't hear her. Oh yes. Still, they're very quiet tonight. Do you think they know? I mean, they might have felt something today. From us. The way we've behaved.

BONNY (*laughs*).

TROUP. Well, she's beating very soft, and the others haven't joined in. How do you explain that?

BONNY. Not by sentiment, anyway. The wonder is she can play at all, after what the Major did to her last night, eh Major?

BARTTELOT (*as if not listening*). Mmmmm?

TROUP. Why does she do it anyway, what do you think, Jameson?

JAMESON. What? Oh — (*coming from the brazier to sit down*) for the magic, I should think. As long as Mrs Minchip plays, the sickness will stay off Mr Minchip.

BONNY. Seems to work. They die around him, but every morning he's as fresh as black paint, except for a few patches of red and blue from the Major's stick or boot, eh Major?

JAMESON. Yes, well it's really very reasonable. Mr and Mrs Minchip are evidently genuinely attached to each other. Her continuing to play the drums for him in spite of the Major's attempts to stop her, only proves it to both of them. And so provides them both with a reason for living.

BONNY. There you are, Major, you're part of her magic too.

BARTTELOT. Mmmm? What do you mean?

BONNY. Well, you're helping to keep their marriage together and that always takes magic. Are you going to go out to them?

BARTTELOT. No, no. Not tonight. It would be wrong tonight.

TROUP. And they *are* very low. I tell you they feel something of what we're feeling. (*Pause.*) There! She's stopped altogether!

WARD *enters through the flap. He is carrying a large tray, on which is an object covered with a handkerchief. Under his arm, a bottle of brandy.*

BARTTELOT. Ah, there you are at last. What have you been up to?

WARD. Gentlemen, my apologies for the delay. There's a little something I gave myself to, in an idle kind of way, during my convalescence that I hesitate to present to public view (*putting the tray on the table*) but I hope that my main contribution (*holds up the brandy bottle*)

Laughs and cheers.

will help to render the other more tolerable. And his own to the evening has been so extreme that, however inadequately, he must be honoured. So gentlemen, Troup old man, if you would — (*hands him the brandy bottle*)

TROUP *pours into glasses.*

While I propose, thank you old man, a toast —

OTHERS (*standing*). A toast!

WARD. To our tender and succulent benefactor! (*He removes*

the hankerchief, to reveal the head of a goat, modelled in clay.)

Exclamations and applause.

WARD. To dear old Nanny!

OTHERS (*laughing*). Dear old Nanny!

JAMESON (*studying it*). But look here, old man, it's a real piece of work, something really done — the mouth is wonderful, quite wonderful — the sardonic grin, the twist there of the lips, the very essence of goatiness —

TROUP (*belches*). The substance being somewhere else.

WARD (*to* JAMESON). I'm not thoroughly shamed by it, I admit.

BONNY. The funny thing is, I shall miss him.

TROUP. That's charitable, Bonny, considering the devil never stopped trying to kick you.

BONNY. The devil's always trying to kick me, in some manifestation or another.

JAMESON. Now the brandy's arrived — (*taking a newspaper packet out of his pocket*) may I present my little — (*Holding it out. They take from it a cigar each, with little exclamations.*)

BARTTELOT (*pocketing his cigar*). I'll hang on to this a little longer, by God, it's good, Troup, damned good! Thank you for it.

BONNY. We all owe Troup thanks for it. He's sweetened the atmosphere around you.

BARTTELOT. What? (*He looks at* BONNY.) Oh. (*He laughs.*) Neat Bonny, very neat.

JAMESON (*who has been about to thrust the cigar newspaper into the brazier, checks himself*). Good Heavens, here's something — the personal column. If the gentleman who waited outside the Savoy on Friday of last week at the appointed hour should care to do so again this week, he will receive a full explanation, and an assurance of —

TROUP. Assurance of what?

JAMESON. It stops there.

BONNY. An assurance of nothing, then.

TROUP. Or of everything.

JAMESON (*looks at date*). Fourteen months ago. Well, let's trust the matter's been settled between them, whatever it was.

TROUP. Oh, it's obvious what it was. The writer is a lady and her message is addressed to a — well, gentleman.

JAMESON. Well, go on, old man. Give us the whole scene.

TROUP. Well, well it's a sacred tryst, what? They meet, let's see, they meet every Friday, for a few precious moments. They don't touch, scarcely speak, look into each other's eyes —

JAMESON. And what happened on that last Friday?

BARTTELOT. I'll tell you what, she has a fierce pater who locked her in, and the gentleman in question's an officer — penniless but true, they're planning something dashing — an elopement — eh?

BONNY. Mark my words, it's either money or — the other thing. If it's the other thing he didn't turn up because he's tired of waiting for it, if it's money she's not giving the other thing until she's got her hands on it.

JAMESON. How does that end?

BONNY. Oh, in the usual way. With an arrangement. The question is how *that* ends?

WARD. How does it usually end?

BONNY. Why, if it's bad, in the law courts. And if it's worse — in church.

BARTTELOT. Careful, Bonny, careful.

TROUP. Oh, I say, why is that worse?

BONNY. Because then it never ends.

JAMESON. Ah, but that song, Bonny — the one you were humming in the shower — I believe you're a sentimentalist at heart, like all cynics.

BARTTELOT. What song?

BONNY. Oh, just a song —

BARTTELOT. Sing it for us.

BONNY. What?

BARTTELOT. Sing it for us. (*Little pause.*) Come on, Bonny!

BONNY, *after a moment, stands, sings a Victorian love song, delicately and with feeling.*

TROUP (*rises, emotionally*). Gentlemen, to a young lady — a young lady in Highgate!

REST. A young lady in Highgate!

BARTTELOT. And a young lady in Sussex!

BONNY. To a young lady in Pimlico. Another in Maidenhead. A third in Greenwich!

BARTTELOT. No no, only allowed one, Bonny.

BONNY. Ah, then I choose — a young lady in Clapham!

REST (*laughing*). A young lady in Clapham!

WARD. To them, all plain and pretty, amiable and otherwise the true, the false, the young, the old — so long as they be ladies!

TROUP. You're worse than old Bonny — you've taken them all!

BONNY. No, he hasn't. Just one. Pretty, amiable, young and true on the way to the altar! Plain, false, old and otherwise from there to the grave!

BARTTELOT. You go too far, Bonny! Too far! Remember Mrs Jameson!

BONNY. Oh, I'm sorry, I didn't mean to give —

JAMESON. Oh good Heavens, I can easily refute our Bonny — by inviting you all to take dinner in my home this day a year hence. Mrs Jameson and I and our (*hesitates*) children will be grateful for the chance to prove that what begins in church can continue ever more happily, please God! Will you come, all of you? Mrs Jameson would be so pleased.

BARTTELOT (*solemnly*). Mrs Jameson!

REST. Mrs Jameson.

A respectful silence.

JAMESON. Or of course, *two* years hence, depending on circumstances known to us all —

Laughter.

WARD. And that's the real interpretation to put on the message in the Personal Column — it's not written by a lady at all, but by some desperate fellow trying to do business with Mr Tippu-Tib. Who is now outside the Savoy —

JAMESON. Or indeed inside it, with his six hundred porters turned waiters.

Laughter.

BARTTELOT. You know what my pater says, he says 'It's a funny old world.' And he's right. Here we all are, we've had our quarrels and our worries, God knows — old Troup and I are a pretty peppery couple of fellows from time to time, eh? But here we are — and somewhere out there, Stanley, please God, as Jamie said — and tonight — well tonight, my spirit's at peace with him. I'll never like him, I can't promise to like him but by God I can't help wishing him safety, and an evening of fellowship like this one. Eh?

REST. Hear, hear!

TROUP. And I'll wager he's wished us the same, eh? And look, I want to endorse everything the Major's said — whatever — whatever the hazards — we are — we remain

BONNY *is quietly pouring himself more brandy.*

united, I mean we've forged a bond — between us — that — that — speaking for myself I know will last to the end of my life. I shall look back on this Christmas together to the — to the end of my life.

There is a pause.

JAMESON. Amen to that.

BARTTELOT. Bonny, give us a carol, there's a chap. My heart yearns for one.

BONNY *begins to sing 'The Twelve Days of Christmas'.*

OTHERS *join in. Half-way through the drums begin, very low, scarcely noticeable.*

BARTTELOT *has put his hand on* JOHN HENRY's *shoulder.*

As they sing, lights and:

Curtain.

Act Three

Scene One

The same. Six months later. It is morning.
The doors are open. Around the room are various pieces of sculpture, in clay, heads of natives, animals, etc; and some sketches, stuffed birds, stuffed snakes.
A NATIVE WOMAN, naked, her arms tied behind her, a halter around her neck and attached to a rafter, is squatting on the floor, right.
WARD is seated on a packing case, modelling her head in clay.
BONNY enters, drifts over, watches WARD, then sits down at the table, close to the woman. There is a silence. He stares at the woman, suddenly smiles at her.
The WOMAN smiles back.
BONNY laughs.
The WOMAN laughs back.
BONNY laughs again.
The WOMAN laughs again.

BONNY. Funny, they squat for hours without an expression until you laugh at them. And they always laugh back.

WARD. Yes, they have very pleasant dispositions. Unless of course she was laughing at you for laughing at her — who can say whether the man is playing with the cat or the cat with the man . . .

BONNY. More like cattle than cats. Although she might have a game or two in her . . . eh, my darling? (*He laughs.*)

The WOMAN laughs.

WARD. Could you, do you think, hold back on your wooing a while — I'd prefer her to keep her head still. Besides, the days when you were the Lothario of Yambuya are over by some months, aren't they — ever since our Commanding Officer delivered his *en passant* homily on what he'd do, by God, to any white man he caught, by God! etc, etc.

BONNY *yawns, puts his feet on the table, his head back. Begins to hum.*

WARD (*glances at him with irritation*). Why don't you join our Commanding Officer, he'd be glad of your company, I'm sure.

BONNY. Where is he?

WARD. Having a word.

BONNY. Who with?

WARD. A couple of Soudanese who fell asleep on watch last night. The second provisions tent, I believe it was. Some of Stanley's medical supplies are in there, so he should be lathering up nicely, you'll catch him at his climax if you run.

BONNY (*after a slight pause*). Anything missing?

WARD. Mmmm?

BONNY. Anything missing?

WARD. Why don't you scamper over and see for yourself, there's a good man.

BONNY *gets up, goes over to the water bucket, tries to pour himself some. It is empty.*

BONNY. John Henry! John Henry!

WARD. Oh for — do stop shouting, Bonny! He won't come. At least, not for you.

BONNY. Well, he'd better, for his sake. If the Major finds out he's forgotten the water — John Henry!

WARD (*throws down the clay in disgust*). He's probably unconscious, you fool.

BONNY. What? (*Little pause.*) Oh.

WARD. Didn't you hear his screams?

BONNY. No.

WARD. Really not? About midnight, from his master's tent?

BONNY. No.

WARD. Nor his master's bellow, stick and boot?

BONNY. No.

WARD. How do you manage those slumbers of yours? You seem

to have found the secret that eludes everyone but the niggers on watch and the dying, of course.

BONNY. Perhaps I've given up worrying.

WARD. But what have you taken up to give up worrying? (*He looks at him.*) Eh, Bonny?

BONNY. The thing about you, Ward, is you can't let up, can you? You set out to make him worse, the way you went on at him in mess, counting off the niggers who'd died or escaped this last month —

WARD. I was merely trying to engage his attention, with a little mental arithmetic.

BONNY. Yes, well you left him in a proper state, then banging your hand up and down to the drums — that's probably why he went off and battered John Henry.

WARD. Ah, I see. And that's why you needn't concern yourself with his health. Don't types of your rank have to take the Hippocratic oath, Bonny?

BONNY (*after a pause*). Oh, shut up, Ward.

WARD. You feel no professional obligation, to minister to him, eh?

BONNY. What am I meant to do? He hasn't consulted me, has he?

WARD. And he won't. He's far too frightened.

BONNY. What of?

WARD. You.

BONNY. Oh very funny, Ward.

WARD. You can have my next year's ration of goat if he isn't.

BONNY. You honestly mean to tell me that Barttelot's frightened of *me* —

WARD. Barttelot? Good God, Bonny, you'd better not go about confusing our Commanding Major Barttelot with his battered little nigger of a serving boy. No, no, get it clear in your head, they're fearfully distinct, you know. The battered little nigger of a serving boy is the one who's frightened of you, even though he needs your skill and bandages. The Commanding Major Barttelot is the one you're frightened of, and with good reason, as he's quite clearly mad. And now you've got something to report to the Major, you'll hurry along, won't you, please, and report it?

BONNY. You want me to tell him that you say he's mad, do you?

WARD. Yes please.

BONNY. Why?

WARD. So that I can tell him what it is you've started taking to give up worrying. Then he'll have you flogged, I should think, and I'd quite enjoy that. Wouldn't you?

BONNY. I warn you, Ward, if you make any trouble for me with Barttelot, I'll make a damned sight more back.

TROUP *enters. He looks very ill, thin and yellow complexioned.*

BONNY. Oh hello, old man, how are you?

TROUP *pays no attention, goes on to the water bucket.*

BONNY. You really shouldn't be up you know.

WARD. There you are, old man, Bonny's just made out his favourite prescription. That should make you feel better.

TROUP *drops the cup, comes back to the table, sits down.*

BONNY. I'll get you some water — (*He rises.*)

TROUP. No, you won't.

BONNY. You're thirsty, aren't you?

TROUP. Yes, but you won't get any water. You'll go out for it, but you won't come back with it.

BONNY. What do you mean?

WARD. You know what he means. He means that you'll go out for it but you won't come back with it.

TROUP. Because you haven't asked him, have you?

BONNY. I haven't even seen him to speak to this morning.

TROUP. But you're not going to ask him, are you?

BONNY. Of course I am. I said I would. But I also said I didn't see the point because we all know what the answer's going to be.

TROUP. What about you, Ward, will you speak up for me?

WARD. Of course. But I won't do any good, old chap. Quite the reverse, I'm afraid.

TROUP. I see. So I'm to die then? Is that it? To die without making a fuss.

BONNY. Look, I don't think it's quite that bad —

TROUP. Oh yes it is. Oh yes it is. I'm weaker every time I come out of it. I shall die all right, I've known it for days now. I shall die. Die here in this place because a lunatic, a lunatic — (*He stops, trembling.*)

WARD. I say, old man, be careful. The faithful Bonny, you know, is at your side.

TROUP. I don't care. I'm past caring. You tell him I saw him, Bonny. He didn't know I was watching, but I saw him, from my tent flap. I saw the lunatic go out and —

BARTTELOT (*enters, carrying his stick and a basket*). Two rotting fish! Two rotting fish!

WARD. Three dying niggers, four flogging gentlemen —

BARTTELOT. What?

WARD. Oh nothing, just what promised to be an amusing anecdote of old Troup's you've interrupted, what were you saying about two rotting fish —

BARTTELOT. That's all her husband thinks she's worth, smirking outside as if he were redeeming from a pawn shop — (*going over to the woman, untying the rope from the rafter*) come on, get up, get up, he's bought you back with two rotting fish — go on, get along with you — and take these with you — (*He hooks basket around her neck*) tell him to choke on them himself — (*He grins at her, she cowers away from him*) go, get along with you — (*He propels her out through the door*) swears there isn't a goat to be had, stinks like a goat himself, a morning wasted catching her for two rotting fish — well, I got them to admit it at last, they'd been asleep all right, thank God they hadn't got into the boxes, none of them opened and they're not cunning enough to put the lids back on — by God if any of the medicine had been touched Stanley'd never have believed it was the niggers — not with a chance like that — Troup, you're closest to the tent, did you hear anything last night?

TROUP. I'm still ill, thank you for asking. Worse, as a matter of fact.

BARTTELOT. What?

WARD. Still ill, thank you for asking. Worse as a matter of fact.

BARTTELOT. I'm talking to Troup, Ward.

TROUP. I said I'm worse.

BARTTELOT. But you're up, aren't you?

TROUP. Oh yes. Yes, I'm up, Barttelot.

BARTTELOT. Slept through the night, did you?

TROUP. No, Barttelot. No sleep. None at all.

WARD. Loyal Bonny did, though, didn't you, Bonny? Slept like a top.

BARTTELOT. Well then, did you hear anything, see anything?

TROUP. Oh yes. I saw and heard quite a lot.

BARTTELOT. What?

WARD. He saw and heard —

BARTTELOT. From the provisions tent?

TROUP. No. Not from there.

BARTTELOT. Well, Ward, what about you?

WARD. Screams, oaths and blows from your tent. From the provisions tent, nothing. So I'm afraid I can't help you either, sir.

BARTTELOT (*goes over to the water*). Well, we've got to find out who's responsible, there's a clutch of Soudanese scum who're up to some mischief — (*Tries to pour water.*)

WARD. How remarkable.

BARTTELOT. What?

WARD (*after a little pause*). Why, that anyone in the compound, apart from your energetic self, of course, could be up to anything as taxing as mischief.

BARTTELOT. Well, you're damned well not are you, been idling in here all day — John Henry, John Henry! Where is the little —

BONNY. Haven't seen hide nor hair of him, Major.

WARD. From which we can conclude, sir, that he must still be out.

BARTTELOT. Out where?

WARD. Of his senses. And after the kind of night you had together, it's not to be wondered at, is it?

BARTTELOT. You drank the last drop of water, I suppose, Ward, but damn if you were going to get some more for the rest of us, eh?

WARD. Damn me, sir, if I was.

BONNY. I'll go, Major, I was just about to fetch some for Troup anyway — (*Getting up.*)

BARTTELOT. Thank you Bonny.

WARD. Before you go, Bonny, would you kindly ask the Major what you promised old Troup here you'd ask him?

BONNY. What?

WARD. Before you go, Bonny, would you kindly ask etc.

BONNY. It's only what I've already mentioned, Major. I explained that the situation being what it is —

BARTTELOT. You know the situation, Troup. You've known it for months. There isn't any.

TROUP. Yes, there is. There is!

BARTTELOT. But it's not ours, Troup. It's Stanley's. We've used up ours.

TROUP. So. So I'm to die —

BARTTELOT. You're not going to die.

TROUP. — because the rest of you used up our stock before I could get ill, is that what it comes to?

WARD. Yes, even you must find that a trifle bizarre, sir. That poor old Troup's superior robustness has had such an unhappy effect on his health. (*He laughs.*)

BARTTELOT. What?

WARD. Yes, even you must find that a trifle —

BARTTELOT. By God, Ward, how sick I am of your jokes.

WARD. Ah, but fortunately — for you — you don't need quinine to recover from them.

BARTTELOT. But I know how to stop you making them.

WARD. So do I, sir. Some humanity, or failing that, a dash of intelligence, in the running of this camp. Or did you mean bellow, boot and stick, as usual?

TROUP. You're just going to stand by, then, and see me die, are you, Barttelot? My death shall be on your head. I've written to MacKinnon, my letter to be conveyed to him with the rest of my effects, Ward, if you'll be so good.

WARD. Of course, my dear chap. Though I should point out that having over a hundred dead blacks on his head already —

BARTTELOT. That's right, Troup. You can die if you want to. I've long wanted you gone, you've never had anything to give to the Rear Column but bluster when you're well and snivelling now you're sick. It's not medicine you lack, Troup, but fortitude.

TROUP (*after a pause*). You refuse me, then.

BARTTELOT. Of course I refuse you.

TROUP. And that's your last word?

BARTTELOT. I hope so. Though knowing you —

TROUP. Very well. I give you warning, Barttelot. I shall help myself from Stanley's supplies.

BARTTELOT. What? (*Pause.*) What did you say?

TROUP. I shall help myself —

BARTTELOT. By God — by God, you already have, haven't you? It was you, wasn't it, in the provisions' tent last night! It was you! I'm going to open every load, every one, and if there's a drop of quinine missing, I'll — by God, Troup, I'll have you flogged for the thieving nigger you are.

TROUP (*runs over to him*). You're mad, Barttelot, a lunatic, a lunatic! I saw you last night, I watched you, I wrote it down, It's in my letter to MacKinnon, don't forget the letter, Ward —

WARD. Certainly not, old man.

TROUP. Everybody'll know you for what you are — do you know what he did last night?

BARTTELOT (*advances on* TROUP, *grinning*). Hah, hah, hah, hah! Hah hah hah hah!

JAMESON *appears at the door. He is carrying equipment, as in Act Two, Scene One. He is not, at first, noticed.*

Hah hah hah hah!

TROUP. You, you —

WARD. Ah, welcome home, old man — oh, the Major and Troup are just sharing a joke on the subject of the Major's sanity.

BARTTELOT. Hah hah hah hah!

TROUP *draws back a fist, to strike* BARTTELOT. BARTTELOT *thrusts his face closer to* TROUP.

Hah hah hah hah!

JAMESON *moves very swiftly, catches* TROUP's *arm, pulls him away. He stands between* BARTTELOT *and* TROUP, *facing* BARTTELOT.

Ah — ah, there you are, Jamie, you're back then are you?

TROUP. He's trying to murder me, murder me, Jameson — well — (*trying to pull* JAMESON *away*) let him do it so everybody can see — go on, Barttelot, kill me, kill me now, in front of everybody —

BARTTELOT. By God I will, Troup, if you don't get out of the Camp and back to England. I'm sending you home, now, this minute.

TROUP. See, see, he's frightened of me because I saw him — Oh, I saw him —

JAMESON. Please. Please, listen to me. (*Little pause.*) I've news. I've seen Tippu-Tib.

BARTTELOT. What? (*As if dazed.*) Seen him?

JAMESON. Yes. He sends his greetings and his apologies for the delay.

BARTTELOT. The delay! For the delay — after a year!

JAMESON. But he solemnly undertakes to be with us shortly, with the porters. He swore it to Allah, and in friendship to Stanley. Apparently he lost his first catch through a series of monstrous misfortunes — escape, sickness, capsizing boats, but he sent messengers to let us know — presumably they were the cannibal victims. But his second lot, with a large guard of his Arabs, are on their way. He's just had word. He's going back to the Falls to bring them up himself.

BARTTELOT. About — about three weeks then! A month at the most!

JAMESON. His own calculation was a month.

BARTTELOT. By God — by God — of all the wonderful — but what was he doing in these parts, if his slaves are at the Falls?

JAMESON. Coming to see you. But I told him that as he'd seen me, you'd prefer him to get back to the porters —

BARTTELOT. By God yes — and Stanley — any news of Stanley?

JAMESON. He must be alive as he'd have heard if he were dead.

He's a rather extraordinary chap, our Tippu, by the way, you'll enjoy —

BARTTELOT (*is pacing about, talking almost as if to himself*). So Stanley's still alive, the porters coming up — can't be more than a month away — we'll meet him on the march, by God — with the loads — with the loads — how d'you do, Mr Stanley, here are your supplies, sir — by God we've beaten you, Stanley — beaten you, sir — (*He goes on out through the doors, and his voice, off.*) Up on your feet, scum, up on your feet, you're going to learn how to walk again — up I say — up with you — by God I've beaten him — march — march along I say — I've beaten the devil — (*His voice fading, but sounding now and then.*)

TROUP. So we'll be moving from this place after all, is that what you mean, Jameson? Is that it?

JAMESON. Yes, old man. That's it.

TROUP. But what about me, what's he going to do about me? I told him, you see, I let him know that I'd seen him — oh why did I, why did I? Now he'll send me home to die in the jungle, or leave me here to perish by myself while you march on —

JAMESON. My dear old chap, there's no question of your being left, or of your being sent home, and certainly not of your dying. I do assure you.

TROUP. Oh, I shall die, Jameson, one way or the other. He'll see to that. Anyway I won't live without quinine, and he won't let me have any of Stanley's, that's how he'll do it —

JAMESON. But there's no need of Stanley's. I've got some. Here. (*He takes a phial out of his equipment.*) I've always kept some of my personal stock in reserve for my expeditions, in case I'm taken with a fever away from base — but I shan't need it now, shall I? Besides, I've never felt so well in my life.

TROUP. Oh, thank you, Jameson. Thank you. God bless you. God bless you. (*He bursts into tears.*) I'm sorry, I'm sorry — (*He sinks to his knees.*) Oh Jameson —

JAMESON *lifts* TROUP *up, holds him.*

BONNY. He should be in bed.

WARD. Well, why don't you put him there?

JAMESON. Yes, I'm sure you're the chap he needs —

BONNY. Yes, come along, old man, let's get you down. (*He puts his arm around* TROUP, *who is in a state of semi-collapse, and leads him off.*)

There is a pause.

WARD. Well. (*Smiling.*) You got back in the nick of time.

JAMESON. I've never moved so fast in my life. (*Little pause.*) How are you?

WARD. I'm anxious to hear about your adventures, what sort of chap is Tippu after all?

JAMESON. Oh very amusing. I kept storing away all sorts of things to tell you, (*going to the water bucket*) he goes in for a grand, not to say flamboyant style of hospitality, I've done one or two sketches of him in characteristic postures, I must show you later, by the way, oh, and I picked up a spectacular lizard and a butterfly I've never seen before, he fluttered over Tippu's head on my second morning and settled in a branch — (*Makes to pour himself water.*)

WARD. I'm afraid it's empty. John Henry being hors de combat, let me get you some.

JAMESON. No, no, I'm not really thirsty, I stopped for a drink when I came in. I wasn't thirsty then either, but one gets into the habit of taking a drink where one can as if it'll make up for the times one can't, which of course it doesn't. (*He laughs.*) But you haven't told me how you are?

WARD. All I can really say is that I'm no worse.

JAMESON. No worse?

WARD. Than the rest of us. I haven't been beating children senseless, for instance. But then that's the Major's way, not mine. Nor have I been stealing morphine from Stanley's supplies. But then that's Bonny's way, as it turns out.

JAMESON. Ah, I did wonder, before I left —

WARD. Troup's way you know about, as you caught the climax of his performance.

JAMESON. Yes, poor old Troup.

WARD. For my part, I've mainly lolled.

JAMESON. Lolled?

WARD. Yes, about and about, you know. Inflaming the

inflammable, goading the goadable and despising the despicable.
That's been my way.

JAMESON. But I see you've made an attempt — (*Indicating the head of the woman.*)

WARD. Yesterday afternoon I dragged myself over to the river-
bank, where I lolled in the hope of catching you in an early
return. But all I saw were the corpses of two drowned niggers,
rolled along by the sluggish current, and a few minutes later
one nigger drowning. He sank some yards from me but bobbed
up half an hour later, his head tangled in weeds, to be rolled off
in his turn. I took him to be a deserting Zanzibari.

JAMESON. I'm sure there was nothing you could have done.

WARD. No, there wasn't, really.

JAMESON. Thank God you didn't go in after him. That current —
you wouldn't have had a chance.

WARD. Not much of one, certainly.

JAMESON. So you mustn't reproach yourself.

WARD. Oh, I haven't been. Nor have I reproached myself for
not reproaching myself, if you see.

JAMESON. Well I don't quite —

WARD. What I'm trying to say is, well, that given our different
forms of degeneration, you were quite right to lie about
seeing Tippu-Tib. False hope is probably our only hope now.

JAMESON. I didn't lie about seeing Tippu-Tib. I spent three days
in his camp.

WARD. I see. Then you lied about what he said.

JAMESON. I reported him absolutely faithfully.

WARD. But you can't have believed him!

JAMESON (*after a pause*). Of course not. It was understood
between us at once that his lies were a courtesy. Kindness, even,
so that I shouldn't feel obliged to accuse him of treachery
when hoplessly outnumbered. As I said, he's an excellent host,
he really went to extravagant lengths to make me comfortable.
(*Pause.*) I hoped you wouldn't be taken in. I shall need your
support more than ever when the month is up and the doubts
return.

WARD. And the whole process starts again. Although we shan't
survive a whole year this time.

JAMESON. But if we can stretch the month into two and then three — until Stanley comes back, or we have news of his death. We have a chance. (*He smiles*.) At least we'll survive until tomorrow.

WARD. Of course if we were all like you, we could survive here for ever. And you could certainly survive without us, couldn't you?

JAMESON. Not quite. (*Pause*.) I say, would you like to have a look (*going to equipment*) at my rendering of Tippu, I think I've caught something of his —

WARD. No! No I wouldn't! (*Little pause*.) I'm sorry, I know it's infernally weak of me, I admire you more than any man I've ever met, and I'm flattered, flattered of course, that you should have counted on me for your support, even though I know you could manage without it, but it's just that — at the moment I wish — I wish you hadn't — no, that's not fair — I hadn't insisted on the truth. I'm sorry. Infernally weak. But then I am. I've learnt that much — (*He turns, goes towards the flap, stops, looks at* JAMESON.)

JAMESON. I'm sorry. If I'd realised —

WARD. Don't worry. You *can* count on me. For what I'm worth. (*He exits*.)

JAMESON *stands for a moment.*

From off, BARTTELOT's *voice, roaring out orders, and the sound of the Soudanese, and the Zanzibaris, calling to each other excitedly, coming near, then turning, going further off.*

JAMESON *goes to the doors, draws them almost closed, but allowing light to enter, comes back, stares at his equipment, then after a moment takes out a dead parakeet, gutted; then a small object, presumably the butterfly; looks at it; takes out several more objects, a bowl and a wooden spoon; finally his sketch pad and note-book. Opens the note-book, sits looking at it.*

JOHN HENRY *enters through the flap, limping bruised, carrying a water-bucket. He looks furtively over at* JAMESON, *who watches him go to replace the empty water-bucket with the full one, and then turn to go out.*

JAMESON. John Henry. John Henry — come here.

JOHN HENRY *comes over.*

Are you all right?

JOHN HENRY *nods.*

Well, you will be from now on. I promise you. No more bruises.
No more. All right? (*He pats his head.*) Now you go and find
your master, eh?

JOHN HENRY *nods, goes out through the flap.*

JAMESON *sits for a moment, looks at the sketches, then puts
his face in his hands, as if tired. The voices off become less and
less distinct. The lights fade slowly down to darkness.*

Scene Two

A couple of hours later.
    *The set is in darkness. There comes from the darkness a low
murmur, an exclamation, silence. Then another exclamation.*
BARTTELOT *enters, left, carrying a lamp.* JOHN HENRY *is at
his side. There is another exclamation.* BARTTELOT *goes over to
the work desk, holds the lamp up.* JAMESON *is slumped over the
desk, asleep. On the desk his note-book. His sketch-pad has fallen
to the floor.* BARTTELOT *lights the lamp near the table, gives
his own lamp to* JOHN HENRY, *who lights the other lamps.*
    JAMESON *groans heavily.*

BARTTELOT (*stands looking down at him. Then puts a hand on*
    JAMESON'*s shoulder.*) All right, Jamie. All right, old boy. It's
    only me.

    JAMESON *lifts his head, sees* BARTTELOT, *lets out a cry of
    terror.*

    Only me, Jamie. Only me.

JAMESON. Oh, I'm — I'm sorry.

BARTTELOT. A bad dream, eh?

JAMESON. Yes.

BARTTELOT. And are you properly awake now?

JAMESON. I'm not sure.

BARTTELOT. Well, I'm no dream, I can tell you. (*He laughs.*)
    I've had them on the march, up and down and around the

compound, then out into the jungle, making them walk, making
them feel their legs again, you see, the halt, the maim,
tomorrow I'll have the strongest moving with loads, some will
have to carry double when Tippu's lot arrive, we've lost so
many, but by God we won't lose another one, not another one
— John Henry — go and get some manioc — manioc, John
Henry — tell you the truth couldn't keep still myself, thinking
of his face — the expression on the devil's face.

JOHN HENRY *has gone out for the manioc.*

— when he finds every one of them intact, eh? Well, Mr
Stanley, what sort of year have you had? Let me tell you about
ours — oh, and here's our Mr Jameson, Mr Bonny, Mr Ward
and even Mr Troup, you do remember us, I take it, or had you
thought us dead, sir. Or deserted even? By God — by God —

JOHN HENRY *returns, pours the manioc.*

That's the boy, John Henry, keep off that bad leg, eh? (*He
drinks.*) Well, Jamie — and what about Emin Pasha, I thought
of him when I was marching them, first time for nearly a year
I remembered him. Make nonsense of the whole business if
Stanley hasn't got him out, if the Mahdi got to him first, eh?
All that we've been through because of Emin Pasha, and none
of it to do with him, just a battle between Stanley and
ourselves, and ourselves and the damned niggers, and ourselves
and ourselves, eh? (*He drinks, looks at* JAMESON.) But I'll tell
you something. He nearly won, old man. He did. If you hadn't
come back God knows what — Troup called me a lunatic and —
by God he was right. Because last night I committed the act of
a lunatic and Troup saw me at it. It was your Mrs Minchip who
drove me to it, on her drums, I sent John Henry out, and they
went silent, then started again, and — I couldn't endure it,
couldn't endure it, but I did, you see, instead of going out and
giving her a cuff myself I endured it, until the others had gone
to bed, and then I went out, walked over them, trampled on
them where they lay, or put my stick into their sides and stirred
them out of the way with the point, walking in a straight line
to their tent, and when I got there I went up to the woman
squatting there, beating away, and I grinned at her, you know
how my grin works, a grin and then a cuff, how they fold before
it, but this time not a bit of it, she kept on pounding away, not
even seeing me, and then I looked up, and there was his face
in the slit of their tent, peering out and grinning back at me,
and beneath that another slit, freshly cut, the barrel of his

rifle sticking out of it straight at me, right at my chest, you see,
and the woman pounding on, so I looked back at him, grinning
at his grin to wipe it off, and I could see him losing his nerve,
the barrel wavered, so I bent over the woman, you see, didn't
know what I was doing until my teeth were in her neck. Sank
them deep into her neck, to stop her on the drums at last. I
looked back at the slit and I thought now — now you nigger,
if you dare — with her blood still around my mouth, and I
laughed into his face. Laughed into his face with his woman's
blood around my mouth and his gun against my chest. It was a
good laugh, a good long laugh, all the time I was waiting for the
rifle to go off, thinking now, nigger, do it now — until I turned
and walked away, stepping on them again, on their arms and
legs and bellies and faces and when I got back to my tent I
remembered the blood was still around my mouth. I licked at
it with my tongue. Licked it off with my tongue. Drank some
manioc to get rid of the taste, and more manioc to keep the
dear old pater, you see, from watching his son lick up nigger
blood from around his mouth — or Stanley seeing — what I
had come to. And there was John Henry — and so he got the
brunt of it, poor little mite. Poor little mite. You see. Had to
tell you myself. Before you hear it from Troup. (*Pause.*) Well,
Jamie — what do you think of me now?

JAMESON. Why, exactly as I've always thought of you, old man.

BARTTELOT. You don't despise me for it.

JAMESON. No.

BARTTELOT. That's a relief. I care what you think of me, you
know. Always have. You, with your strength — well, you know
that. (*Pause.*) By God, you know, I may be the wrong man for
the Rear Column, that's why he chose me, but I did one good
thing, right at the beginning, I had the beating of Stanley right
at the beginning, when I made him give you over to me.

JAMESON. Give me over to you?

BARTTELOT. One of Parke, Jephson or Stair will remain behind
with you, Barttelot, he said. You may choose. And I said,
None of them, thank you, Mr Stanley, the man I want is
Jameson. Jameson, Jameson, he said, but Jameson isn't an
officer, he's a paying gentleman. And I said, It's Jameson I
want, Mr Stanley. And he gave me a Stanley look, and I
readied myself for a row, instead he whinnied out some
laughter, Very well, he said. Very well. But I advise you,

Major Barttelot, for the sake of harmony between you, not
to tell him he's staying behind at your request. Even Jameson,
gentleman though he is, might come to hate you for it. Stanley,
the great judge of men! Didn't know you as I knew you, even
then — and that's where I had the beating of him. And beaten
him all over again by telling you. Although I've waited until
today to do it, I admit, and probably wouldn't have today if —
if —

JAMESON. Fate hadn't worked things otherwise.

BARTTELOT. That's it, old man! That's it!

JAMESON. But then fate, being fate, never does. At least in as
much as you've been mine, and didn't.

BARTTELOT. All I can say is, in spite of everything, I wouldn't
have had it different.

JAMESON. Amen to that!

BONNY *enters through the flap.*

Ah, Bonny, here you are then — Jameson and I were just
having a glass — John Henry, a glass for Mr Bonny —

JOHN HENRY *pours* BONNY *a glass.*

Off, the drums start, with a flourish.

BARTTELOT. There they go, eh Jamie? So that's all right then —
well, they've something to celebrate tonight, John Henry, go
tell them with the Major's compliments that tonight they
may play their drums — but low, tell them — low.

BONNY (*meanwhile, spotting* JAMESON's *fallen sketch-pad,
picks it up*). Brought back some drawings too, eh?

JAMESON. Yes.

BONNY. So quite a successful trip, what with one thing and the
other.

JOHN HENRY *goes out.*

BONNY (*looking through the pad*). Any of Tippu-Tib?

BARTTELOT. What, Tippu, I must have a look at those, get to
know the devil on different terms, eh? By God, it'll be hard to
keep a check on my tongue when he comes in here — How
d'you do, Mr Tib, glad to make your acquaintance at last, sir —

WARD *enters through the flap.*

Ah, here you are, Ward — here's a glass of Yambuya

champagne for you — and *I've* got good news — fish stew
tonight.

BONNY. What?

BARTTELOT (*laughs*). No, it's all right, Bonny, three I picked
up down-river when I was marching the men, not the rotting
pair this morning — Jamie, you haven't heard about that yet,
Bonny and I caught ourselves a woman yesterday, hobbled her,
brought her back, her man came in this morning with two
stinking fish —

The drums have quietened.

TROUP *enters through the flap.*

Troup, by God, you've come — here — a glass for Troup — but
should you be up, even for Yambuya champagne, old man —
here — (*pouring him a glass*) should you be?

TROUP. Thank you. Jameson's quinine, you know — (*He clears
his throat.*) Um Major, I want to say — say before everybody
— that — I said some things this morning I — I deeply regret,
accused you of all sorts of nonsense, which Bonny tells me — I
realise was just — just delirium —

BARTTELOT (*pause*). Well — you and I have had our — our —
what's passed is passed, eh? That's the thing — let's drink
instead — drink to, to —

WARD. Tippu-Tib. (*He glances at* JAMESON.)

BARTTELOT. Why, yes — Tippu-Tib, damn his soul!

REST. Tippu-Tib, damn his soul!

BONNY. I saw him a minute ago, yes, here he is — (*Flicking
open the sketch pad.*)

BARTTELOT. What, let's see, why that's as good as your famous
A Faithful Zanzibari says his Farewell, Jamie — what slyness,
what pomp, eh, and his rifle — the one Stanley gave him —
over his chest — hah, hah, hah!

JAMESON *puts his hand to his forehead.*

BARTTELOT *goes to get the manioc jug.*

WARD (*to* JAMESON). Are you all right?

JAMESON. Yes, yes — just a touch tired —

BONNY *is casually turning over pages of the pad.*

TROUP (*to* JAMESON). I'm very conscious of my debt to you, Jameson. For the quinine — and everything else.

JAMESON. Oh.

JOHN HENRY *enters.*

BARTTELOT. Ah, there's a good boy — well done John Henry, well done — (*Coming back with the jug.*)

BONNY (*lets out an exclamation*). What's this?

JAMESON (*looking up*). Mmmm?

WARD *saunters over to look.*

BARTTELOT *comes over with the jug, offers to pour for* TROUP.

TROUP. No thank you, Major, feeling a bit — a bit — (*Goes, sits down.*)

BONNY. A little girl tied to a tree.

JAMESON. Oh. (*Little pause.*) Yes.

BARTTELOT *comes over, looks over* BONNY'*s other shoulder.*

BARTTELOT. What, what is it, Jamie?

BONNY *turns another page, stares at it.* WARD, BARTTELOT *also stare.*

WARD. But she's — they're —

BARTTELOT. Can't make it out, what's going on?

There is a pause.

JAMESON. It's a cannibal feast. (*Pause.*) I happened to mention to Tippu that once or twice I'd come across the remains of one, but never the beginnings or middle of one. So the next morning he invited me to accompany him and some of his chaps to a village where a couple of Tippu's men had been doing a bit of slaving. Among their merchandise was a girl of about thirteen, I suppose — that girl. I bought her from them, at Tippu's suggestion, for five brass-rods, and then we took her off to a cannibal chief Tippu knew of, who was told he could have her for lunch on the understanding that I did drawings of him while he was at it, and Tippu got a goat for our supper. (*Pause.*) To my knowledge it's the first time the whole process has been recorded. (*Pause.*) He was my host.

WARD. You bought the girl, then watched her being killed and prepared for the pot and cooked and eaten. And made sketches of it?

BONNY. And here, asleep under a tree, that's him is it, afterwards?

JAMESON. Yes.

BARTTELOT (*quietly*). What have you done?

JAMESON. What? (*He looks around at their faces.*) Nothing very terrible, surely. The girl had already been caught by slavers, she was bound to end up in the pot — they have no other use for them at that age. Good Heavens, we've flogged them to death, we've watched them die by the score, what does it matter, one nigger girl — (*He stops, looks at* WARD.) Yes. I see. I suppose I've slightly lost my — my — My curiosity and the uniqueness of it evidently blinded me to the — the — (*stops*) I'm sorry.

BONNY. Tippu-Tib doesn't have any of these, by any chance, does he?

JAMESON. Some rough versions, yes.

BONNY. Did you sign them for him?

JAMESON. Yes.

BARTTELOT. Do you know — do you know — what he'll do with them? Why, he'll head straight back to the Falls and show them — show them around to everyone, everyone. The story will be all over the Congo, in England, in London, on the first steamer — that we participated — participated in a cannibal — a cannibal —

BONNY. They'll say you ate your share of her, too.

BARTTELOT. All these months — this year — of waiting and hoping — and then just as the end is in sight you — you — with your damned — your damned — collection — you bring us down!

The drums increase, and increase, through BARTTELOT's *next speech, almost drowning it towards its end.*

Why, it's all been for nothing, nothing! Worse than nothing, to dishonour, to disgrace — by God man, after all this you've destroyed us, worse than death, worse than desertion, in England, with Stanley, here, destroyed — destroyed — is that why Stanley gave you to me, because he knew, he knew you'd — you'd — (*he is shaking, as if in a fit*) do his work for him, you and Stanley, is that what it was, — (*he holds his*

stick towards JAMESON, *makes as if to thrust it into him,
then wheels around, sees* JOHN HENRY) I told you — I told
you to stop them, told you, (*gouges the stick into* JOHN
HENRY) little black — scum — scum — (*as the pounding of the
drum is at its fullest pitch*)

WARD *runs over to stop* BARTTELOT.

BARTTELOT *shakes him off savagely, then rounds on him
raises his stick, makes to thrust it into* WARD, *then turns,
flings open the doors, on the darkness, with fires burning,
drums pounding, strides off.*

BONNY *goes over to the door, stares out.*

WARD *goes to* JOHN HENRY, *bends over him, then
straightens.*

TROUP *is sitting, motionless.*

JAMESON *is sitting, motionless.*

The drums stop. There is silence.

BARTTELOT (*off*). Hah, hah, hah, hah! Hah, hah, hah —

There is a shot.

Silence.

WARD *moves towards the doors.*

There are sudden cries, shouts, off.

BONNY *pushes the doors closed before* WARD *reaches them,
locks them. Turns his back to them.*

BONNY. If you go out there they'll do the same to you. And
then come on in and do the same to us. (*Pause.*) We'll get him
in the morning.

WARD *hesitates, then turns away. Looks at* JAMESON. *He
goes over to him, looks at him.*

JAMESON *looks slowly up at* WARD.

There is a pause.

TROUP (*in a dull voice*). Now perhaps you'll listen to me. Now
perhaps we can go home.

BONNY *goes over, helps himself to manioc from the jug.*

WARD *puts his hand on* JAMESON's *shoulder.*

Go home at last, eh?

BONNY *drinks.*

*Lights fade slowly on this tableau, to darkness, as the drums
start up again excitable, unrhythmic.*
The same. Some days later.
  *The doors are slightly open. From off, the sound of voices,
Zanzibari, Soudanese. BONNY is moving about, doing an
inventory of the boxes, but slowly. The sound of STANLEY's
voice, off, commanding. BONNY straightens, listens.*
  STANLEY *enters through the doors, pulling them wide.*

STANLEY. Well Bonny, Parke is back from the Falls, with
  some news. He spoke to Mr Troup, who is in excellent health,
  and has booked his passage back to Southampton. He is also
  in excellent voice. His self-justifications and denials have fuelled
  the scandal, God knows what form the story will finally take
  when it appears in *The Times*, but it will certainly have
  precedence with the public over my own poor efforts, who
  will want to read of the successful relief of Emin Pasha when
  there are tales of Barttelot's lash and Jameson's experiments
  in slaughtering, cooking and consuming infant girls to wallow
  in, eh? Mr Jameson, by the way, is dead.

BONNY. Oh.

STANLEY. He died at a Mission House between here and the
  Falls. He went too fast, in no state to travel, though if he'd
  had quinine with him he would probably have survived, why
  he didn't have quinine is another of the incomprehensible — as
  there is quinine here — is there not? But let us be charitable
  and assume that his neglect of himself had something
  Roman in it. If not Roman, then at least English. He was
  buried by Mr Ward, some nonsense about a Union Jack
  draped over a coffin rough-hewn from a tree — no doubt a
  bugle carved on the spot to sound a lament, eh? Pshaw! The
  good people at the Mission were much moved, being
  ignorant at the time that they were officiating over the
  remains of a celebrated cannibal, with his good friend, the
  opium fiend.

BONNY. I can't be sure it was Mr Ward who took the laudanum —
  all I know is that some is missing —

STANLEY (*looks at him*). Mr Ward left the Mission House, and
  has completely vanished. You, on the other hand, Bonny, are
  here, the only survivor, in the moral sense, of the Yambuya

fiasco. So let us make sure that your reputation is unsullied, eh?

BONNY. Thank you, sir. I felt somebody had to stay behind until you —

STANLEY. I'm not interested in your motives, Bonny. One can't plan motives only results. But there's no way of planning for gentlemen like Jameson, or a maniac like Barttelot. I did my best. I knew him to be a danger to us all, that's why I left him behind, in this place, where he could do no harm. (*Laughs.*) With an English gentleman to keep a check on him. And a set of orders that couldn't have been simpler, clearer or more flexible. All he had to do was to follow my orders. Easy enough, easy enough, even for a maniac, eh?

BONNY. At least you rescued Emin Pasha.

STANLEY. Who resents it bitterly, being comfortable and probably safe where he was. By the way, Bonny, where did you bury my John Henry?

BONNY. Outside the compound, with all the other — um —

STANLEY *looks at him, then bends, begins to pull off one of his boots.*

BONNY *waits.*

STANLEY. Be so kind as to take those damned turtles to the kitchen, would you?

BONNY *releases the turtles, takes them out through the flap.*

STANLEY *straightens for a moment, then begins to take off the other boot.*

Curtain.

Quartermaine's Terms

For Beryl

Quartermaine's Terms was first presented by Michael Codron at the Queen's Theatre, London, on 30 July 1981, with the following cast:

ST. JOHN QUARTERMAINE	Edward Fox
ANITA MANCHIP	Jenny Quayle
MARK SACKLING	Peter Birch
EDDIE LOOMIS	Robin Bailey
DEREK MEADLE	Glyn Grain
HENRY WINDSCAPE	James Grout
MELANIE GARTH	Prunella Scales

Directed by Harold Pinter
Designed by Eileen Diss
Lighting by Leonard Tucker

Quartermaine's Terms was taken on tour by Full Steam Ahead Productions from 24 May to 31 July 1982, with the following cast:

ST. JOHN QUARTERMAINE	Michael Williams
ANITA MANCHIP	Lynne Miller
MARK SACKLING	Michael Bertenshaw
EDDIE LOOMIS	Ernest Clark
DEREK MEADLE	Clive Francis
HENRY WINDSCAPE	Ronald Hines
MELANIE GARTH	Polly James

Directed by Kevin Billington
Designed by Eileen Diss
Lighting by Frederick Curtis

The Set: The staff-room of the Cull-Loomis School of English for foreigners, Cambridge, or rather a section of the staff-room — the last quarter of it. On stage are French windows, a long table, lockers for members of the staff, pegs for coats etc. and a number of armchairs; on the table a telephone, newspapers and magazines. This is the basic set, to which, between scenes and between the two Acts, additions can be made to suggest the varying fortunes of the school. Off stage, left, a suggestion of hard-backed chairs, and off left, a door to the main corridor of the school, where the class-rooms are.

The period: early 1960s.

Act One

Scene One

Monday morning, Spring term. The French windows are open. It is about 9.30. Sunny.

QUARTERMAINE *is sitting with his feet up, hands folded on his lap, staring ahead. From off, outside the French windows, in the garden, the sound of foreign voices excited, talking, laughing etc; passing by. As these recede:*

ANITA *comes through the French windows carrying a briefcase.*

QUARTERMAINE. Hello, Anita.

ANITA. 'Morning, St. John.

QUARTERMAINE. But I say, you know, you look different, don't you?

ANITA. Do I? Oh — my hair probably. I've put it up.

QUARTERMAINE. Oh yes. Well, it looks — looks really terrific!

ANITA. Thank you.

QUARTERMAINE. Of course I liked it the other way too, tumbling down your shoulders.

ANITA. It hasn't tumbled down my shoulders for three years St. John.

QUARTERMAINE. Oh. How was it then before you changed it?

ANITA. Back in a pony tail. (*She indicates.*)

QUARTERMAINE. That's it. Yes. Well, I liked it like that, too.

ANITA. Oh by the way, Nigel asked me to apologise again for having to cancel dinner. He was afraid he was a little abrupt on the 'phone.

QUARTERMAINE. Oh Lord, not at all, it was lucky he was, you know how my landlady hates me using the 'phone, but I understood exactly what he was getting at, um — something to do with his new magazine, wasn't it?

ANITA. He still hasn't got enough material for the first issue even. He was up until four, going through all the unsolicited poems and essays and short stories and bits of plays and God knows what. Without much luck, too. He's in despair, poor darling. Anyway, he felt really rotten about messing up *your* evening.

QUARTERMAINE. Oh, do tell him, no need to worry about that. Because as it happened, a few minutes after he 'phoned to cancel, old Henry 'phoned to invite me round there. So that was all right.

ANITA. How smashing! For dinner, you mean?

QUARTERMAINE. Well no, to baby-sit actually.

ANITA. Oh.

QUARTERMAINE. They suddenly remembered there was a film at The Arts, some old um, um German classic that they seem very fond of, about — about a child-murderer as far as I could make out from what Henry said.

ANITA. Still St. John, how boring for you!

QUARTERMAINE. No, no, I enjoyed it enormously, I used to baby-sit for them all the time. It was lovely seeing them again. Children are such . . . And they were as good as gold really, no trouble at all, except that Susan would keep screaming at the little ones. She's working for her 'O' levels you see. The least little bit of noise seems to upset her concentration. But the one they call little Fanny — very charming, very charming. . . . once she'd got used to me again. As for Ben — my word, what a little devil, full of mischief, he told me little Fanny had drowned in the bath and when I ran in, there she was . . . lying face down — hair floating around — and I stood there thinking, you know, (*He laughs.*) Lord, what am I going to say to Henry and Fanny when they get back. Especially after seeing a film like that — but it turned out it was only one of those enormous dolls, you know. (*They both laugh.*)

ANITA. Still St. John, I hope at least you had a bit of an evening with Henry and Fanny when they got back.

QUARTERMAINE. Oh yes. *Rather.* Well, except poor old Fanny had a bit of a headache from straining to read the subtitles — a very poor print apparently — and Henry got into a tussle with Susan about going to bed, so I felt you know — that they rather wanted me out of the way —

The sound of the door opening, during the above. Footsteps.

Oh hello Mark, top of the morning to you, have a good weekend?

SACKLING *appears on stage. He is carrying a briefcase, is unshaven, looks ghastly.*

ANITA (*looking at him in concern*). Are you all right?

SACKLING. Yes, yes, fine, fine. (*He drops the briefcase, slumps into chair.*)

ANITA. Are you growing a beard?

SACKLING. What? Oh Christ! (*Feeling his chin.*) I forgot! Haven't been to bed you see. All weekend.

QUARTERMAINE. Ah, been hard at it, eh?

SACKLING. What?

QUARTERMAINE. Hard at it. The old writing.

SACKLING. Oh yes — hard at it.

QUARTERMAINE. Terrific!

ANITA. Oh, I've got a message from Nigel, by the way, he asked me to ask you to hurry up with the extract from your novel, they're desperate to get it into the first issue, he says don't worry about whether it's not quite ready, they can always shove it in as 'Work in Progress' or something.

SACKLING. Right.

ANITA. You look to me as if you've over-done it — are you sure you're all right?

QUARTERMAINE. I say, how's old Camelia?

SACKLING (*barks out a laugh*). Oh fine! just — fine!

QUARTERMAINE. Terrific, and little Tom too?

SACKLING. Tom too, oh yes, Tom too.

QUARTERMAINE. The last time I saw him he was teething, standing there in his high chair dribbling away like anything, while Camelia was sitting on old Mark's lap making faces at him with orange peel in her mouth —

SACKLING *bursts into tears.* ANITA *goes to* SACKLING, *puts her hand on his shoulder.*

QUARTERMAINE. What? Oh — oh Lord!

ANITA. Mark — what is it?

SACKLING. Sorry — sorry — I'll be all right — still digesting.

QUARTERMAINE. Something you had for breakfast, is it?

ANITA *shakes her head at him.*

Mmmm?

ANITA. Do you want to talk about it?

SACKLING. I don't want anyone — anyone else to know — not Thomas or Eddie — don't want them dripping their — their filthy compassion all over me.

ANITA. We're to keep it to ourselves, St. John.

QUARTERMAINE. Oh Lord yes. Of course. (*A pause.*) What though

SACKLING. She's left me.

QUARTERMAINE. Who?

ANITA. Camelia, of course.

QUARTERMAINE. What! Old Camelia! Oh no!

SACKLING. Taking Tom — taking Tom with her.

QUARTERMAINE. Oh, not little Tom too!

SACKLING. Tom too.

ANITA. Well, did she — say why?

SACKLING (*makes an effort, pulls himself together*). She — (*He takes an envelope out of his pocket.*) I was upstairs in the attic — writing away — as far as I knew she was downstairs where she usually is — in the kitchen or — ironing — with the television on. And Tom in bed, of course. So I wrote on and on — I felt inspired, quite inspired, a passage about — about what I'd felt when I saw Tom coming out of her womb — so shiny and whole and beautiful — a wonderful passage — full of — full of my love for her and him — and when I finished I went downstairs to her — to read it to her — as I always do when it's something I'm burning with — and this was on the pillow. (*He opens the letter.*) 'I'm sorry darling, but it seems after all that I wasn't cut out to be a writer's wife. I can't stand the strain of it, the lonely evenings, your remoteness, and most of all the feeling that your novel means more to you than Tom and I do. Perhaps that's what being an artist is. Not caring about those who love you. I'm going back to mother's, I'll take the car' — yes, taken the car — she'd take that all right, wouldn't she! — 'until you've passed your driving test' and begin proceedings as soon as I've got a lawyer. Take care, my love, look after yourself, I wish you such success and I know that one day I'll be proud to have been your first wife, just as Tom will be proud to be your father.'

There is a pause.

QUARTERMAINE. Um, son, surely.

SACKLING. What?

QUARTERMAINE. Um, Tom's your son. Not your father. You read out that he was your father. Not your son.

SACKLING. Oh, if only I'd been able to read her that passage — she would have understood my feelings, she'd have known — but what do I do, I can't give up my novel now, not when I'm so close to finishing — my fourth draft — my penultimate draft — I *know* it's the penultimate — then one final one — and — and — so what do I do —

LOOMIS *enters through the French windows. He walks awkwardly, has thick glasses, is carrying a file.*

LOOMIS. Good morning, good morning, Anita my dear, Mark, St. John. I trust you all had a good weekend?

QUARTERMAINE.
ANITA. } Yes, thank you Eddie.
SACKLING.

LOOMIS. I'm just on my way through to do my little welcome speech to the new students, with a small dilation this time on the problems of our Cambridge landladies, we've just heard that our faithful Mrs Cornley is refusing to take any of our students except what she calls traditional foreigners, all over some dreadful misunderstanding she's had with those three really delightful Turks we sent her, over the proper function of the bathroom — such a nuisance, Thomas has been on the 'phone to her for hours — but still, I suppose the problems of a flourishing school — nine Japanese have turned up, by the way, instead of the anticipated six, and as it was three last time we can hope for a round dozen next — Mark, is it these fast-fading old eyes of mine, or did you forget to shave this morning, and yesterday morning, even?

SACKLING. No, no — I'm thinking of growing a beard, Eddie.

LOOMIS. Alas! And what saith the fair Camelia to that?

SACKLING (*mutters*). I don't think she'll mind, Eddie.

LOOMIS. Good, good — Anita, my dear, may I pay you a compliment?

ANITA. Yes please, Eddie.

LOOMIS. I like your hair even more *that* way.

ANITA. Well, thank you Eddie, actually I had it cut for a dinner party we had last night — so I suppose I'm stuck with it for a bit — it was a sort of editorial dinner, you see — (*Realising.*)

LOOMIS. Ah! And the magazine's progressing well, or so we gathered from Nigel. We bumped into him on the Backs, on Saturday afternoon, did he tell you?

ANITA. No. No he didn't.

LOOMIS. He was having a conference with one of his co-editors, I suppose it was.

ANITA. Oh. Jeffrey Pine.

LOOMIS. No no, I don't think Jeffrey Pine, my dear, but co-editress I should have said, shouldn't I, one can't be too precise these days.

ANITA. Oh. Was she — blonde and — rather pretty?

LOOMIS. Oh, very pretty — at least Thomas was much smitten, you know what an eye he's got.

ANITA. Ah, then that would be Amanda Southgate, yes, I expect he was trying to persuade her to take on all the dog-bodying — you know, hounding contributors, keeping the printers at bay — she's terrifically efficient. She's an old friend of mine. We were at school together. (*Little pause.*) She's smashing, actually.

LOOMIS. Good good — now St. John, what was it Thomas asked me to tell you — or was it Henry and Melanie I'm to tell what to? Oh yes, this postcard of course, from one of your old students. (*He hands him a post-card from the file.*) We couldn't resist having a look, post-cards being somehow in the public domain, one always thinks. At least when they're other people's. (*He laughs.*) Do read it out to Mark and Anita, don't be modest St. John.

QUARTERMAINE. Um, I must writing to thanking you for all excellent times in your most glorified classes, your true Ferdinand Muller. Lord! (*He laughs.*)

LOOMIS. And which one was he, can you recall?

QUARTERMAINE. Oh. Well, you know a — a German —

LOOMIS. Post-marked Zurich, I believe, so more likely a Swiss.

QUARTERMAINE. Oh yes, that's right, a Swiss, a — a well, rather large, Eddie, and with a round face — in his forties or so, with his hair cut en brosse.

LOOMIS. — and wearing lederhosen, perhaps, and good at yodelling, no no, St. John, I don't think I quite believe in your rather caricature Swiss, I suspect you must have made rather more of an impression on Herr Ferdinand Muller than he managed to make on you, still, I suppose that's better than the other way round, and his sentiments are certainly quite a tribute — would that his English were, too eh? But do try to remember them St. John, match names to faces. (*He laughs.*) And on that subject, you haven't forgotten Mr Middleton begins this morning, have you?

QUARTERMAINE. Who, Eddie?

LOOMIS. Middleton. Dennis Middleton, St. John. Our new part timer. Thomas told you all about him at the last staff meeting. He should be here any minute — so whilst I'm making the students welcome, perhaps you'd do the same for him, and tell him that either Thomas or I will be along before the bell. Mark?

SACKLING. Mmm?

LOOMIS. Middleton, Mark.

SACKLING (*blankly*). Yes. Yes. Right Eddie.

LOOMIS. Good good. See you all at the bell then — (*He walks off, stage left. Sound of him stopping. Slight pause.*) Oh Mark, there is one other thing — If I could just have a quick private word — May I put in my personal plea against the beard, I do think they make even the handsomest chaps red-eyed and snively looking, I don't want to end up begging Camelia to be Delilah to your Samson, eh, and think of poor little Tom too, having to endure Daddy's whiskers against his chubby young cheeks at cuddle-time —

SACKLING *rushes past him, out of the door.*

But — but — what did I say? It was only about about the beard, I couldn't have been more playful.

QUARTERMAINE. Oh, it's not your fault, Eddie, is it Anita, the poor chap's had a — a horrible weekend — you see —

ANITA (*warningly, cutting in*). Yes, up all night, working at his novel. I'll go and see if he's all right. (*She goes off, left.*)

LOOMIS. I see. Well that's all very well, after all nobody could respect Mark's literary ambitions more than Thomas and myself, but we really can't have him running about in this sort of state, what on earth would the students make of it if he were to gallop emotionally off in the middle of a dictation —

MEADLE *appears at the French windows.*

MEADLE. Um, is this the staff room, please?

He is hot and flustered, wearing bicycle clips, carrying a briefcase.

LOOMIS. Yes, what do you want?

MEADLE. I'm the new member of staff.

LOOMIS. Oh, of course, it's Mr Middleton, isn't it?

MEADLE. Well, yes — well, Meadle, actually, Derek Meadle.

LOOMIS. Yes, yes, Derek Meadle, well, I'm Eddie Loomis, the Principal. One of two Principals, as you know, as you've met Mr Cull of course, and this is St. John Quartermaine who's been with us since our school started, and you've come down to join us from Huddersfield, isn't it.

MEADLE. Yes sir, well Hull actually.

LOOMIS. Hull, good good — and when did you arrive?

MEADLE. Yesterday afternoon.

LOOMIS. And found yourself a room?

MEADLE. Yes, yes thank you, sir.

LOOMIS. Good good, and found yourself a bicycle too, I see.

MEADLE (*who throughout all this has been standing rather awkwardly keeping face on to* LOOMIS). Yes, sir. My landlady — I happened to ask her where could be a good place to buy a second-hand one, not being familiar with the shops, and she happened to mention that her son had left one behind in the basement and I could have it for two pounds, but unfortunately —

LOOMIS (*interrupting*). Good good, most enterprising — at least of your landlady. (*He laughs.*) But Mr Meadle I've got to have a little talk with the students, and Mr Cull is still looking after enrolment, but one of us will be back at the bell to introduce you to your first class — intermediary comprehension isn't it —

MEADLE. Dictation sir.

LOOMIS. Quite. So I'll leave you in St. John's capable hands —

MEADLE. Yes sir. Thank you.

LOOMIS. Oh, one thing, though, Mr Meadle — sir us no sirs, we're very informal here — I'm Eddie, Mr Cull is Thomas and you're Dennis.

MEADLE. Oh, well thank you very much —

LOOMIS *goes off left.*

Derek actually —

QUARTERMAINE. Well, I must say — jolly glad to have you with us — I think you'll enjoy it here — the staff is — well, they're terrific — and the students are — well, they've very interesting, coming as they do from all quarters of the globe, so to speak — but look here, why don't you sit down and make yourself at home.

MEADLE. Yes, thanks, but — well, you see the trouble is I've had a bit of an accident.

QUARTERMAINE. Oh really? Oh Lord.

MEADLE. Yes, well — you'd better see for yourself.

He turns. His trousers are rent at the seat.

How bad is it actually?

QUARTERMAINE. Well — they're a bit of a write off, I'm afraid. How did it happen?

MEADLE. Some bloody Japanese! I rode into a little pack of them coming up the school drive. They were laughing and chattering so much among themselves they didn't hear my bell until I was almost on top of them, and then a big, bald one stepped right out in front of me and of course I lost control on the gravel and skidded.

QUARTERMAINE. Oh dear.

MEADLE. And as there was the minutest bit of spring sticking out of the seat — I suppose it must have worked its way into my trousers on the way here — the worm in the apple, eh?

But anyway — what do you think I should do about it?

QUARTERMAINE. Well you know, old chap, I think the best thing would be to go back and change.

MEADLE. Ah yes, but into what is the question.

QUARTERMAINE. Well — into another pair of trousers, I — I suppose.

MEADLE. Yes, but you see, I haven't got another pair is the problem. An elderly gentleman on the train yesterday spilt hot chocolate out of his thermos right over the pair I happened to have on, so the first thing I did when I got in — irony of ironies — was to take them to the cleaners. And my trunk, which I'd sent on from Hull and which contained my suit and my other two pairs, hasn't arrived yet. So there it is. What do I do? Any suggestions? I mean if I pull them really high — like this — and leave my clips on — well how do I look?

QUARTERMAINE. Well, well, jolly formidable, actually.

MEADLE (*takes a few more steps*). No, no, I can't go round like this! I'm meant to be teaching — people will think I'm sort of — some sort of — my first day of my new job — oh, this is the sheerest, the sheerest — !

WINDSCAPE (*enters through the French windows. He is carrying a brief-case, wears bicycle clips, smokes a pipe. Seeing MEADLE*). Ah —

QUARTERMAINE. Hello Henry — um, come and meet our new chap —

WINDSCAPE. Oh yes, of course. Merton, isn't it?

QUARTERMAINE. Middleton, actually.

MEADLE. Meadle, as a matter of fact.

QUARTERMAINE. Meadle. That's right. So sorry. Dennis Meadle.

WINDSCAPE (*comes over*). Well, whatever yours happens to be — mine's Windscape. Henry Windscape. How do you do.

MEADLE. How do you do.

WINDSCAPE. Very glad to have you with us.

MEADLE. Thank you.

QUARTERMAINE. Henry's our academic tutor — syllabus and all that.

MEADLE. Oh.

WINDSCAPE. Oh, St. John, I didn't thank you properly last night for baby-sitting. It was most kind.

QUARTERMAINE. Oh, not at all — I enjoyed it. I say, how were they in the end — Susan, little Fanny and old Ben?

WINDSCAPE. Oh fine thank you, St. John, fine. I didn't get Susan to bed until midnight of course. (*To* MEADLE:) She's studying for her 'O' levels — a couple of years in advance.

QUARTERMAINE. And what about Fanny's headache?

WINDSCAPE. Oh fine thank you, fine. Though she did have rather a bad moment actually, when she went to have her bath and thought little Fanny was lying in it — drowned.

QUARTERMAINE. Oh yes — that blessed doll.

WINDSCAPE. Yes, Ben told me you'd put it there. St. John was good enough to come over and sit with our three last night — we went to see *M* you know — such a fine film — so delicate and human in its treatment of a — a sexual freak, and Peter Lorre — unfortunately the print was a trifle worn — but still — memorable — memorable — but isn't it interesting — on another subject — this English thing about names, how we forget them the second we hear them. Just now, for instance, when St. John was introducing you. Unlike Americans for instance. (*He puffs and pulls on his pipe throughout this speech.* MEADLE *nods and chuckles tensely.*) I suppose because we — the English that is — are so busy looking at the person the name represents — or *not* looking, being English (*He laughs.*) that we don't take in the name itself — whereas the Americans, you see, make a point of beginning with the name — when one's introduced they repeat it endlessly. 'This is Dennis Meadle. Dennis Meadle, why hello Dennis, and how long have you been in this country Dennis, this is Dennis Meadle dear, Dennis was just telling me how much he liked our fair city, weren't you Dennis . . . ' (*All this is an execrable imitation of an American accent.*) And — and so forth.

MEADLE (*tacit*). Derek actually.

WINDSCAPE. And in no time at all they've learnt what you're called by even if not who you are (*He laughs.*) while we, the English, being more empirical, don't learn your name until you yourself have taken on a complicated reality — you and your name grow, so to speak, in associated stages in our memories, until what you are as Dennis Meadle and the sounds Dennis Meadle are inseparable which is actually — when you think about it, a radical division in ways of perceiving that goes back to the Middle Ages in the Nominalists — the name callers — calling the name preceeding the object, so to speak, and the realists —

During this, MELANIE *has entered through the French windows. She puts her briefcase on the table.*

— who believed the object preceeded the name — but one could go on and on; and, there's Melanie, come and meet (*A pause.*) our new chap —

MELANIE. You're in top form for a Monday morning Henry, how do you do, I'm Melanie Garth.

MEADLE. Meadle. Derek Meadle.

MELANIE. And you've come to reinforce us, well we certainly could do with you, Thomas was just telling me about the enrolment chaos, you'll be getting a lot of overspill from my groups, I can tell you.

WINDSCAPE. Melanie's our Elementary Conversation specialist, by the way.

MELANIE. Oh, I don't know about specialist, Henry, Henry's our only real specialist here, he specialises in — well, everything, doesn't he, St. John, from pronounciation to British Life and Institutions, but what I enjoyed most about the sight of you two philosophising away here was that you both still had your bicycle clips on — as if you'd met on a street corner —

WINDSCAPE (*laughing*). Good heavens, so they are. Thank you

for reminding me, my dear, whenever I forget to take them off
I spend hours after school hunting for them — (*He bends, to
take them off.*)

MEADLE *grinning and distraught, makes a gesture towards
taking his off.*

QUARTERMAINE (*taking this in*). I say — I say, Melanie, how's
— um, how's mother?

MELANIE. Top form, thanks, St. John, her left leg's still giving
her bother, and the stairs are a dreadful strain, you know,
because of this sudden vertigo, but yesterday she managed to
hobble down to the corner-shop all by herself, and was
halfway back by the time I got there to pick her up.

QUARTERMAINE. Oh, that's terrific! Melanie's mother's just
recovering from a thingemebob.

MELANIE. Stroke, if you please, St. John. She insists on the
proper term, she hates euphemisms.

WINDSCAPE. Not surprisingly, as Melanie's mother was
Cambridge's first lady of philology — I had the honour of
being supervised by her in my second year as an undergraduate.
A remarkable woman who seems to be coming to terms with
her little upset in a characteristically — characteristically
indomitable — fashion.

MEADLE. I have an aunt who had a stroke a year ago. She was
the active sort too.

MELANIE. And how is *she* coping?

MEADLE. Well, she was doing splendidly until she had the
next. Now she's pretty well out of it altogether, my uncle
has to do virtually everything for her. But then that's one of
the usual patterns, they said at the hospital. First a mild
stroke, followed by a worse stroke, and then, if that doesn't
do the job — (*He gestures.*)

MELANIE. Yes, well, Mr Meadle, I'm sorry for your aunt — and
for your uncle — but sufficient unto the day, sufficient unto
the day. (*She picks up her briefcase and goes to a locker.*)

WINDSCAPE. Of course that's only *one* of the possible patterns —

there are many cases of complete — or — or more than merely partial recovery — Dennis, if I might — might just — Melanie puts on a remarkably brave front, but don't be led astray, she's an intensely feeling person who knows very well the likely outcome of her mother's — her mother's - she's deeply attached to her, as you probably gathered.

I hope you don't mind my er —

MEADLE. No, no. Thank you. Thank you.

WINDSCAPE. Good man! (*He puts his hand on* MEADLE's *shoulder.*) Well, I'd better unpack my own — (*He goes over to a locker, looking towards* MELANIE, *who is still standing still by hers.*)

MELANIE (*whispered*). Well naught out of ten for tact, I thought!

WINDSCAPE (*whispered*). Yes well, it is his first day, Melanie my dear — he didn't really understand.

MEADLE (*crossing to* QUARTERMAINE). I don't think I can stand much more of this. I hardly know what I'm saying. Look, what I need is some safety pins and a few minutes in the toilet.

QUARTERMAINE. Yes, of course, you come along with me.

LOOMIS (*comes through the French windows*). Good morning, Melanie, my dear. Good morning Henry — good weekend, I trust?

MELANIE. ⎫
WINDSCAPE. ⎬ Yes thanks, Eddie.

QUARTERMAINE (*to* MEADLE). Better hang on a tick.

LOOMIS. All well with mother, I trust?

MELANIE. Yes thanks Eddie. Top form.

LOOMIS. Good, good — and Fanny and the children?

WINDSCAPE. Yes, thanks Eddie — all splendid.

LOOMIS. Good good —

As ANITA *and* SACKLING *enter from right.*

Ah, and here you are, you two, and quite composed again
Mark, I trust —

ANITA. Well Eddie, actually I'm not sure that Mark's quite up
to it.

SACKLING *feebly gestures silence to* ANITA.

LOOMIS. And Mr Meadle, I don't know which of you had
the chance to meet him yet, but those who haven't can make
their separate introductions, in the meanwhile I'll say a welcome
on all our behalves, we're delighted to have you with us — I
see you've still got your clips on, by the way.

MEADLE. Oh yes.

LOOMIS. Perhaps you'd better remove them or you'll create the
impression that you're just pedalling through — (*He laughs.*)

MEADLE *bends, to take them off.*

Good — now as we're all here and there are a few minutes
before the bell, I'd like to say a few words, if I may. So,
gather ye round — gather ye round. (*They all do so.*) As you've
no doubt realised, we have an exceptionally high enrolment
for the month, the highest in the school's career, as a matter
of fact. (*Little murmurs.*)

QUARTERMAINE. I say, terrific!

LOOMIS. Yes, very gratifying. You all know how hard Thomas
has worked for this. Though he'd loathe to hear me say it.
But what he wouldn't mind hearing me say is that in his turn
he knows how hard you've worked. I think we all have a right
to be proud of our growing reputation as one of the best
schools of English — not one of the biggest but one of the
best — in Cambridge. Which, when it comes down to it, means
in the country.

ALL. Murmur.

MELANIE (*murmurs*). Solemn thought.

LOOMIS. Well and good. Well and good. But success will
bring — has already begun to bring — its own problems. (*He
gestures to* MEADLE.) As Mr Meadle's presence here testifies.
But even with Mr Meadle — or Dennis, as I've already told

him I intend to call him — with Dennis to help us, there is
going to be a considerable strain on our resources. Perhaps
a few too many students to a classroom, more work to take
home and correct, more difficulties in developing personal
contact — that so crucial personal contact —

QUARTERMAINE. Absolutely crucial.

LOOMIS. Many of whom are only here for a short time — well, as
I say, you've already become familiar with the problems, the
problems, as Thomas remarked 'midst the chaos this
morning, of a flourishing school —

SACKLING *faints*.

ANITA. Oh my God!

ANITA *cries out*.
WINDSCAPE *gets to him*.

WINDSCAPE. The thing is to — (*He puts his hand on
SACKLING's heart*.) His heart — I can't feel his heart —

A pause.

QUARTERMAINE (*also looking down*). Oh Lord!

The bell rings.

Lights.

Scene Two

QUARTERMAINE. Oh Lord! Hello Eddie.

LOOMIS. You're in sprightly mood, St. John.

QUARTERMAINE. Friday evening you know — and I'm off to
the theatre tonight with old Mark and Anita.

LOOMIS. And what are you going to see?

QUARTERMAINE. Oh that — that Strinberg, I think it is. At
The Arts.

LOOMIS. I believe it's an Ibsen, Hedda Gabler — I believe.

QUARTERMAINE. Oh, is it really?

LOOMIS. But tell me, the bell's gone then, has it, I didn't hear it — but then these old ears of mine —

QUARTERMAINE. Ah yes, well I let them out a little early, you see Eddie.

LOOMIS. Why?

QUARTERMAINE. Well, it was my turn to give the advance British Life and Institutions Lecture, and I chose Oxford Colleges — to give them the other point of view, for once — illustrated with slides, but I'd only just got going, and blow me tight — the old projector broke.

LOOMIS. Broke? But we've only just bought it. It's the newest model.

QUARTERMAINE. Yes, I think that's part of the problem, all those extra bits to master — anyway, one of the colleges went in upside down and wouldn't come out so I had to — to abandon technology and do it all off my own bat — you know, reminiscences of my time at the House and — and anedotes — and — you know — that sort of thing. The personal touch. But of course I ran out of steam a little, towards the end, I'm afraid.

LOOMIS. And how many turned up?

QUARTERMAINE. Oh well — about a handful.

LOOMIS. A handful!

QUARTERMAINE. A good handful.

LOOMIS. But there are meant to be twenty-three in the group that that special lecture's designed for.

QUARTERMAINE. Yes, well I think you know — it's being Friday and — and the sun shining and the Backs so lovely and the Cam jam-packed with punts and — but the ones who did come were jolly interested — especially that little Italian girl — you know um — um — almost midget sized, the one with the wart —

LOOMIS. If you mean Angelina, she happens to be Greek. Her father's an exceptionally distinguished army officer. Thomas will be very disappointed to hear about all this, St. John, he devised that lecture series himself, you know, it's quite an innovation, and if you can't keep attendances up — and you know very well how important it is to keep classes going until at least the bell — ah, hello my dear, you've finished a trifle on the early side too, then?

ANITA. Oh, isn't it past five?

LOOMIS. Well, the bell hasn't gone yet, even in your part of the corridor — intermediary dictation, wasn't it, and how was your attendance?

ANITA. Oh, nearly a full complement, Eddie, they're a very keen lot, mostly Germans, in fact that's why I thought the bell had gone, one of them said he'd heard it.

LOOMIS. Which one?

ANITA. I think it was Kurt.

LOOMIS. I see.

ANITA *makes to go to her locker.*

LOOMIS. My dear, have I told you what I think about your sandals?

ANITA. No, Eddie.

QUARTERMAINE. I think they're smashing.

LOOMIS. Well, when I first saw you in them I wondered if they were quite *comme il fault,* Thomas and I had quite a thing about them — but I've been quite won around, I've come to the view that they're most fetching. Or that your feet are. Or both. (*He laughs.*)

ANITA. Thank you, Eddie.

LOOMIS. And Nigel's still in London, is he, with his co-editress?

ANITA. Yes, he comes back on Saturday or Sunday.

LOOMIS. Quite a coincidence Thomas seeing them on the train like that, he's scarcely been out of his office this many a month, as you know — and it's all working out all right, is it?

ANITA. Yes, Amanda's been absolutely wonderful, quite a surprise really, because when I first met her at a party a few months ago, I thought she was — well, absolutely charming, of course, but rather — rather feckless, if anything. But it turns out she's got a really good tough brain. Her boyfriend's being a great help too. He's invaluable.

LOOMIS. But you met her at a party. How odd, I had an idea you went to school with her?

ANITA (*slight hesitation*). No no — with her sister, Seraphina.

LOOMIS. Ah yes — but I was really asking about the magazine itself, how that was coming?

ANITA. Oh, they've finally settled on a title. It's going to be called *Reports*.

QUARTERMAINE. Terrific!

LOOMIS. *Reports*.

The bell rings.

Reports, mmm, well, tell Nigel when he gets back that Thomas has decided to take out *two* subscriptions, one for ourselves and one for the student common room, so we'll be showing a great personal interest —

ANITA. Oh thank you, Eddie, Nigel will be so pleased —

From the garden, the sound of WINDSCAPE, *off.*

WINDSCAPE (*off*). I can't stay too long, I'm afraid, just to start you off and explain the rules — but first let's get the mallets and balls —

The voices recede.

LOOMIS (*going to the window*). Ah, the croquet's under way again, good, good, — and who's playing — ah, Piccolo and Jean-Pierre, Gisela — Teresa — Okona — Liv and Gerta — you know, I always feel that if ever our little school had to justify itself, we could do it by showing the world the spectacle of an Italian, a Frenchman, a German, a Japanese, a Swedish girl and a Belgian girl, all gathered together on an English lawn, under an English sky to play a game of croquet —

ANITA *through this has gone to her locker.*

QUARTERMAINE. Absolutely, Eddie, absolutely — croquet —

I must try my hand again — haven't for years — not since my
aunt's when I was a child — she had such a lawn, you know, and
I remember, oh Lord, (*Shaking his head, laughing.*) Oh Lord,
I say, I forgot, Thomas told me to tell you he was looking
for you.

LOOMIS. Thomas? When?

QUARTERMAINE. Oh, just at the end of my lecture — he
popped his head in.

LOOMIS. Really, St. John, I wish you'd mentioned it straight
away, it would have to be something urgent for Thomas to
interrupt a class — was he going back to the office?

SACKLING *enters, during this. Carrying books, etc. He sports
a moustache.*

QUARTERMAINE. He didn't say, Eddie.

LOOMIS. Mark, have you happened to glimpse Thomas —

SACKLING. Yes. I think he and Melanie were going up to your
flat —

LOOMIS. Oh. Well, if he should come down here looking for me,
tell him I've gone upstairs to the flat — and that I'll stay there
so that we don't do one of our famous boxes and coxes —
(*He goes out left.*)

SACKLING. Right Eddie. (*Going to his locker.*)

ANITA, *during the above, has finished packing, is leaving.
There is an air of desperate rush about her.*

QUARTERMAINE. Wasn't he in a dodgy mood — but I say, where
shall we meet, Anita, shall Mark and I come and pick you
up at your place, or shall we go to Mark's place, or the foyer,
or — or we could go to The Eagle — or you two could come
to my place —

ANITA. Oh, I'm sorry, St. John, I completely forgot — you see
I'm going to London. It suddenly occurred to me that as Nigel
can't get back until tomorrow or Sunday, why not pop down
and spend the weekend with him.

QUARTERMAINE. What a good idea. Much more fun than some

old Ibsen thing.

SACKLING. Does he know you're coming?

ANITA. No, it's a surprise.

SACKLING. Shouldn't you 'phone him first? I mean he may be going out or — you know.

ANITA. I haven't got time. Look, I've got to dash if I'm going to make the five-thirty — damn Eddie! (*Rushing off.*)

SACKLING. Oh Christ! Poor old Nigel.

QUARTERMAINE. Mmmm?

SACKLING. Well, surely you know?

QUARTERMAINE. What?

SACKLING. About Nigel and Amanda Southgate. They're having a passionate affair. He only started the magazine because of her — she's got literary ambitions.

QUARTERMAINE. Oh — oh, Lord, poor old Anita! But they always seemed so happy —

SACKLING. You know, St. John, you have an amazing ability not to let the world impinge on you. Anita's the unhappiest woman I know, at the moment. And has been, ever since she met Nigel. Amanda's his fifth affair in the last two years, even if the most serious. But Anita covers up for him, pretends it isn't happening, or tries to protect a reputation he hasn't got and probably doesn't want anyway, he's made her have three abortions although she's desperate for children — haven't you had the slightest inkling of any of that?

QUARTERMAINE. No.

SACKLING. But what I don't understand is why she's suddenly gone down to confront him. She's only survived so far by not daring to have anything out with him — she's never once mentioned even the most blatant of his infidelities, actually that's one of the things about her that drives him mad. Anyway, there's nothing we can do about it, is there? I haven't even got his number, so I can't warn him.

QUARTERMAINE. Don't you like Anita?

SACKLING. Of course I do. Far more than I like Nigel, as a matter of fact.

QUARTERMAINE. Oh. Oh well it all seems — all seems — I mean these things between people — people one cares for — it's hard to bear them — but, but I say, what about this evening then, how would you like to play it? Eagle or — shall we meet at the theatre?

SACKLING. As a matter of fact, St. John, I'm going to have to bow out of the theatre, too.

QUARTERMAINE. Oh. Oh well —

SACKLING. You see, last night I went back to it again. My novel. The first time since Camelia left. And there was the old flame aflickering as strongly as ever. So I've got to get back to it this evening. Look, you haven't actually bought the tickets, have you?

QUARTERMAINE (*makes to say yes, changes his mind*). No, no, never any need to at the Arts, so don't worry about that but — but it's terrific that you've starting writing again, that's far more important than going to see some — some old Ibsen thing.

SACKLING. Thanks. And St. John, thanks also for your companionship these last weeks. It must have been bloody boring for you, having me grind on and on in my misery.

QUARTERMAINE. Lord no, I've enjoyed it enormously. Not your misery I don't mean but your (*He laughs.*) — your — but I say, have you heard from Camelia?

SACKLING. Yes, this morning. She's allowing me a few hours tomorrow afternoon. With my son.

QUARTERMAINE. But that's wonderful, Mark. Look, when will you be back?

SACKLING. Tomorrow evening, I suppose.

QUARTERMAINE. Well, perhaps we could have lunch on Sunday or dinner or meet for a drink — and you could tell me how things went with little Tom — I'd really love to know.

During this, the sound of the door opening, closing, followed by a yelp.

MEADLE (*off*). Blast!

QUARTERMAINE. You all right, old man?

MEADLE (*he is wearing a suit, has a bump on his forehead, covered by a piece of sticking plaster*). Yes, yes — (*Rubbing his hand.*) It's that door-knob, a bit too close to the door-jamb — at least for my taste — (*He laughs.*) I'm always scraping my knuckles on it — hello, Mark, haven't seen you around for a bit, I suppose because you're usually gone before I finish.

SACKLING. Don't worry, I do my time. Right to the bell.

MEADLE. Oh, I didn't mean any reflection — (*He laughs.*) Good God, I only meant that I always seem to get caught by students who want to practise their English after hours too — of course it doesn't help to be carrying a conversation piece around on your forehead — What 'appen 'ead, Mr Mittle, whasa matter weet de het, Meester Meetle, Mister Mittle vat goes mit der hed b- (*Laughing.*) up the corridor, down, in the classroom, in the garden — by the time I'd gone through all the details, with pantomime, landlady calling to the telephone, toe stubbing in cracked linoleum, body pitching down the stairs and bonce cracking down on tile I'd have settled for serious internal injuries instead.

SACKLING (*smiles*). Goodnight. (*He goes out through the French windows.*)

QUARTERMAINE (*who has been laughing with* MEADLE). Oh, night old man, but oh, just a minute, we haven't fixed our meeting — (*He goes to the French windows, stares out.*)

MEADLE (*who has registered* SACKLING's *manner*). He's a hard chap to get to know, isn't he?

QUARTERMAINE. Who? Old Mark? Lord no — oh, well perhaps to begin with but once you do know him you can't imagine a — a better friend.

MEADLE. Oh. Well, I'll keep working on it then. (*Going to his locker.*)

QUARTERMAINE. I say, I've managed to get hold of some tickets for the theatre tonight. They're doing an Ibsen! Would you like to come?

MEADLE. To tell you the truth, Ibsen's not quite my cup of tea, thanks, but anyway as a matter of fact Oko-Ri's taking me out to dinner tonight with the rest of the boys.

QUARTERMAINE. Oko — what?

MEADLE. Ri. Oko-Ri. My Japanese chum.

QUARTERMAINE. Oh, old baldy, you mean? Taking you out to dinner — well, that's — that's — I didn't know you'd hit it off so well with them, after your trouser —

MEADLE. Well, I never thought they'd made me skid deliberately — and we've had lots of good laughs about it since — now that I'm on their wave-length — Oko-Ri's got a splendid sense of humour. Loves a drink too, I gather, from some of their jokes.

QUARTERMAINE. Oh, well, you'll have a good evening ther —

MEADLE. It's really just to say thank you for all the extra hours I've put in with them. They left it to me to decide where we'd go, and I've chosen that French place that's just opened opposite Trinity, Eddie and Thomas were saying it's very good.

QUARTERMAINE. So I hear.

MEADLE. Anyway, I'd better get back. I'd ask you to come along too, but it's not really my invitation —

QUARTERMAINE. No, no — I quite understand.

The sound of the door opening and closing, feet.

MEADLE. Oh. Here. Let me give you a hand with those, Melanie —

MELANIE (*off*). No, it's quite all right, I've got them —

MEADLE (*off*). Well, let me just take this one —

MELANIE. No, no, really — there's no need —

The sound of books dropping on the floor.

MEADLE (*off*). Oh, sorry, Melanie —

MELANIE (*irritably*). Oh — really! I had them perfectly well — and Thomas has just lent me that one with great warnings to be careful, it's a rare edition —

MEADLE *coming on stage, carrying a distinguished volume,
along with a briefcase, exercise books and further books.)*
If you could just put it on the table — Have either of you seen
Eddie, Thomas has been looking for him.

QUARTERMAINE. Now what did Eddie say — oh yes, that he
was going to wait for Thomas in the — in the office, it must
have been.

MELANIE. Oh, good, well that's where Thomas has gone — so
you're the last two then, are you?

QUARTERMAINE. Yes, well apart from old Henry, that is, he's
playing croquet —

MELANIE. Is he, jolly good! (*She goes to her locker.*)

MEADLE (*who has been looking through the book*). No, no
damage done, Melanie. (*He looks at his watch.*) So Thomas
is in the office, is he?

MELANIE. Yes, why, what do you want him for?

MEADLE. Oh — well — well actually he said something about
seeing if he could get me some extra pronunciation classes —
as I'm part-time, I need all the hours I can get, you see.
(*He laughs.*)

MELANIE. I wouldn't go disturbing him now, if I were you,
he's had a particularly fraught day. He's got a dreadful
headache. The only person he'll want to see is Eddie.

MEADLE. Oh. Well, in that case, goodnight, Melanie.

MELANIE. Goodnight — oh, that reminds me, I'd be very
grateful if you'd stop putting your bicycle against the wall
where I park my car — there's not enough room for both.

MEADLE. Oh, sorry about that — right Melanie — well, see you
Monday then.

QUARTERMAINE. See you Monday, old man. (*As* MEADLE
goes out through the French windows.)

MELANIE. I really think I'd get on much better with Mr Meadle
if he didn't try so hard to get on with me.

MEADLE (*meanwhile, off*). 'Night Henry, see you Monday.

WINDSCAPE (*off*). Oh. 'Night Derek. Have a good weekend.

MEADLE (*off*). Thanks, Henry — same to you.

MELANIE. Still, apparently he works very hard at his teaching, from all accounts. Thomas and Eddie are both rather thrilled with him. And really I had no right to stop him from seeing Thomas — not my business at all. But Thomas really is in a terrible state. He's spent the whole afternoon on the telephone because of that wretched Jap — the big, bald one, you know — apparently he got drunk and ran amok in that new French restaurant last night, and the owners are demanding damages and threatening to call the police, if he shows up again, and then one of the other Japanese turned up at lunch-time to book a table for tonight — Goodness knows what's going to happen if the bald one appears too. Well, St. John, and what are your plans for the weekend, something on the boil, I'll bet!

QUARTERMAINE. Oh, well I thought I might take in a show tonight — that Ibsen thing at the Arts —

MELANIE. Isn't it *The Cherry Orchard*?

QUARTERMAINE. Oh, is it? Well — something terrific like that. And then a bit of supper, I suppose. I might try that French place in fact. Might be rather — rather amusing. (*He laughs.*)

MELANIE. It must be jolly nice being a bachelor and having the weekend before you. Especially in Cambridge.

QUARTERMAINE. Yes, terrific fun.

MELANIE. Well, I'd better get on with this. I don't think Thomas really wants me to take it off the premises. (*She pulls the book towards her.*)

QUARTERMAINE. Oh. Righto. (*He begins to wander up and down, gaze out of the French windows etc.*)

MELANIE *writing, glancing occasionally at him. She is, in fact, anxious for him to be gone. There are occasional cries and sounds of* WINDSCAPE's *voice from the garden, 'Oh yes,*

yes, right to the very beginning,' to which MELANIE
responds by lifting her head, or stopping writing.

QUARTERMAINE. I say, Melanie — do you like *The Cherry
Orchard*?

MELANIE. Loathe it.

QUARTERMAINE. Oh. Why?

MELANIE. All that Russian gloom and doom and people
shooting themselves from loneliness and depression and that
sort of thing. But then mother says I don't understand
comedy. I expect she's right.

QUARTERMAINE. How is mother?

MELANIE. Oh, top hole, thanks. (*Automatically.*)

QUARTERMAINE. Well, if there's ever anything I can do —
you know — if she wants company when you want to go
out —

MELANIE. That's very thoughtful of you, St. John, thank you.

QUARTERMAINE. No, no — I'd enjoy it — I say, that is an
impressive tome old Thomas has lent you, what are you
copying out exactly?

MELANIE. Recipes. This one's for roasted swan.

QUARTERMAINE. Oh. For a dinner party?

MELANIE. No, no, St. John, it's for my British Life and
Institutions lot, to give them some idea of a Medieval
banquet. Swans are protected birds, you know, these days.

QUARTERMAINE. Oh yes, of course they are. (*He laughs.*)
Fancy thinking you'd give them for a — a — oh Lord! But
aren't they the most — most beautiful creatures. I was
looking at one — oh, just the other day, you know — on the
Cam — drifting behind a punt — and they were all shouting
and drinking champagne and — and it was just drifting
behind them — so calm — and I remember there used to be
oh! a dozen or so — they came every year to a pond near my
aunt's — when I was — was and I could hear their wings —
great wings beating — in the evenings when I was lying in bed

— it could be quite — quite frightening even after I knew
what was making the noise — and then the next morning
there they'd be — a dozen of them or so — drifting — drifting
around — and it was hard to imagine — their long necks
twining and their way of drifting — all that — that power —
those wings beating — I wonder where they went to. I'd like
to know more about them really. Where they go, what they —

MELANIE. St. John, please don't think me fearfully rude, but
I must try and finish this and I can't write and talk at the
same time, you see.

QUARTERMAINE. What? Oh — oh sorry, Melanie, no, you're
quite right, I can't either. Anyway, I ought to be getting
on —

MELANIE. Yes, with such a full evening. I do hope you enjoy it.

QUARTERMAINE. Well — well 'night Melanie, see you Monday.
And don't forget about your mother — any time —

MELANIE. I won't, St. John, goodnight.

QUARTERMAINE *goes.*

MELANIE *sits, not writing, as:*

QUARTERMAINE (*off*). I say, Henry, any chance of a game?

WINDSCAPE (*off*). Actually, I've just finished, I'm afraid —
perhaps next week.

QUARTERMAINE (*off*). Right, I'll hold you to that. 'Night.

WINDSCAPE (*off*). 'Night.

QUARTERMAINE (*off*). Oh, by the way, if you want any
baby-sitting done during the weekend, I'll try and make myself
available —

WINDSCAPE (*off*). Righto, I'll put it to Fanny — I know she's
quite keen to see the *Uncle Vanya* at the Arts — perhaps
tomorrow night —

QUARTERMAINE (*off*). *A votre disposition.* 'Night.

WINDSCAPE (*off*). 'Night.

MELANIE, *during this, has got up, gone to the French windows and during the latter part hurries back to the table, sits down, pretends to continue transcribing.*

WINDSCAPE *enters through the French windows. He stops on seeing* MELANIE, *braces himself, then enters properly, jovially.*

WINDSCAPE. Hello Melanie, my dear, I thought everyone had gone.

MELANIE. How are they taking to the croquet?

WINDSCAPE. At the moment they find it a bit sedate, I think, but another time or two around and they'll discover just how much — how much incivility is possible on our tranquil English lawns. (*He laughs, embarrassed.*) Now I must sort myself out — I promised Fanny I'd be home by six — now where's my briefcase — ah, yes — and a pile of unseens I seem to remember — (*Going to his locker.*) to be marked by Monday —

MELANIE. How is Fanny?

WINDSCAPE. Oh, very well, thanks, very well — a bit tired in the evenings, what with the children on the one hand and her two hours voluntary with the O.A.P's — but she's enjoying every minute of her day —

MELANIE. Good! — And the children — are all well?

WINDSCAPE. Oh yes — they're fine! Susan's a little tense at the moment, actually, with her 'O' levels — a pity she's taking them so early, I think, but she insists — she's in with a particularly bright lot and doesn't want to fall behind or let herself down so she works away until all hours. Quite often after Fanny and I have gone to bed. But she's developing quite an interest in — in — well, philosophical speculation, I suppose it is, really — the other evening — (*Bending down during this to put on his clips.*) she suddenly insisted — in the middle of supper — she'd been very quiet until then — she suddenly insisted that we couldn't prove that other people existed — and that perhaps when we thought about them or remembered them or saw and heard them even — we were actually just making them up — and of course I took her up on this and attempted to explain how it is we do know that other people exist including people we don't know exist, if you follow — (*Laughing.*) and she kept saying 'But you can't prove it, Daddy, you can't actually prove it!' And she was right. I found myself getting quite tangled in my own arguments.

MELANIE. I've always thought she was the one who takes most after you.

WINDSCAPE. Yes, yes — perhaps she does, perhaps she does — I'm afraid I rather like to think so anyway — but you haven't seen them for ages have you, you really must come over sometime soon — Fanny would love to see you again. We all would.

MELANIE. That would be lovely.

WINDSCAPE. I'll get Fanny to give you a ring over the weekend or —

MELANIE. Good.

WINDSCAPE. Right — well, oh, by the way, I've been meaning to ask — how is your mother's day-nurse working out, with the name out of Dickens?

MELANIE. Nurse Grimes. Well enough so far — she seems a very efficient, cheerful little soul — a little too cheerful for my taste perhaps, as apparently she belongs to one of those peculiar revivalist sects that seem to be springing up all over the place now — you know, meeting in each other's homes and chanting prayers and dancing about in their love of God.

WINDSCAPE. Oh Lord.

MELANIE. At least that's how she describes it — but Mother seems to like her.

WINDSCAPE. Well, that's the main thing, isn't it?

MELANIE. Yes. Yes it is.

WINDSCAPE. Well do give her my — my very best — see you Monday, Melanie, my dear.

MELANIE. See you Monday, Henry.

> WINDSCAPE, *carrying papers, books, etc., goes off left. The sound of the door closing.*

> MELANIE *sits. She lets out a sudden wail, and then in a sort of frenzy, tears at the page of the book from which she's been copying, sobbing. She checks herself as: the sound of the door opening.*

WINDSCAPE (*laughing*). What on earth can I be thinking of — going off with all these in my arms and leaving my briefcase behind — I do that sort of thing more and more now — perhaps it's premature senility — (*Entering, going to the briefcase, shovelling the papers and books in.*) or did I get switched on to the wrong track and think I was going off to teach a class — I must have as I went out that way — (*He looks at her smiling. Little pause.*) Melanie — Melanie — (*He hesitates, then goes to her, leaving the briefcase on the desk.*) Is something the matter?

MELANIE. She hates me, you see.

WINDSCAPE. Who?

MELANIE. Mother.

WINDSCAPE. Oh Melanie, I'm sure she doesn't.

MELANIE. When I get home in the evenings — do you know what she does? She sits there for hours refusing to speak — then when I get her supper on the table — she refuses to eat. I know she can only work one side of her face now, but she can eat perfectly well. And when I try to feed her — she lets the food fall out of her mouth, and — and stares at me with such malevolence, until suddenly she'll say something — something utterly — Last night she said 'It's not my fault you've spent your life in my home. I've never wanted you here, but as you're too stupid and too unattractive to make any reasonable man a wife, I accepted the responsibility for you. And now I need you at last, you refuse to pay your debt.' And coming out of the side of her mouth like a — like a gangster in one of those films you used to take me to. And she wets herself. She wets herself all the time.

WINDSCAPE. Oh Melanie, I'm so sorry. Of course I realised
   that last attack must have left her more — more incapacitated
   — and — possibly even a little incontinent —

MELANIE. She's not incontinent, Henry. She does it on
   purpose. Out of spite. She never does it with Grimes. Only
   with me. She says that as I'm behaving like a neglectful
   parent, she'll behave like a neglected child. The only child
   I'll ever have. Of course, she adores Grimes — or at least she
   pretends to. And she's started giving her things — things
   that belong to me she knows I love. The buttons from
   Daddy's uniform or, the other day, a silly lithograph of a
   donkey that's hung in my room all my life almost — of
   course Grimes gives them back but — but — the worst thing is
   I'm beginning to hate her. To hate going home or when I'm
   there have such dreadful feelings. Because the thought of
   years — it could be years apparently — years of this — and so
   wishing she would have another attack and die now —
   dreadful — too dreadful — almost imagining myself doing
   something to — get her out of the way.

WINDSCAPE. She must love you really, mustn't she, or she
   wouldn't — wouldn't resent your being away from her so
   much —

MELANIE. But I can't give up my teaching, Henry, I can't.
   Your getting me this job was the best thing that ever
   happened to me. Of course she always despised it. Even
   before she was ill she used to say teaching foreigners was a
   job for failures — but I love it and I'm not going to give it up.

   A pause.

WINDSCAPE. I only wish I could give you some comfort, my
   dear.

MEALNIE. You do, Henry. Your just being here and knowing
   that you — that you care about me makes all the difference.
   All the difference. It always has. (*She begins to cry.*) What a
   fool I was not to — not to marry you when you gave me the
   chance — I keep thinking of it now — and what she said
   about your being too young and not knowing what you were
   doing — and blighting your career — even then she was my

enemy — my real enemy. Of course I'm happy that you're so happy — I wouldn't have been able to make you so happy, I know — (*Sobbing.*) I'm sorry, sorry —

WINDSCAPE (*hesitates, then with reluctance puts his arms around her*). There there, my dear, there there — mustn't think of the past — it's the — the future — the future — there there —

The telephone rings.

(*After a moment.*) Perhaps I'd better — perhaps I'd better — um — (*Releasing himself, he picks up the telephone.*) Hello. Oh Hello Nigel, yes it is! No Anita's gone I'm afraid — at least I think she has — have you seen Anita in the last half hour —

MELANIE, *now handkerchiefing her tears, shakes her head.*

Melanie hasn't seen her either so I'm fairly sure — yes of course I will. (*He listens.*) You're 'phoning from Liverpool Street and you're about to catch the 6.13 so you'll be home before eight, right, got that — but if Melanie or I do see her by any unlikely — yes, right, goodbye — and oh, Nigel, good luck with your first issue. We're all looking forward to it enormously — yes — goodbye. (*He hangs up.*) That was Nigel — for Anita — as you probably realised and — and anyway she's certainly left, hasn't she — Look Melanie, you must come around, and have a real — a real talk with Fanny — take you out of yourself — away from your problems —

MELANIE. Thank you, Henry.

WINDSCAPE. No, we'd love to see you, I'll get her to ring you. All right? And now I must — I really must —

MELANIE. Yes, you must get back.

WINDSCAPE. Yes. See you Monday, my dear.

MELANIE. Monday, Henry.

WINDSCAPE *looks around vaguely for a moment, then goes out through the French windows.*

MELANIE *stands for a moment, then sees the briefcase, registers it, takes it to* WINDSCAPE's *locker, puts it in, goes*

ACT ONE, SCENE TWO 245

back to the book, looks down at it, tries futiley to sort it out,
pressing the page flat with her hand, as she does so.

The sound of the door opening, footsteps.

MELANIE (*closes the book quickly, gathers herself together*). Oh,
hello Eddie! (*Brightly.*)

LOOMIS. Thomas is not here then — I can't make out — I've
been everywhere, everywhere, up to the flat, all the class-rooms
and in the office — and the 'phone going all the time about
some of our Japanese and that French restaurant, and they're
not even French. It turns out they're from Wiltshire — and I
don't know what Thomas has said to them, I didn't even know
about it — he knows I can't deal with that sort of thing — and
he's booked a table for the two of us tonight at their request,
forcing us to take responsibility, I don't see what it's got to do
with the school if a few Japanese can't hold their drink, I don't
know why he agreed — it really is too all too —

MELANIE. Now Eddie. Now. (*Going to him.*) You mustn't worry.
You'll make yourself ill, and it's not worth it. Why don't you
go upstairs to the flat and have a rest, I'm sure it'll all sort
itself out, you know Thomas, he'll get it completely under
control, he always does, in the end.

LOOMIS. Yes, yes, of course you're right, my dear, thank you,
thank you. And a little rest — and I'll try and make Thomas
have one, too —

MELANIE. That's right, Eddie, you both need it — oh, and would
you give this back to him when you see him, and tell him I'm
terribly sorry (*As she collects her briefcase and hands* LOOMIS
the book.) a page of it seems to have got torn — our Mr Meadle
insisted on snatching it out of my hands and then dropped it — he
was only trying to be helpful of course — but you know how
clumsy he is —

LOOMIS. Oh — oh dear, Cussons' — one of our favourite books,
Thomas will find it difficult to forgive Meadle. Oh, by the
way, how's mother?

MELANIE. Oh, top hole, thanks Eddie.

LOOMIS. Good, good.

MELANIE. See you Monday.

LOOMIS. See you Monday. (MELANIE *goes off, left*. LOOMIS *looks at Cussons' and turns to see* QUARTERMAINE *standing at the French windows.*

QUARTERMAINE. Hello Eddie.

LOOMIS. Hello St. John. I thought you'd left.

QUARTERMAINE. No — I just thought I'd see if there was anyone still about.

LOOMIS. No, they've all gone.

QUARTERMAINE. Ah.

LOOMIS. Goodnight then, St. John.

QUARTERMAINE. Goodnight, Eddie. See you Monday.

LOOMIS. See you Monday.

LOOMIS *goes off, left*. QUARTERMAINE *stands for a moment. A distant spire chimes.* QUARTERMAINE *goes to his chair, sits, crosses his legs and lies back.*

Lights.

Curtain.

Act Two

Scene One

The following year, towards summer. It is a Monday morning, about nine-thirty.
  There have been a few improvements, different pictures perhaps; a record player, with a record rack consisting of poetry readings and Shakespeare plays. There is also a large new tape-recorder, sophisticated for the period.
  QUARTERMAINE is seated, staring ahead.
  WINDSCAPE enters through the French windows, carrying a briefcase, smoking a pipe, wearing bicycle clips.

WINDSCAPE. Hello St. John. (*He goes to his locker.*)

QUARTERMAINE (*doesn't respond at first, then takes in* WINDSCAPE). Oh, hello — um (*He thinks.*) Henry.

WINDSCAPE (*turns, looks at him*). Deep in thought?

QUARTERMAINE. Mmmm? Oh. No, no — just — just — you know.

WINDSCAPE. Ah. Did you have a good half term?

QUARTERMAINE. Oh. Yes thanks. Yes.

WINDSCAPE. What did you do? Did you go away? (*Going to his locker.*)

QUARTERMAINE. Well, I — I — no, I stayed here.

WINDSCAPE. Here!

QUARTERMAINE. Yes.

WINDSCAPE. Oh, in Cambridge, you mean? Just for a moment I thought you meant actually *here* — in this room — I think, perhaps because the last time I saw you, you were sitting in exactly the same place in very much that position — as if you haven't moved all week.

QUARTERMAINE. Oh. (*He laughs*.) But I say — good to be back, isn't it?

WINDSCAPE. Well, I could have done with a little longer myself.

QUARTERMAINE (*watches* WINDSCAPE *at the locker*). I say, Henry, what did you do for the half?

WINDSCAPE. Mmmm? Oh nothing very exciting really, we packed ourselves into the caravan and took ourselves off to a spot we'd heard about in Norfolk —

QUARTERMAINE. That sounds terrific!

WINDSCAPE. Yes — yes — well, the trouble was that it rained fairly steadily — all week, in fact — so we didn't get out as much as we would have liked — a shame really as among other things we were hoping that a few jaunts would cheer Susan up.

QUARTERMAINE. Oh — is she a bit low then?

WINDSCAPE. Yes yes — well she's still brooding over her 'O' level results — we keep telling her that at her age six positive passes — I mean threes and fours — is jolly good — but she seems to feel she's let herself down — but I'll tell you what we did see — it really was most — extraordinary — one morning at about six it was, I was up trying to plug the leak — it was right over little Fanny's bunk — and so she was awake and so was Ben — and Susan hadn't slept at all — so it was all rather — rather fraught, with tempers fraying — but Fanny she'd gone outside to the loo, as a matter of fact — and suddenly she called us — all of us — told us to put on our wellies and macs and come out and look — and we did — and there — silhouetted against the sky was the most — the most —

MEADLE *enters through the French windows in bicycle clips, carrying a briefcase.*

MEADLE. Greetings, Henry, St. John.

QUARTERMAINE. Hello, old chap.

WINDSCAPE. Hello, Derek. Have a good holiday?

MEADLE. Yes, thanks, Henry, very, very good indeed. What

about you? (*He goes to his locker, taking off clips, etc.*)

WINDSCAPE. Yes, I was just telling St. John, we went to Norfolk, a little wet, but there really was one very remarkable — well, moment is all it amounted to really. In temporal terms.

MEADLE. Sounds marvellous. Thomas isn't around yet, is he?

WINDSCAPE. He wasn't in the office when I came through, have you seen him, St. John?

QUARTERMAINE. Mmmm?

WINDSCAPE. Thomas. Have you seen him?

QUARTERMAINE. No no — but I expect he's here somewhere. I say — I say, Dennis, did you have a good holiday?

MEADLE. Who's Dennis, St. John? (*He laughs.*)

QUARTERMAINE. Mmmm?

WINDSCAPE. You said Dennis, instead of Derek. And he's already said he had a very good holiday.

QUARTERMAINE. Oh. What did you do?

MEADLE. I went to Sheffield, as a matter of fact.

WINDSCAPE. Sheffield, I know it well, Fanny and I went there the year before Susan was born, we were doing a tour of out-of-the-way urban domestic architecture, I've got great affection for Sheffield, what were *you* doing there?

MEADLE. Um — oh. Attending my aunt's funeral, as a matter of fact.

QUARTERMAINE. What?

WINDSCAPE. Oh Derek, I'm so sorry. How upsetting for you.

MEADLE. Yes, it was. Very. Very.

WINDSCAPE. But when I asked you just now you did say — I suppose it was merely social reflex — that you'd had a good half-term —

MEADLE. Yes, well actually I met someone there I used to know. And I managed to see quite a lot of her. That was the good part of it. Not my aunt's death, I need hardly say. (*He laughs.*)

WINDSCAPE. Ah.

QUARTERMAINE. Who was she?

MEADLE. Oh, just a girl St. John — we were at Hull University together, as a matter of fact, she was doing the library course but we — we lost contact, for various reasons. Although I hadn't forgotten her. And when I had to take back all my poor aunt's books — there she was. Behind the counter.

QUARTERMAINE. What was she doing there?

MEADLE. Well, stamping the books in and out of course. What do you think she was doing? (*With a mitigating laugh.*)

WINDSCAPE. Oh don't worry about St. John, one of his absent days, eh St. John?

QUARTERMAINE. What Henry?

WINDSCAPE. But how nice for you to bump into her like that, especially under those circumstances, eh?

MEADLE. Yes, I can't tell you what a — a blessing it turned out to be. As soon as she was off work she'd come over and sit with me and my uncle, and on a couple of evenings when I had to go out and console some of my aunt's friends, she came and sat with him anyway, by herself. He's very keen on football, but he can't follow it in the newspapers as his eyesight's nearly gone and they're too quick for him on the radio. So she'd read out all the teams and their scores. Which was very tiring for her, as she's got a bit of a speech impediment actually.

WINDSCAPE. What a nice girl she sounds, eh, St. John?

QUARTERMAINE. What, Henry?

WINDSCAPE. What a nice girl Derek's friend sounds.

QUARTERMAINE. Oh — oh yes, smashing, smashing. Um, tell me — tell me — what — what are her legs like?

MEADLE. What!

WINDSCAPE. Good heavens, St. John, what an extraordinary question!

QUARTERMAINE. Oh yes, — oh — I'm sorry — I was just trying to imagine — I have a sort of thing about girls' legs, you see.

(*He laughs apologetically.*) I can't stand them if they're dumpy or stumpy.

MEADLE. Well, let's just say, shall we, St. John, (*Manifestly exercising smiling control.*) that Daphne's legs happen to be my sort of legs.

A pause.

QUARTERMAINE. Your sort of legs. (*He looks at* MEADLE's *legs.*)

MEADLE. The sort of legs I happen to like. But I don't want to dilate on the subject of Daphne's legs (*He laughs.*) at least just at the moment — look, St. John, I wonder if you'd mind, there's a matter I was very much hoping to have a conversation with Henry about. As a matter of fact, it's rather urgent.

QUARTERMAINE. Oh. No. Sorry. Go ahead.

MEADLE. Well the thing is, St. John, it's — it's of a confidential nature.

QUARTERMAINE. Oh — oh well, I'll go and have a little stroll then, in the garden. (*Getting up.*) To tell you the truth my head feels a little — a little — as if it could do with some air.

MEADLE. Thanks very much, St. John, very decent of you.

QUARTERMAINE (*going off*). Oh, not at all — but I say — I say — (*Exiting.*) what a beautiful morning! (*He goes out.*)

MEADLE (*smiling*). You know, I can't help wondering sometimes about old Quartermaine. I can't imagine a more charming fellow but from the students' point of view — do you know what one of the advanced Swedes was telling me just before half-term —

WINDSCAPE (*interrupting*). I think it would be better really — really much better — if we didn't find ourselves talking about a colleague and a friend — I know that your concern is entirely — entirely disinterested, but — but — these little conflabs can do unintended harm. I hope you don't mind my — er —

MEADLE. Not at all, Henry, you're quite right, one can't be too careful, needless to say I meant no — no slur on St. John —

WINDSCAPE. I know you didn't, I know you didn't. But now. You said you had something urgent —

MEADLE. Yes, well, the thing is — well look, Henry, I've been here a year now and Thomas said when I started that it wouldn't be long before I'd be made a Permanent — and yet here I am, you see, still on part-time. The only one of the staff on part-time, as it happens.

WINDSCAPE. And part-time isn't really very satisfactory for you, then?

MEADLE. Well, no, it isn't, Henry, frankly. I get paid one pound two and sixpence for every hour I teach.

WINDSCAPE. But surely, Derek, one pound two and sixpence an hour isn't such a bad rate, is it?

MEADLE. Ah yes, Henry, but you see I don't get paid during the vacations, you see. I only get paid by the hour for the hours I'm allowed to do, while the rest of the staff get paid an annual salary. So even though I'm currently doing twice as many hours again as — well, St. John for example, I in fact get slightly less than half of what St. John gets, over the year. I mean, take this half-term we've just had, Henry, a week of paid holiday for everybody else but a week of no money at all for me, it was just luck that my aunt died in it, or I might have had to miss an earning week to go to her funeral and sort out my uncle you see. — And last Christmas, well, I've kept this very quiet, Henry, but last Christmas I had to be a post-man. (*He laughs.*)

WINDSCAPE. Oh dear!

MEADLE. Yes, and let me tell you it wasn't simply the work, Henry — being up at six, and trudging through the snow and sleet we had the whole of those three weeks — it was also the sheer embarrassment. Twice during my second round I nearly bumped into some students. I only got away with it because I kept my head lowered and once Thomas himself went right past me in the car — it was a miracle he didn't see me, especially as I'd slipped on some ice and I was actually lying on the pavement with the letters scattered everywhere — and now the summer holiday's looming ahead — I simply don't know how I'm going to get through that. Or at least I do. I've already sent in my application to be an Entertainments Officer at a holiday camp in Cleethorpes.

WINDSCAPE. Oh, have you?

MEADLE. Yes. And now that Daphne's back in the picture — well you probably gathered from what I said that we're pretty serious about each other — and I don't want to keep her waiting around with a long engagement — there's been a lot of tragedy in that family, Henry.

WINDSCAPE. Oh dear!

MEADLE. Yes, I won't go into it, if you don't mind. Not that Daphne tries to conceal it. She's too straightforward for that.

WINDSCAPE. Well, she really does sound a most — a most remarkable —

MEADLE. Yes, I consider myself a very very lucky man. So what do you think, Henry — I know how much Eddie and Thomas respect you — I'm going to try and nab Thomas for a few minutes this morning — how should I go about it, with him?

WINDSCAPE. Well, Derek, I think there's no doubt that you have a very strong case. Very strong. And as we all know, Thomas and Eddie are very fair, always. I know they'd respond most sympathetically — to all that you've told me about yourself and Daphne — but you see Derek, the thing is —

The sound of the door opening, footsteps.

SACKLING (*off*). 'Morning. (*He enters somewhat jauntily, his moustache now accompanied by a beard.*) Henry — Derek —

WINDSCAPE. Oh hello, Mark, good holiday?

MEADLE. You didn't notice if Thomas was in his office as you went by, did you?

SACKLING. Yes, he was. Just come down. I like the chin. A comparatively unexplored area, isn't it? How did you come by it, not shaving, I trust.

MEADLE (*who has been getting up*). No, not shaving, don't worry — (*Attempting a chuckle*.) I'll tell you all about it later — and thanks, Henry, for your advice. It was most helpful —

WINDSCAPE. Oh, not at all, I'm glad if — if —

MEADLE *goes out during this, and as the door closes:*

WINDSCAPE. Oh — no — Derek! Oh — blast!

SACKLING. What's the matter?

WINDSCAPE. I think we had a slight misunderstanding — he's under the impression that I was advising him to go and see Thomas about being put on a more — a more permanent basis, and the truth is I was going on to explain to him that in spite of the — the strong claim he has — he should — well, in my view anyway — hold his horses for the moment — Of course — I do sometimes feel, strictly between ourselves, that it *is* hard on Meadle as the only part-time teacher — and we must be careful in the staff-room not to show any — any — well, make fun of him more than is absolutely necessary — if you see, Mark.

SACKLING. Oh, I shouldn't worry about Meadle. (*He's been at the locker during all the above.*) even St. John's observed that he's one of those people who always lands on his feet — even if he damages a toe in the process. The thing is to make sure it's his and not yours. Well, Henry, peace-maker, apostle and saint, what sort of half did you have?

WINDSCAPE. Oh, we did the usual sort of thing, took the caravan to a spot near the Broads. The weather wasn't too splendid but as I was telling — St. John, I think it was — there was one rather exceptional experience. To tell you the truth I've never seen anything quite like it. Fanny actually wrote a small sort of prose poem about it.

SACKLING. Really? I didn't know Fanny wrote!

WINDSCAPE. Oh yes, you see —

SACKLING. But on that subject — listen — I must tell you. I've finished.

WINDSCAPE. Finished?

SACKLING. My novel, old cheese.

WINDSCAPE. Oh Mark — well, congratulations, congratulations!

SACKLING. Thanks Henry. Of course, it's still only the first draft. But the point is I feel — in my guts — that it's the first draft of the final version and damned near the thing itself, actually. Because of the way it happened, you see. What I did was — I put everything I'd previously written — round about three thousand pages — into a box and lugged it into the cellar and started again. Completely from scratch. Just me, the typewriter and a carton of paper. I was actually quite — quite frightened. But it was all perfectly simple. No strain. No effort. Almost no thought. Just a steady untaxing continuous flow of creation. For a whole week. It was the nearest I've come, will probably ever come, to a mystical experience.

WINDSCAPE. I envy you. I once tried to write a novel — but as Fanny said my forte — if I have a forte — (*He laughs.*)

SACKLING. The thing is, though — the thing is — it proves to *me* that I'm a novelist. The doubts I've had since Camelia left — and worst of all, the envy! I'd read the reviews and seen the photographs of other novelists — the real ones, who'd been published — some of them people I knew, had been up with — God, there's a man at Trinity — an absolute imbecile — his *second* novel came out last month, well received too — and when I saw his face in the middle of some interview he'd given — the same imbecile face, with a smirk added — that I used to see opposite me in Hall I — I — well, I'd better not go into what I wanted to do to him. And all those women that are getting published everywhere — everyone, everyone but me, that's what I began to think — as if they'd got something, through some genetic accident — like an extra gland or double joints — that I hadn't. And so they could do it, again and again while I was working away like some — some drudge — some lunatic drudge who'd given up his wife and child and hours and hours of his life — and would go on and on drudging, through thousands and thousands of pages, not one of them publishable, to the end of my life — so I suppose that what I've discovered at last is my — well, let's use the word. My talent. Perhaps it's been growing down there, in the dark, all this time — until finally it's strong enough to take over, eh? Anyway, now all I've got to do is a bit of pruning, no doubt some tightening up — correct the spelling and the typing mistakes, and float an extract or two in Nigel's currently fashionable little magazine — I've been promising him for years — (*He laughs.*)

QUARTERMAINE *enters through the French windows.*

QUARTERMAINE. All clear, then?

WINDSCAPE. What — oh good Heavens, St. John — yes, yes, I forgot that you were still out there.

QUARTERMAINE. Oh no — I enjoyed it — to tell the truth it seems to have cleared my head.

WINDSCAPE. Oh good.

QUARTERMAINE. Hello Mark.

SACKLING. Hello St. John. Have a good holiday?

QUARTERMAINE. Yes — yes — terrific thanks. Terrific. And how were they?

SACKLING. Who?

QUARTERMAINE. Camelia. And little Tom too. Weren't you going to see them over the half term?

SACKLING. St. John, I'd be grateful if you'd stop referring to him as little Tom, and little Tom too — it makes him sound like something out of the workhouse.

QUARTERMAINE. Oh right — right.

WINDSCAPE *during this goes to his briefcase, takes out books, puts the briefcase and other books into his locker.*

SACKLING. Actually, they were unavailable. He was getting over mumps, or so at least Camelia claimed, so she took him to a friends' to convalesce. They have a cottage by the sea, and of course I couldn't offer him that, could I?

QUARTERMAINE. Um — but what a pity I didn't know you were stuck in Cambridge over the half, we could have got together.

ANITA *enters through the French windows.*

SACKLING. Hi, Anita!

QUARTERMAINE. Hello, Anita!

WINDSCAPE. Anita, my dear —

ANITA *takes off her coat.*
She is pregnant.

SACKLING. — you're swelling along pleasantly. Rapidly too.

ANITA *laughs.*

QUARTERMAINE. But you look — you look — (*Gazing at her in a sort of reverence.*) I mean (*He gestures.*) in just a week, good Lord!

ANITA. Well, it's taken a bit longer than a week, St. John.

QUARTERMAINE. No, no, but I mean —

WINDSCAPE. Just like Fanny, nothing shows for ages and then one day there it is — for the world to see —

SACKLING. And how's Nigel getting on in New York?

ANITA. Oh, he decided not to go. He suddenly became convinced — he had a dream, or something — that I'd spawn prematurely, so he stayed at home and mugged up on all the texts — Spock for practicals, and Blake and D.H. Lawrence and some Indian writer he's discovered and is going to publish, for significance — which was lovely for me as I didn't have to go to my parents, I spent most of the time in the bath reading thrillers. It was lovely.

QUARTERMAINE. Oh, I wish I'd known you were here, so was Mark, as it turned out, weren't you Mark, we could have got together — but I say, I say, it's good to be back in a way, isn't it — I mean, after a good holiday of course —

SACKLING. Tell him I'm going to give him a ring, will you — (*To* ANITA.)

The sound of the door opening, closing, during this.

— there's something I've got for him. At last.

QUARTERMAINE. You don't mean you've finished your novel?

SACKLING. Yes!

QUARTERMAINE. Oh wonderful!

ANITA. Oh Mark, really! He'll be so thrilled — he keeps
refusing to 'phone you because he says it's like soliciting —

QUARTERMAINE. Hello, Derek, have you had a good half —

MEADLE *enters.*

(*Laughing.*) But of course I've seen you already, I'm sorry if
I was a bit — off-colour, don't know what was the matter with
me — but oh Lord, what have you done to your chin, you do
get in the wars, though, don't you, old man. Was it shaving?

ANITA. Derek, are you all right?

MEADLE. Yes, yes thanks — well — (*He laughs.*) apart from
finding out that I won't be joining you as a full-time member
of the staff. In fact, my hours are going to be cut. By over
a quarter. Which won't give me enough money to survive on.
Furthermore, I may not have any hours at all next month.
So I'll — I'll probably be leaving you then.

QUARTERMAINE. Leave! Oh no! That's rotten!

WINDSCAPE. I'm very sorry. I blame myself. I should have
explained more fully. But you were out of the room so
quickly —

SACKLING. Look, we must have a word with Thomas, with
Eddie — we can't allow him just to be chucked out — Henry,
perhaps you could speak to them on behalf of us all —

ANITA. Yes. Henry, you will, won't you?

WINDSCAPE. Of course I'll — I'll do my best. But whatever
happens, Dennis — it's no reflection on your teaching. None
at all.

MEADLE. Oh, I know that. It's Derek, by the way, Henry.
(*Laughing.*) But that's life, isn't it? That's the joke. How hard

I've worked. I mean, old Quartermaine here — well, according to one of the Swedes I'm not allowed to mention because it's a fraction on the unethical side to speak ill of a colleague — well, he sometimes sits for a whole hour not speaking. Even in dictation classes or if he does condescend to speak, goes off into little stories about himself they can't make head or tail of.

There is a pause.

QUARTERMAINE. What, a Swede, did you say? What does he look like?

MEADLE. Oh, what does it matter? Everybody knows that for you one Swede is like another German, one Greek is like another Italian, you can't tell them apart and you don't know what they're called — unlike me, you see — because do you know what I do? I memorise their names before their first class, and then study their faces during it, and then when I go home I close my eyes and practise putting the two together so that by the second class I know every one of my students *personally,* and do you know what else I do, I keep a look-out not only in term-time but also in my holidays — my *unpaid* holidays — for any item that might interest them for British Life and Institutions and actually make a note of them — here — in my notebook, which I always keep especially in my pocket (*Wrestling with it with increasing violence, jerking it out of his pocket, tearing his pocket as he does so.*) along with any of the out-of-the-way idioms and interesting usages I might happen across — and do you know what *else* I do — I — but what does it matter what else I do, that's what I mean by joke or life or whatever it is, because I'm the one that's facing the push, and you're the one that's on Permanent. (*During this speech* MEADLE's *accent has become increasingly North Country.*) Not that I begrudge you — it's just that I reckon that I've earned it. Look — look, I don't mean — I don't mean — the last thing I mean is — (*He turns away, possibly in tears.*)

There is silence, into which MELANIE *enters, through the French windows.*

WINDSCAPE. Hello Melanie, my dear.

QUARTERMAINE. Hello Melanie, have a good half?

SACKLING. Melanie.

ANITA. Hello Melanie.

MELANIE goes to the table, puts down the briefcase, takes off her coat.

QUARTERMAINE. Um — um — how's your mother?

WINDSCAPE. Yes, how — how is she?

MELANIE. She's dead. She died last Tuesday.

There is silence.

WINDSCAPE. Oh Melanie — I'm so sorry — so sorry —

Murmurings from the others.

Was it another attack, my dear?

MELANIE. No, she fell down the stairs and broke her neck. We don't quite know how it happened as it was after I'd gone to bed. Nurse Grimes found her there in the morning, I still hadn't got up, the first I knew of it was Nurse Grimes calling me — and — and — that's really all there is to tell. I'd be grateful if we could dispense with condolences and that sort of thing, because what I really want most of all is to get on in the usual fashion, without any — any fuss.

The sound of the door opening. The sound of footsteps, rather odd, though.

LOOMIS. Hello everybody, hello, all rested up I trust, welcome back, welcome back — but first, is Melanie here?

MELANIE. Yes.

LOOMIS. Ah there you are, Melanie my dear. (*Appearing on stage. He has a stick, his glasses are tinted, and his voice and manner are frailer.*) There are a couple of policemen in the office with Thomas, who want a word with you. They refuse to say what about, but not to worry, not to worry, because I asked whether it was illness or accident, and they assured me it wasn't so your mother's perfectly all right, my dear, which is the main thing, isn't it, it's probably some nonsense to do with your car, anyway if you'd go along to the office and flirt with them — and whatever you do, don't let Thomas lose his temper. (*He laughs.*) Mmmm?

MELANIE. Right Eddie.

>MELANIE *stands for a moment, then braces herself, walks off, left as:*

LOOMIS. Really! Our Cambridge bobbies, they always have to make such a solemn meal out of the most trivial business — Anita, my dear, how blooming you look, how blooming — and how did Nigel find New York?

ANITA. Oh fine, thank you Eddie, fine —

LOOMIS. Good good good, well tell Nigel how much we're looking forward to the first Anglo-American edition, and how sorry we are we've had to cut back to just the one subscription but *semper fidelis*. Henry, what sort of half term did you have — one of your adventurous caravan treks, where to this time?

WINDSCAPE. Yes Eddie — to Norfolk.

LOOMIS. Weather all right, I trust?

WINDSCAPE. Oh yes, Eddie, yes, lovely thank you, except when it rained and — and even then we had one — one amazing moment at sunrise —

LOOMIS. Good, good, especially for Fanny, little Fanny, Ben and Susan eh — and how did Susan get on with her 'O' levels, results as expected?

WINDSCAPE. Yes, Eddie, thanks, lots of 'threes' and 'fours' — and so forth.

LOOMIS. I'm not surprised, with you and Fanny behind her, give her our congratulations do, and Mark — if that is Mark I see behind a week's further fuzzy-wuzzy, lots of tap, tap, tapping?

SACKLING. Oh, well, as a matter of fact Eddie, as I was just telling —

LOOMIS. Well keep at it, we know that one day — ah, there's our Derek, but I've already said my welcomes to him, haven't I Derek, in the corridor — I gather you found Thomas?

MEADLE. Yes thank you, Eddie, yes yes.

LOOMIS. And that you got whatever it was you were so anxious to get sorted out, sorted out, at least Thomas seemed very pleased with the fruits of your deliberations.

MEADLE. Well — well yes, thank you, Eddie, all sorted out, yes.

LOOMIS. Good, good — and St. John — yes well — gather ye round — gather ye round. (*They all do so.*) I'd like to take the opportunity of saying to you, just between ourselves, and a little behind Thomas's back, so to speak, I expect you've all noticed the very distinct drop in student enrolment these last few months. This business of the Japanese suddenly deserting us has really hit us very hard — and what with all the recent renovation expenses — anyway — Thomas is slightly more worried than perhaps he's let any of you realise. We all know how dedicated he is to the future of the school — and to the future of the staff —

QUARTERMAINE. Hear, hear!

LOOMIS. — we've long thought of you as part of a family, I think you all know that we do our best to care for you in that spirit —

QUARTERMAINE. Absolutely!

LOOMIS. — and I'm sure you're all wondering what you can do to help us through this little rough patch — and the answer is, to go on giving of your very best to your teaching, and to show what students we've got that while we may not be as grand as some schools in Cambridge, we yield to no school in the country in the thing that matters most, our devotion to their devotion to their learning of our language. That's how —

QUARTERMAINE (*amid murmurs*). Hear, hear!

LOOMIS. That's how we can best serve our school at this time of slight crisis, and as I say, this strictly *entre nous*, without reference to Thomas — thank you everybody and bless you all — the bell will ring in a minute or so I believe, so — (*He gestures.*)

And as all except QUARTERMAINE *move to lockers, etc.*

QUARTERMAINE. Eddie that was — that was terrific!

LOOMIS. St. John a word of warning, I'm afraid there have been a number of complaints about your teaching — Thomas, I regret to say, received a round robin before half-term.

QUARTERMAINE. Oh Lord, that Swede, you mean?

LOOMIS. What Swede?

During this, the sound of door opening, footsteps.

Ah — Melanie, my dear, you've cleared it up, have you, what was it all about?

MELANIE. Oh yes, Eddie. All too preposterous. Apparently a group of French girls — from my intermediary Life and Institutions got hold of the wrong end of the stick. They didn't realise my recipe for roasting swan was for a medieval banquet, and actually tried to kill one on the Cam, can you believe it! Club one to death from a punt, with the intention of taking it back to their rooms and cooking and eating it! And then when they were reported to the police, blamed me. I'm glad to say that the swan, being a swan, survived. And gave one of them a badly bruised arm. Typically French.

Towards the end of this speech, MELANIE begins to laugh. All remain still. The laugh — now almost hysterical — builds. ANITA half moves towards MELANIE.

The bell rings.

Lights.

Scene Two

A Friday evening, some months later. The French windows are open. QUARTERMAINE is asleep in an armchair, papers and books on his lap, in which he is visible to the audience, but not to anyone on stage who doesn't look specifically in it.
    QUARTERMAINE suddenly groans.
    There is a pause.

QUARTERMAINE (*in sleep*). Oh Lord! (*Pause.*) I say! (*Pause, laughs. Sleeps.*)

The sound of the door opening. Footsteps.

MELANIE *enters from left. She goes to her locker, puts her books in.*

QUARTERMAINE, *not heard, or perhaps half heard, by* MELANIE, *lets out a groan.*

MELANIE *takes out of her locker an over-night bag.*

QUARTERMAINE (*lets out another groan*). Oh, Lord!

MELANIE (*starts, turns, sees* QUARTERMAINE). St. John! (*She goes towards him.*) Are you all right?

QUARTERMAINE (*blinks at her*). Oh — oh yes thanks — um — Melanie — next class, is it?

MELANIE. Heavens no, we've finished for the day. For the week, in fact.

QUARTERMAINE (*clearly confused*). Oh, I — I didn't hear the bell.

MELANIE. It hasn't gone yet. Don't worry, Eddie's having one of his very out-of-sorts days, poor lamb, and Thomas is in the office. We're safe.

QUARTERMAINE. Oh. Oh yes — I suppose I must have let them go early — always restless on a Friday, aren't they, and then sat down and — and —

MELANIE. St. John, what are you doing tonight?

QUARTERMAINE. Oh — usual — nothing very —

MELANIE. Then I'd like to introduce you to some very special friends of mine. Would you like that?

QUARTERMAINE. Well yes — yes — thank you, Melanie.

MELANIE. I'm sure you'll enjoy it — we always end up with singing and dancing, the food's delicious and the people are — well you'll see for yourself.

QUARTERMAINE. Well, it sounds — sounds terrific!

The sound of the door, footsteps.

MELANIE. Right, you wait for me here, and I'll come and collect you when I'm ready —

QUARTERMAINE. Right oh.

MELANIE. Oh hello Derek, you too — what a bunch of skyvers we're all turning out to be, eh?

MEADLE. Yes, well, it's only a few minutes off — besides Daphne's coming down for the weekend, I don't want to miss her train —

MELANIE (*exiting*). Jolly good — give her my love —

MEADLE. Right, Melanie, right — but I had a bloody near one in the corridor I can tell you. I was sloping past the office — terrible din coming from it, sounded like a gang of Germans, all bellowing away and Thomas trying to calm them down — anyway I'd just got past the door when Eddie came round the corner.

QUARTERMAINE. Phew!

MEADLE. Yes. I began to mumble some nonsense about wanting to check up on a student — but he didn't see me — went right on past — I mean, we were like that! (*Showing.*)

QUARTERMAINE. He didn't even see you, you say? Well, I hope he's all right —

MEADLE. Oh, by the way, Daphne and I have got an invitation for you — to celebrate our engagement. Now that I've got my Permanency, we've decided to make it official.

QUARTERMAINE. Oh congratulations!

MEADLE. We're getting married on the first day of the summer vac', and I'm going to ask Thomas and Eddie to be the best man. I mean, let them decide which — I don't want to upset one by choosing the other.

QUARTERMAINE. Oh terrific! And then off on your honeymoon, eh?

MEADLE. Yes. We've settled for Cleethorpes. Not very exciting, I know, but there may be a way to pick up a little money as well as have a good holiday ourselves. Daphne's keen to start saving for a house — you know how it is, there's a very practical head on those little shoulders of hers. There's a good

chance she might even come and do a bit of teaching here
— to replace me as the part-time, you see. I've already
dropped a little hint to Thomas — I think he was worried by
her speech impediment, but I pointed out that in some
respects that could be an asset.

QUARTERMAINE. Absolutely — and she'd be — a great asset
here, wouldn't she, in the staff room, I mean — she's a
wonderful girl, Derek.

MEADLE. Yes, well, I think you'll like her even more when you
meet her. Because frankly she's — she's — (*He shakes his head.*)
And I'll tell you something — I don't know whether you've
noticed but since she came back into my life I've stopped
having all those ridiculous accidents. They were the bane of
my life, even though I was always trying to make light of
them. I suppose it's — it's something to do with needing —
well, well, the right person, eh? Love. Let's face it. Love. Oh,
I'd better get going. So see you at seven for supper. It'll be
nothing special.

QUARTERMAINE. Derek, I'm very — I'm very honoured —

MEADLE. Actually, you'd better make it 6.30, as it'll be more
on the lines of a high tea. And if you could bring along a
couple of bottles of wine —

QUARTERMAINE. My dear chap, I'll bring — I'll bring *champagne*
— and — and — oh Lord, I'd forgotten! Oh no! I've already
accepted an invitation for this evening.

MEADLE. Oh. What to?

QUARTERMAINE. Well, I can't make out, quite — I was in a bit
of a haze when Melanie asked me, but she said something
about friends and singing and dancing —

MEADLE. And you accepted?

QUARTERMAINE. Well yes.

MEADLE. But it's — it's — one of those evenings. What they sing
is hymns and the dancing up and down and around and about
and then that Nurse Grimes declares for Jesus — and then the
rest of them follow suit, and then they all stand around and
wait for you to do it.

QUARTERMAINE. Oh Lord!

MEADLE. At least, that's how it went the night she got me along. She's trying to convert you.

QUARTERMAINE. Oh Lord!

The bell rings.

MEADLE. But I told you all about it —

QUARTERMAINE. Yes, but I'd forgotten — I mean she didn't mention Jesus —

MEADLE. Well, she won't let you get out of it now. (*During this, he has been getting ready to go, putting on bicycle clips, etc.*)

SACKLING *enters.*

Well, I'll get you and Daphne together very soon — don't worry — (*Making to go.*) Here, Mark, guess what St. John's got himself into — one of Melanie's evening.

SACKLING (*in a hurry, with books etc.*). Christ, you haven't, have you? (*He is clean-shaven, by the way.*) You *are* a chump, St. John, you must have heard her going on about Nurse Grimes and her dark night of the soul, after her mother died. Don't you take anything in!

QUARTERMAINE. Yes, yes I did, but —

SACKLING. But you didn't know how to say no. Which, if I may say so, is both your charm and your major weakness.

QUARTERMAINE. Well, you never know — it may be — may be quite interesting — one has to — has to have a go at anything really — and I wasn't doing anything else this evening.

SACKLING (*who is now ready to go*). This evening! Yes, you bloody *are* doing something else this evening. You're going out to dinner.

QUARTERMAINE. What — where?

SACKLING. At my place — oh Christ! Don't say I forgot to invite you. Well you're invited. So there you are, saved from salvation. All you have to do is to tell Melanie that you'd forgotten —

QUARTERMAINE. Oh, this is terrible. You mean I'd be having dinner with you.

SACKLING. You *are* having dinner with us. It's obligatory. For one thing, I told Camelia I'd asked you — she's counting on you -- we all are — even Tom, I promised him he could stay up an extra half an hour especially to see you again.

QUARTERMAINE. But what about Melanie? I promised her —

SACKLING. Oh, to Hell with Melanie! It's all a load of pathetic nonsense — and probably blasphemous, too, if one believed in God. Look, speaking as one of your best and oldest and dearest, etc., — it's *crucial* that you come. Of the greatest importance. To me. You see. O.K.? Look, I've got to dash, I'm picking Tom up from school —

The sound of the door opening, sound of footsteps.

Make sure (*To off.*) that he turns up tonight, won't you? He's got himself into one of his usual messes — see you both at eight. (*Going out as:*)

ANITA enters. She has a look of weariness about her, is subtly less well-turned out than in previous scenes.

QUARTERMAINE. Oh don't say you and Nigel are going to be there too — oh dear.

ANITA. Why can't you come?

QUARTERMAINE. Well I fell into one of those dozes again — you know how they keep coming over me suddenly — for a minute or so — and — and when I came out of it, there I was, right in the middle of this — this Melanie business.

ANITA. Poor St. John.

QUARTERMAINE. Well, I can't just turn around to her now and say — 'Sorry Melanie, something much more amusing's turned up'. She was so — well — her eyes — I can't explain — oh, if only Mark hadn't forgotten! — but then I suppose he knows I'm usually free and thought — but what do I do, Anita, what do I do?

ANITA. Oh do come if you can. It's meant to be a reconciliation

dinner, and you know how they usually turn out. So you'd
be a great help, as the perfect outsider.

QUARTERMAINE. Well, you know I'd do anything — anything —
to make sure that old Mark and his Camelia stay together.

ANITA. Oh, it's not them that need reconciling. They already
are. It's Mark and Nigel.

QUARTERMAINE. Mark and Nigel — but they're such friends,
what happened?

ANITA. Oh, it was all a couple of months ago. They had the
most appalling row, because Nigel turned down an extract
from Mark's novel. About seven extracts, actually.

QUARTERMAINE. Oh no. Oh, poor Mark!

ANITA. Of course, Nigel made everything worse by deciding
to be completely honest for once. I suppose he thought Mark,
being an old friend, had it coming to him. He said that
everything Mark had sent him was imitative and laboured, and
anyway who really cared any more about the mysteries of
sex, the wonders of childbirth, the delicacies of personal
relationships — it had all been done and done and done to
death, there were far bigger issues. And then of course when
the magazine folded, and Nigel was going through his rough
patch, with the printers threatening to sue and various other
things, Mark wrote him a gloating letter — and added a P.S.
about the old Amanda Southgate affair, claiming to be
indignant on my account. I must say, I rather wish he'd
resisted that.

QUARTERMAINE. But still — but still — he has asked Nigel to
dinner —

ANITA. Oh, that was probably Camelia. She never took literature
seriously. I loathe the thought of it — for one thing we haven't
been able to find a baby-sitter, so we'll have to bring Ophelia
in her carry-cot — she's still got six weeks colic, after
four months — so it would be nice if you came, St. John,
you'd make the whole thing more bearable.

QUARTERMAINE. Oh, I'd love to — and to see Ophelia — I've
only seen her the once, in hospital — what hair she had!

ANITA *laughs. In fact crying slightly.*

Oh Anita — what is it — oh, I hate to see you unhappy —
more than anyone else — (*He makes to make a move towards
her. Checks himself. Makes a move again.*) Oh Lord! (*He
stands before her, helplessly.*)

ANITA. I'm all right, St. John, honestly — it's just that — oh,
the way things go, I mean. Or don't go. Nothing seems to
come out right. All the years I adored him and he couldn't
bear me. And now he adores me and I can't bear him. You
see. (*She looks at him.*) What a — what a nice man you are.
(*She begins to cry again.*) I'm sorry — I'm tired, I expect, I'm
just tired — (*Turning away, blowing nose, wiping eyes, etc.,
as:*)

The sound of the door opening, footsteps.

QUARTERMAINE (*turning*). Oh — oh hello Henry, you've
finished late — um —

WINDSCAPE (*appearing rather heavily*). Yes, I got into a bit of
a tangle with my Intermediary British Life and Institutions,
over our parliamentary system. Usually it's perfectly clear to
me but this time it all came out rather oddly. Or it must
have done, as I had the whole lot of them dismissing it with
contempt — the three or four from the Eastern bloc, all the
ones from Fascist countries — the French were the loudest,
as always — but even the Japanese — normally such a polite,
reticent man — and I don't see quite how it happened or
what I said, but it was rather hard being lectured at on — on
political decencies — and shouted at by — by — still, I
suppose it's better they should all join up for a wrangle with
me than with each other — although to tell you the truth I
found it rather hard to keep my temper (*Sitting down.*) but
I think I managed to — with the result that I've got a — a
slight heachache. After all, I was only *explaining* our
constitution, not boasting about it. I've got my own — own
distinct reservations — no system's perfect, as I kept having
to say to Santos. His father's a Bolivian cabinet minister.

ANITA (*who has been discreetly composing herself during the
above*). It's awful when they get like that, isn't it? I always

make them explain our politics to me, and then just correct their English, whatever they say — one of the advantages of being female, I suppose — (*She attempts a little laugh.*) well, goodnight, Henry, see you Monday —

WINDSCAPE. 'Night, Anita, my dear. Best to Nigel, and little Ophelia —

ANITA. And St. John, see you later I hope. Do come if you can.

QUARTERMAINE. Yes, well — I'll — I'll — right, Anita. Right. If I can.

ANITA *goes out through the French windows.*

There is a pause. WINDSCAPE *is sitting in the chair, stroking his forehead.*

QUARTERMAINE (*is staring in a state of desperation*). I say, Henry — I say — I wonder if you could give me some advice.

WINDSCAPE. Mmmm?

QUARTERMAINE. I'm in a bit of a pickle, you see.

WINDSCAPE. Oh, St. John, is there any chance you could come over tonight?

QUARTERMAINE. What?

WINDSCAPE. I'm sorry it's such short notice, it wouldn't have been if I'd remembered. The thing is that Fanny's really very down in the dumps, very down, she really does need a — So do I, come to that. It's Susan, you see. She's taken a turn for the worse.

QUARTERMAINE. Oh, I am sorry.

WINDSCAPE. Oh, it's probably just withdrawal from all the tranquilising drugs they put her on in hospital, and then her friends will keep coming over in the evenings and talking about their plans and their blasted 'A' Levels and of course there's no possibility that Susan — at least for a few years — anyway. You see — last night — we heard her shrieking with laughter at something on television. A good sign, Fanny and I thought. The first time she's laughed since her breakdown.

So we went into the living-room and laughed with her — until
we realised that what we were laughing at was a news flash to
do with some particularly hideous atrocity in — in — (*He
gestures*.) and what followed was a bit of a nightmare,
especially for Ben and little Fanny — it ended with the
doctor having to sedate her — almost forcibly, I'm afraid —
so — so I noticed *La Regle du Jeu* was on at the Arts, one of
our favourite films, so decent and — and humane — and
then a quiet dinner afterwards at the French place — just the
two of us — if you can manage it. You're the only person
Susan will allow to baby-sit, you see. She seems to feel some
— some reassurance from you. And of course little Fanny and
Benjamin love it too, when you come.

QUARTERMAINE. I'd love to, Henry — love to — but could it
be tomorrow?

WINDSCAPE. No, Saturday's no good — we have our family
therapy session in the afternoon and we all feel so exhausted
afterwards. Demoralised, really. I've still to be persuaded that
they serve a — a useful — though of course one mustn't
prejudge —

QUARTERMAINE. Sunday, then?

WINDSCAPE. Unfortunately Fanny's mother's coming on
Sunday. Rather against our inclinations as — as she's rather
insensitive with Susan — advises her to pull her socks up — that
sort of thing — you can't manage this evening then.

QUARTERMAINE. Well — I — I — you see the problem is — Henry
the problem is —

The sound of the door opening. Footsteps.
*MELANIE appears. She has changed her dress, is wearing
high-heeled shoes, some make-up, and has taken much
trouble with her hair.*

MELANIE. Well, there we are then, St. John — sorry to have
been so long — oh, hello, Henry, I didn't know you were still
here.

WINDSCAPE. Hello Melanie (*Slightly awkward.*) Oh, I've meant
to say all day how much I like that dress.

MELANIE (*smiles*). Thank you. I'm taking St. John to one of my evenings --

WINDSCAPE. Oh. Oh I see. I'm so sorry that Fanny and I have been unable to come so far —

MELANIE. Oh, I know how difficult things are for you at the moment — as long as you both realise that any time you want to come along, I've been thinking that perhaps Susan might —

WINDSCAPE. Yes, yes, thank you, Melanie. (*Cutting her slightly.*)

MELANIE. Are you all right, you look a little fraught.

WINDSCAPE. Oh just tired, Friday eveningish, that's all.

QUARTERMAINE. And a bit of a headache — eh Henry?

MELANIE. Oh? Where?

WINDSCAPE. Well — in my head.

MELANIE. Yes, but which part?

WINDSCAPE. Well, it seems to be — just here — (*Rubbing his brow.*)

MELANIE. Ah, well then it's a tension headache, Nurse Grimes showed me a marvellous trick for dealing with that, let me have a go at it. (*She comes over to* WINDSCAPE, *behind the chair.*) Now put your head back — right back —

WINDSCAPE *does so, with perceptible lack of enthusiasm.*

MELANIE. There. Now. (*She proceeds to knead her fingers into the back of* WINDSCAPE's *neck.*)

QUARTERMAINE. So that's how they do it — looks jolly relaxing, Henry.

WINDSCAPE *endures for a few seconds, then suddenly lets out a cry, leaps up.*

WINDSCAPE. No!

There is a pause.

I'm — Melanie, I'm sorry — I — don't know quite what —

MELANIE. I expect I hurt you, pressed the wrong nerve or — I still haven't quite got the trick of it, with my clumsy —

WINDSCAPE. Well — well actually it feels a little better. (*He tries a laugh.*) Thank you.

MELANIE (*smiles*). Well, St. John, we'd better be on our way. It's quite a drive. Goodnight, Henry, and rest yourself during the weekend, won't you?

WINDSCAPE. Yes, yes — the same to you (*A slight hesitation.*) my dear. Goodnight, St. John, see you Monday.

QUARTERMAINE. See you Monday Henry and — oh, if it turns out that Saturday or Sunday — well, I'm sure I'll be free —

WINDSCAPE *smiles, nods.*

MELANIE. Off we go, St. John.

QUARTERMAINE. Right.

As they go out through the French windows there is the sound of the door opening and feet, a stick.

WINDSCAPE. Oh hello Eddie, I didn't know you were about today.

LOOMIS (*enters. He is much frailer than when last seen*). Well, there was a frightful schmozzle in the office — and Thomas asked me to come down — but was that St. John's voice I heard just now?

WINDSCAPE. Yes. His and Melanie's —

LOOMIS. Ah. Well, I would have quite liked a word with our St. John. He's caused us quite an afternoon. He appears to have missed his last class entirely. His students waited doggedly through the whole hour for him to turn up, and then went to the office and berated poor Thomas — they were mostly Germans, and you know what they're like if they think they're not getting their money's worth of syllabus.

WINDSCAPE. Oh dear.

LOOMIS. Though I doubt whether they'd get much more

sensible English from St. John present than from St. John
absent — as far as I know that Swiss Ferdinand Müller was
the only student who ever felt he got value for money from
St. John, thank goodness he's stopped sending those
postcards at last, they made Thomas quite upset — but I
wonder what it was he enjoyed so much about St. John's
classes — perhaps the lack of — of — I don't know what
we're going to do about him in the end, though, if we turned
him out where would he go, who else would have him, one
does look after one's own, I suppose, when it comes to it. I
agree with Thomas on that, after all the school's our — our
family, the only family Thomas and I have between us, so
one has a responsibility for them — but a responsibility for
the students too —

*There should be a slightly rambling quality in the delivery of
this speech.*

it's so difficult to get the balance right — so difficult —
St. John's forgetting to teach them, and now Melanie's
starting up her missionary work amongst them — Thomas is
going to have a word with her too — the Catholic countries
won't stand for it, and why should they, and now our
Meadle, taking to slipping away before the bell now he's got
his Permanency, trying to bluff his way past me in the hall
as if I couldn't see him — ha — well, at least Mark's pulling
his weight now he's got his Camelia back, I never thought for
a moment there was a writer in that lad, did you? — and
Anita — really I don't know how these modern young
couples cope — but I gather Nigel's taken to fatherhood quite
wonderfully, Thomas and I saw the three of them on the
Backs the other day, a very pretty sight it was too — so — so
— good, good, — just the problems of a flourishing school,
eh? (*He laughs.*)

WINDSCAPE. Yes. Yes indeed, Eddie.

LOOMIS. Well, I'd best get back up to bed, or Thomas will have
a fit, goodnight Henry, see you Monday, bless you, bless you.

WINDSCAPE. Yes, see you Monday Eddie.

LOOMIS (*goes off, stops*). Oh, I haven't asked for a while — how's
our Susan?

WINDSCAPE. Oh, responding I think — slowly — slowly responding.

LOOMIS. Good, good. (*The sound of the door closing.*)

During this, the sound of students' voices, young, distant, in the garden. They get closer as the scene concludes.

WINDSCAPE *stands for a moment, touches his forehead.*

Students' voices, probably two girls, two boys, now laughing, calling out to each other in some sort of game.

WINDSCAPE *gets out bicycle clips, bends to put them on, as he does so looks towards the French windows. He smiles slightly, continues putting on the clips, as sounds of voices, still raised in laughter.*

Lights.

Scene Three

Eighteen months later. It is around Christmas. Not yet dark, but darkening slightly. The French windows are closed, but the curtains are opened. There is an atmosphere of chill. One table-light is on.
    SACKLING, QUARTERMAINE, MELANIE, ANITA,
WINDSCAPE, MEADLE *are variously sitting and standing.*
    SACKLING *is smoking a pipe, has a beard.*
    WINDSCAPE *is also smoking a pipe.*
    ANITA *is pregnant.*
    MEADLE *has a plaster neck-brace.*
    QUARTERMAINE *is in a dinner-jacket.*
    MELANIE *is sitting, rather hunched, nervously smoking a cigarette. It is the first time in the play that she smokes, of course. She smokes throughout the scene, lighting one after another.*
    After a pause.

SACKLING. It's always at Christmas, somehow, isn't it?

WINDSCAPE. Yes.

SACKLING. Oh Henry, I'm sorry —

WINDSCAPE. No, you're right. I was thinking much the same thing. Both my parents too, but — but of course in Susan's case I don't think the season was — was relevant. At least to her. The blinds were always down, you see. Because any brightness hurt her mind. Natural brightness, that is. She could tolerate artificial light. Until the last — last bit.

ANITA (*there is a faint touch of querulousness in her voice*). Look, I'm sorry, but I'll have to go soon, I'm afraid. I promised the *au pair* she could have the night off, and Nigel's probably not coming back from London until tomorrow —

MEADLE. Yes, I've got to get back pretty soon. Daphne's not too grand, what with her morning sickness and all the redecorating — she's been over-doing it and I promised — I don't want to leave her alone too long.

WINDSCAPE. Of course — of course — there's really no need for all of us when it comes to it — it's just that — that — as soon as I heard I had some idea that you would want — well — without perhaps enough consideration — it was a bad idea, perhaps —

QUARTERMAINE. Oh, I say Henry — well, I'm jolly glad you got in touch with me — though of course I wasn't doing anything in particular —

SACKLING. Well, I must say it St. John, (*Smiling.*) you do look as if you might have been about to be up to something —

QUARTERMAINE. What? Oh — (*He laughs.*) well, no, no, not really — it was just — just —

During this, the sound of the door opening.

They all look towards it, as footsteps, dragging feet, a stick.

LOOMIS (*in an over-coat, with his stick, and with a deaf-aid attached to his glasses*). I saw the lights on so I guessed that some of you — one or two perhaps — had come. But I didn't expect all of you. Not at this time of year, with your families and responsibilities. Thomas would have been so touched. So touched. My thanks on his behalf. My thanks. (*Little pause.*) He died an hour ago. They did everything they could, right to the end, but of course, as we've all known for some time, there was nothing to be done. (*Little pause.*) You

know how much you all meant to him. He talked of every
one of you, every evening, until — (*He gestures.*) But you'll
also want to know what its future is to be, this school's that
he loved so much. I know what his wishes are, we discussed
them quite openly once we both knew that he was bound to
leave us. I've also talked to Henry. I'm sure it will be no
surprise to all of you that I asked Henry some time ago to
take over the school as its sole Principal. I've no desire to take
an active part in it, now that Thomas is no longer here. I loved
it for his sake, you see. I'll make no secret of that. Not this
evening. (*Pause, he nearly breaks down, pulls himself
together.*) Not this evening. I shall be leaving the flat as soon
as possible — it has too many memories — and settle
somewhere by the sea. As we'd always planned to do. I hope
that some of you will come and see me — (*Little pause.*)
Bless you. Bless you. (*He turns. Goes. The sound of his feet
dragging slowly. The sound of the door shutting.*)

There is a pause.

WINDSCAPE. I — I really don't want to speak at such a moment
about plans or changes. We'll have a meeting at the beginning
of term to go into those, but I should just say that I've
already talked to Mark about his following me as the academic
tutor. I am happy to say that he has accepted.

There are murmurs.

So until next term — which has a very reasonable enrolement,
I am glad to report, let me merely assure you that I intend
to do my best, as I know you will, to maintain our reputation
as a flourishing school. I know — I know — Thomas and Eddie
wouldn't want me to let you part without wishing you all a
Happy Christmas.

Murmurs of 'Happy Christmas'.

Well, see you all next term!

They rise to go, putting on coats, etc.

QUARTERMAINE. Henry — I say, well you and Mark — that's
quite a team, you know.

WINDSCAPE. Thank you, St. John.

SACKLING (*coated*). Well, night Henry — we'll speak. And St. John — over the Christmas, eh? You must come round. (*Gesturing with his pipe.*)

QUARTERMAINE. Oh, I'd love that — thanks Mark. See you then. Love to Camelia and Tom and little Mark too.

ANITA. Sorry if I was a little edgy earlier Henry, (*Also coated.*) put it down to my current condition and Yugoslav *au pairs*! (*She laughs.*)

WINDSCAPE. You get home to your Ophelia, my dear, and make Nigel look after you.

ANITA. Oh, I will, Henry — see you over Christmas, St. John, I hope.

QUARTERMAINE. Oh Lord yes — lovely — lovely — 'night, Anita and love to little Ophelia and Nigel too.

MEADLE (*coated*). Sorry Daphne couldn't make it, Henry. She wanted to, of course. But I'll fill her in, don't worry, she's very much looking forward to her courses next term —

WINDSCAPE. And I'm looking forward to having her join us. Goodnight, Derek.

MEADLE. Drop around when you feel in the mood, St. John. Lots of paint-brushes for you to wield — (*He laughs.*)

QUARTERMAINE. Terrific! I love the smell of paint — love to Daphne —

MELANIE (*comes up, hunched, smoking*). 'Night Henry. 'Night.

WINDSCAPE. Night Melanie my dear. And perhaps we can all get together after Christmas — Fanny was saying how much she'd like to see you, after all this time.

MELANIE. Love to, love to, and St. John, if you're free pop around and have a drink. (*She laughs.*)

QUARTERMAINE. Oh yes please Melanie — I'd like that.

WINDSCAPE. Well St. John where were you off to tonight by the way?

QUARTERMAINE. Oh Lord, nowhere Henry. (*He laughs.*) You

see, there was a suitcase I still hadn't unpacked — it's been
down in Mrs Harris' cellar all these years. But suddenly she
wanted the space, so she made me take it upstairs, and of
course I opened it and there was this. (*Indicating the dinner-
jacket.*) So I decided to try it on, to see if it still fits. And
then you 'phoned, so — so I came straight over here, forgetting
I had it on. Stinks of moth-balls, I'm afraid, but not a bad
fit, eh? Might come in useful sometime. But I say, poor old
Eddie, poor old Eddie. Wasn't he — wasn't he terrific!

WINDSCAPE. Yes. Indeed. (*A slight pause.*) St. John. St. John.
I've been worrying about this for — oh, ever since I realised
I was to take over from Eddie and Thomas. If I'm to be
Principal, I have to run the school in my own way, you see.

QUARTERMAINE. Oh, I know that, Henry. We all do.

WINDSCAPE. And — and — I don't see, you see — however fond
of you I happen to be — we all happen to be — that there's
any room for you any more. You see?

A pause.

I thought it only right to tell you at the first — the very
first possible moment. So that you can — well, look around —

QUARTERMAINE. No, that's — right, thank you Henry. I — oh
Lord, I know that I haven't got much to offer — never had,
I suppose — and recently it's got even worse — it's a wonder —
a wonder people have put up with me so long, eh? (*He
attempts a laugh.*)

WINDSCAPE. If I could see any way —

QUARTERMAINE. No, no — I mean it's no good being all
right in the staff room if you're no good in the classroom, is
it? They're different things.

WINDSCAPE. I can't tell you how much I'll miss you. We all will.

QUARTERMAINE. And I — I'll miss it. All of you.

WINDSCAPE. Yes, I know. Would you like a quick drink — or —
or — come back and see Fanny.

QUARTERMAINE. Oh, no — no thank you Henry, I'll stay here

for a while — if I may — you know — and get myself used to — and — I'll go in a minute.

WINDSCAPE (*hesitates, looks at* QUARTERMAINE). Well, goodnight, St. John.

QUARTERMAINE. Goodnight, Henry, see you next — (*He gestures.*)

WINDSCAPE *goes off. The sound of feet, door opening and closing.*

Oh Lord!

Well — I say —

Oh Lord!

Lights.

Curtain.

The Common Pursuit

For Ben and Lucy

This version of THE COMMON PURSUIT was first presented by
Joseph Stern, Actors for Themselves at the Matrix Theatre, Los
Angeles on 8th February 1986, with the following cast:

STUART	Kristoffer Tabori
MARIGOLD	Judy Geeson
MARTIN	Wayne Alexander
HUMPHRY	John de Lancie
NICK	Nathan Lane
PETER	Christopher Neame

Directed by Sam Weisman

Act One

Scene One

STUART's *room in Cambridge. Twenty years ago. The gramophone is playing.*
 STUART *is seated at his desk, a letter in his hands.*
 MARIGOLD *is lying on the bed reading a book.*

STUART (*referring to letter*). I just don't know.

MARIGOLD (*looking up at him*). What is it?

STUART. A letter from Leavis. I wrote telling him I was thinking of calling the magazine *The Common Pursuit*. In homage to his book. He says I can publish it in my first issue, if I want.

MARIGOLD. That's terrific.

STUART. Yes, but he says I have to publish the whole letter, and the trouble is it's full of qualifications, rather long and depressing qualifications actually, about my chances of making a success of it — full of words like 'embattled' and 'beleaguered' — it makes the magazine seem on the point of surrender before it's even begun. But on the other hand, to have his name in the very first issue would certainly attract a lot of attention, wouldn't it?

MARIGOLD. Yes, I'm sure it would. (*Smiles at him.*)

 STUART *smiles back. Picks up a typescript, then looks towards* MARIGOLD *again. She has turned away. He continues to look at her, then opens a drawer, takes a letter out, looks it over.*

 Hey what's that?

STUART. I rather think from the way that it goes into all sorts of details about my private person, that it must be a letter from you. (*Turns the last page over.*) Ah yes. It is from you. You're the only person in the world who knows enough about me to have written this postscript. And here's your name. Marigold Watson. That *is* your name, isn't it?

MARIGOLD. You're meant to be reading poems and articles and such stuff. Not sex-crazed communications from the likes of me.

STUART (*leaving letter on desk, he crosses and sits next to her on the bed*). I just wanted to make absolutely sure that I was trapped in my room with the most disgusting girl in Cambridge. You *are* Marigold Watson, aren't you?

They kiss.

MARIGOLD. Oh Stuart, Stuart, Stuart. If you are Stuart Thorne, that is.

They kiss again, he starts to unbutton her shirt.

STUART (*remembering*). Oh Christ, we can't. I've got some people coming.

MARIGOLD. What people?

STUART. All the types I've invited to help me with the magazine. Nick, and Captain Marvel, and the chap who sent me those terrific poems, Humphry Taylor, and some peculiar freak who actually *wants* to work on the financial side, I can't remember his name — I've invited them all for coffee (*Looks at his watch.*) in ten minutes.

MARIGOLD. That's all right. We'll be extremely quick. Like lightning. We'll be finished long before they arrive.

STUART. But I don't want to be extremely quick. Like lightning. I want to be extremely slow. (*Pause.*) For ever, in fact.

MARIGOLD (*after a small pause*). For ever?

STUART. For ever. But that doesn't mean I can't be extremely quick too.

They start to make love.
MARTIN appears at the doorway, stops.

MARIGOLD. Oh, the door.

MARTIN *withdraws hurriedly.*

STUART. Oh, yes.

STUART *crosses to door, closes it.*

MARIGOLD. And the curtains.

STUART. Prude. (*Crosses to curtains, makes to draw them, looks out of window, stops.*) Christ! (*Small pause, staring out.*) Christ!

MARIGOLD (*coming over*). What is it?

STUART. It's — it's Stout! (*Pointing.*)

MARIGOLD. Stout?

STUART. Hubert Stout!

MARIGOLD. The poet? Really. He looks rather jolly. Like Father Christmas. Or a child molester. Who's the lady, she doesn't look at all jolly, except possibly jolly cross.

STUART. That must be his wife — Charlotte. They've just married. But where are they going? Oh, into one of the guest rooms. They must be staying the night. Marigold, come on!

MARIGOLD. What?

STUART. Let's talk to him. Tell him about the magazine. Actually to see Hubert Stout. Today of all days. It's like an omen. A portent!

MARIGOLD. But I thought that you were going to ravish my body.

STUART. Yes, well I will. Ravish and ravish and ravish. You are the master-mistress of my passions, etc., and so forth. Later. But now — (STUART *crosses to his desk to get his jacket.*)

MARIGOLD. Do you want me to come like this, or would he prefer me with clothes on?

STUART. Probably like that given his reputation. (*She crosses to the bed and starts to dress, he checks papers on his desk, speaking to himself.*) I'll show him this; Humphry Taylor's poems, where are they — I know he'll like them. And this. (*To her.*) Marigold come on. (*He exits, runs into MARTIN in hallway, backs into room speaking to* MARTIN.) Oh — hello. Um — um — come in.

MARTIN *enters as* MARIGOLD *is still dealing with buttons.*

This is um, um this is —

MARTIN. Martin Musgrove.

MARIGOLD (*embarrassed*). Hello.

MARTIN. Isn't there going to be a meeting about the magazine then?

STUART. Yes but look, I'm terribly sorry, we won't be a minute actually, but there's somebody we've got to see urgently, make yourself at home. And tell anyone else who shows up we'll be right back.

MARTIN. Oh right.

STUART (*gestures*). Put a record on, if you want. (*He goes off with* MARIGOLD.)

MARTIN *stands uncertainly. He leans the folder he is carrying against the bureau and looks at the gramophone, on top of which is a record sleeve. He reads the title of the work, nods, puts the record on. Holding on to the cover, wanders over to the desk, glances at the typescripts, etc., sees a letter, picks it up and furtively begins to read it. He goes to the window to read it by the light, glances out of the window, dashes in a panic to the desk, puts the letter on it, dashes to the bureau, picks up folder, starts to sit on bed, rushes back to window, sits down, assumes a listening posture.*

HUMPHRY *appears at the door.* MARTIN *is enacting too absorbed to be aware of him.*

HUMPHRY (*entering properly*). Stuart Thorne not here then?

MARTIN (*starting*). Oh. No, they've just dashed off somewhere. But they'll be back in a moment. He said to wait.

HUMPHRY *sits down. There is a pause.*

MARTIN. Marvellous stuff, isn't it?

HUMPHRY *grunts.*

Do you like Vivaldi?

HUMPHRY. Yes. But I like Bach more. Which this is.

MARTIN. Really? Are you sure?

HUMPHRY. Yes.

MARTIN. Oh. Well, you're probably right. I had some idea it was that Vivaldi piece in F major — which Bach is it then, do you know?

HUMPHRY. No.

MARTIN. It sounds terribly like Vivaldi to me.

HUMPRHY *gets up, goes over to it. He deftly stops the gramophone, removes the record and looks around for the sleeve.*

What is it precisely?

HUMPHRY (*glances at the record*). The suite No. 3.

MARTIN. Vivaldi, you mean?

HUMPHRY (*he picks up the correct sleeve from the bureau and slips the record in*). No, Bach of course.

MARTIN. Really! You must have a terrific feeling for music. I only recognize stuff when I've heard it hundreds of times before. And then I get it wrong, it turns out. (*He laughs.*) You're Humphry Taylor, aren't you?

HUMPHRY. That's right.

MARTIN. And you're doing history, aren't you?

HUMPHRY. Moral sciences.

MARTIN. Oh, of course. But in your *last* year, aren't you?

HUMPHRY. Second year.

MARTIN. Ah. Well, I'm Martin Musgrove. I'm second year too. In English. Stuart told me you were interested in his new literary magazine. I think it's a terrific idea, don't you? Just what Cambridge needs, a new literary magazine. He said he was thinking of calling it *The Common Pursuit* after that book — you know — called — uh —

HUMPHRY. *The Common Pursuit.*

MARTIN. That's the one, yes. (*Little laugh.*) Are you going to help him edit it?

HUMPHRY. I doubt it. One editor is usually more than enough. (*Pause.*)

MARTIN. Oh, I see what you mean. Quarrels and things like that. Have you written something for it?

HUMPHRY. I sent in some poems. What about you? Have you written anything?

MARTIN. Oh, no — well, I did submit a little thing. A sort of prose poem about well, cats, actually. (*He laughs.*) But Stuart sent it back saying I had far more grasp of cats than I did of poetry — or prose, so I'd better stick to those. Quite right, of course. It was pretty embarrassing when I read it through. I haven't got any talent at all, you see. But I'm interested in publishing, so I want to work on the magazine from that point of view. The business side, you know, helping with subscriptions, advertising, raising money, anything of that sort. Is he going to publish your poems?

HUMPHRY. No. I've come to get them back.

MARTIN. Oh. What didn't he like about them?

HUMPHRY. He liked them. It's me. I don't like them.

MARTIN. Really, why not?

HUMPHRY. Because they make me feel sick. In fact, I've decided to give up writing. Poetry, anyway.

MARTIN. But mightn't you eventually write some that don't make you feel sick?

HUMPHRY. Possibly. But it's not worth the risk. Besides I'm going to be a professional philosopher. So I'll have to concentrate on thinking until I've got my First Class degree and a job in a university.

MARTIN. That's what you want, is it?

HUMPHRY. I haven't any choice. As you can't be a professional philosopher except in a university.

MARTIN. Do you want to be in any particular university?

HUMPHRY. This one will do.

MARTIN (*laughs slightly*). Any particular college?

HUMPHRY. This one will do.

MARTIN. Well — that's quite a prediction, really.

HUMPHRY. It wasn't meant to be. More like an obituary in fact. But if I'm going to institutionalize myself, I suppose I might as well do it in one of the better institutions.

MARTIN. I wish I had that sort of confidence about my own future. I only thought of publishing because I can't think of anything else.

NICK *enters, coughing slightly. Looks around.*

NICK. Where's Stuart?

MARTIN. He'll be back in a minute. He said we were to wait.

NICK. Well. Isn't there any coffee on the go or anything? I've got a hangover.

MARTIN. Really? How did you get it?

NICK. I think it might have been because I drank too much. In fact, look, what's that stuff; slimy, thick and yellow?

HUMPHRY. That covers a large number of revolting substances.

MARTIN. Oh, it must be advocaat, mustn't it? A sort of egg nog.

NICK. That explains it. I'm allergic to eggs. Probably allergic to nogs too. If they're what they sound like. It was that bloody girl from Girton — Harriet what's-it?

MARTIN. Hofstadt?

NICK. Yes, she produced it. I was perfectly all right until then. Coasting along on white wine, martini, rum, Scotch, that sort of thing. But then that's Harriet, always there when you least want her, passing out egg nogs when you least want them, she should have been a nurse. (*He laughs and coughs slightly.*)

MARTIN. Did Harriet give the party?

NICK. Do you think I'd go to a party given by Harriet Hofstadt?
No, no, it was some prick, prickette from King's, secretary of
their literary society, Jeremy —

MARTIN. Jeremy Prince.

NICK. To meet that woman who's written a novel about her
menstrual cycle, *Murdering*.

MARTIN. *Mothering,* isn't it?

NICK. What?

MARTIN. Isn't it *Mothering,* not *Murdering*?

NICK. I thought they were synonyms.

MARTIN (*laughs*). Angela Thark.

NICK. What?

MARTIN. That's her name. The novelist isn't it? Angela Thark.
I wish I'd met her. I got the novel just yesterday, I haven't
read it yet. What's she like?

NICK. Much sexier than her prose. Bit of a knock-out really. If
you like long legs, big breasts, that sort of thing. I do. But I'm
not very selective yet. I'm still a virgin. What about you two?
Actually, this room reeks of passion. What were you two up
to before I came in? (*Laughs, coughs slightly and meets*
HUMPHRY's *eye.*)

MARTIN. Did she have anything interesting to say?

NICK. Who?

MARTIN. Angela Thark. Did she talk about novel writing, that
sort of thing?

NICK. Look, could you hold on the incisive questions, just for a
moment? I'm about to do something exceptionally difficult.
(*He takes out a cigarette, lights it and inhales.*) Oh, yes, here
they come, the little buggers, bobbing from iris to pupil and
back again. Now the ripples of giddiness — turning into tidal
bloody waves of nausea. (*He groans. Coughs.*)

MARTIN. Is it always like this when you smoke a cigarette?

NICK. Only the first.

HUMPHRY. Why have it then?

NICK. So I can get on to my next. By the third or fourth I won't
even notice I'm smoking.

MARTIN. But if the first few are so ghastly, and you don't even
notice the rest of them, why don't you just give up?

NICK. What for?

HUMPHRY. For one thing you might live longer.

NICK. Oh, you don't live longer, it just seems longer. As Sam
Goldwyn said. (*To* HUMPHRY.) One of the poets anyway.
(*He wanders to the table, picks up the typescripts, etc.*)

MARTIN. You know sometimes I think I'm missing out on
addiction. I've never been addicted to anything in my life. Not
even when I was a child. I mean, I'm normal all the time,
which is very boring. For everyone else as well as me. While
for you I suppose normal's something you accelerate away
from with drinks and cigarettes —

NICK. Good God, there's a letter here from old Leavis! (*Reads
out.*) 'Can't persuade myself that in the current literary and
indeed cultural climate, when the decline in our Cambridge
values . . .' No, too early for that — (*Drops it, picks up
another one.*) — Ah, I like the handwriting. (*Reads.*) 'Boys on
their river banks, naked in the sad and dewey dawn.' (*Laughs,
coughs slightly.*) God, I hate queer literature. (*Reads again.*)
'The enclosed poems are not for publication, at least at this
stage, but glad to hear of new magazine, hope it will be noted
not only for its critical rigour, vigour, rigour, but also for its
delicate insensitive poetry' — delicate insensitive — (*Looks
closer.*) — oh, delicate *and* sensitive — pity, who's it from? Ah,
James Harrop, New College, *Oxford*! Oh, that explains it,
probably not even queer, just Oxford, I knew a Harrop at
prep school, Nappies we used to call him. Alias Panties, alias
Bladders, but mainly Nappies. He had to wear them in bed at
night because he was an inveterate bed wetter. Wonder if it's
the same one, he was a creep, too. (*Picks up another letter.*)
Ah, hah! Stuart's got a fan letter already. No, no, it's a love
letter. Who's it from? Oh, old Marigold, of course. (*This is the
letter* MARTIN *read earlier.*)

HUMPHRY. You shouldn't do that.

NICK. I say. She can really turn it on, old Marigold. A little over-written, if you ask me, but I suppose that's the problem with having an affair with a literary editor. Keeping her prose up to snuff.

HUMPHRY. I said don't do that.

MARTIN. Yes, well — I must say I've never seen anyone read anyone's private letters before, you know.

NICK. Of course, you haven't. This is a notable breakthrough. Doing it in public, so to speak. (*Turns the last page.*) Hey this postscript! Wow!

HUMPHRY. That's two warnings. You don't get a third.

NICK. Actually it's from the Dean inviting him to pay last term's wine bill.

MARTIN. No, it's not.

NICK. How do you know?

NICK *and* HUMPHRY *look at* MARTIN.

MARTIN. Well it's handwritten! And pages long.

NICK. Well, you know the Dean. Anything to make a conquest. Or settle an account.

HUMPHRY (*stands*). Are you going to put it down?

NICK. Are you going to make me?

HUMPHRY. If I have to. (*Crosses toward* NICK.)

NICK *quickly tosses the letter on the desk.*

NICK. It's time I introduced myself. I'm Nick Finchling, special agent. I've adopted this flamboyant personality as a disguise. I'm trying to find ways of persuading Stuart to publish my 'Poems of Passion' written in my late adolescence. But he says I'm still too close to them to be able to revise them properly. So, I'll do the theatre criticism, as I intend to be the *Sunday Times* theatre critic when I grow up. Would you really have hit me a moment ago?

HUMPHRY. That moment hasn't passed.

NICK. You're Humphry Taylor, aren't you, the philosopher poet,
    I've decided we're going to be friends. It's safer. (*He laughs.*)
    Actually Stuart says your poems have genius. And that you're
    a real find. (*To* MARTIN.) Who are you — Oh, I know, the
    millionaire orphan, aren't you?

MARTIN. Well, I'm not a millionaire.

NICK. But everybody says you're quite rich and if you're an
    orphan, you'll need a friend. (*He embraces* MARTIN.) I'm
    your man. I'm the opposite of an orphan. I've got six parents
    in all, if you include the steps and ex-steps.

    PETER *enters.*

NICK. Shazam! Captain Marvel.

PETER. Sorry I'm late. I had a supervision. Where's Stuart then?

NICK. We're patiently waiting for him. Meanwhile — meet the
    poet, philosopher and pugilist, Humphry Taylor, and that chap
    who wrote the charming little piece about cats that Stuart
    showed us. Before returning it to him.

MARTIN. Martin. Martin Musgrove.

NICK. And this is Peter Whetworth. Known as Captain Marvel
    from the American comic book because of the way he handles
    the ladies. Senior scholar in history, Future Fellow of the
    college, and consequently one of my closest friends. Why
    didn't you come Angela Tharking last night?

PETER (*who has smiled and nodded at* HUMPHRY *and*
    MARTIN). Oh yes. Sorry. I met up with some people.

NICK. Female people, I suppose. More than one female people?

PETER. There were two to begin with, but I whittled them down
    to one. Actually, I got the wrong one, as the one I whittled
    turned out to be the one I wanted — given the one I ended up
    with.

NICK. Not ghastly Erika?

PETER. Ghastly Erika?

NICK. Well, I think her name is Erika, and she's certainly ghastly.
    You met her in my room last week, when I was rounding up

some hopefuls, to sacrifice my virginity to.

PETER. Oh yes, I remember. Very, very pretty.

NICK. Exactly. In fact your usual type. Would you like to meet her again?

PETER. I wouldn't mind.

NICK. Right. I'll arrange it.

PETER. Thanks.

MARTIN. Are you going to write for *The Common Pursuit*?

PETER. I don't know if Stuart would be interested in the kind of stuff I write.

HUMPHRY. I heard your paper. The one you gave to the college History Society.

PETER. Really? What did you think?

HUMPHRY. It had one or two good things in it. Even some originality. Especially in the first few pages.

PETER. Oh, you objected to the stuff on Professor Woodruff at the end, then, did you? I was afraid some people would. Perhaps I went a bit too far —

HUMPHRY. You didn't go nearly far enough.

PETER. Yes I know, but there's a slight problem you see. Old Woodruff's been very nice to me — in fact, he got me my scholarship — and I do really admire his work, in a way.

HUMPHRY. Yes, well that's the wrong way, isn't it? If you admired him in the right way you'd have paid him the compliment of arguing with him properly, wouldn't you? Besides, you introduced Schopenhauer when it was too late to count, made one or two striking points about him, and then just closed the whole argument down.

PETER. Yes, wasn't that terrible. Thank God, nobody else seemed to notice. The trouble is I kept getting interrupted before I'd finished, by this person and that, you know how it is, so I had to scribble out the last few paragraphs an hour before I actually gave the paper — a pity really. I'd liked to have thought it through more thoroughly.

HUMPHRY. If you want to discuss it further, my rooms are just around the corner; Neville's Court, C staircase —

NICK (*interrupting*). Have you two finished? Because I want to hear about last night. (*To* PETER.) What you did with that girl. I'm anxious to acquire any information I can on this sex business. All I'm sure of at the moment is that I'm not queer. So what did you do with her? Did you take her back? Or get her to take you to her place? Or what? How? When? Where? With illustrations. If you don't tell me, I won't invite Ghastly Erika back for you, after all. So, come on then! What did you do with her?

PETER. Oh, nothing special.

NICK. But you took her to bed?

PETER. Of course. What else could I do with her?

NICK. Well, how did you manage it?

PETER. Manage what?

NICK. How did you persuade her? That's what I need to know. I mean, what sort of thing does one say?

PETER. Well, I gave her a cup of tea and a biscuit, and said, 'Let's go to bed'.

NICK. A cup of tea and a biscuit! What did you put in the tea? Or was it in the biscuit?

HUMPHRY. Excuse me, can we have some music? If we're going to wait, could we at least do something worthwhile?

NICK. I advise you not to resist him. He has a powerful personality. He nearly knocked me down just before you came in. What would you like to hear, sir?

HUMPHRY. Wagner would probably be the most inappropriate. So let's have him.

NICK. I don't know if Stuart goes in for Wagner, sir. (*Hunting.*) Or anything musical really, sir. Except for seducing Marigold with, sir. Ah — here's some, sir. (*Puts it on the gramophone, lights a cigarette, coughs, sits on bed. They settle back and start to listen.*)

PETER (*to* NICK). So tell me some more about Ghastly Erika —

NICK (*makes to speak, is frozen by a look from* HUMPHRY, *looks at* PETER). Sssssh! (*Putting a finger to his lips.*)

Wagner fills the room. NICK *lies back on bed.* HUMPHRY *listens.* MARTIN *assumes his listening posture.* PETER *listens idly, smiling pleasantly.* MARIGOLD *appears in the doorway, breathless.*

They remain in that position as the set goes off, the music still playing while STUART's *office moves on.*

Scene Two

Late spring. Early summer.
    STUART's *office in Holborn. Nine years later. Late morning. The office is large, and could be handsome. But it is dingy. There is a desk with a telephone on it. An armchair, a sofa, a cupboard. A few glasses and half-filled bottles of wine are on the shelves, as if left over from a party.*
    STUART *is sitting at his desk, reading a typescript.*
    STUART *thinks, checks the front of the manuscript he's been reading for a number, finds it, dials the phone.*

STUART. May I speak to Mr Stout, please. Oh Charlotte, hello. It's Stuart Thorne, here. I was just wondering if I might have a word with Hubert. Oh is he, I'm sorry to hear that. No, I won't keep him long I promise. (*Pause.*) Hubert, it's Stuart. Charlotte says you're still a bit under the weather, and I mustn't keep you long, so I'll come straight to the point. I've just been re-reading the poems you sent me, and I was wondering whether you'd consider letting me publish them. (*Stops.*) What! Where did you hear that? (*Pause.*) No, that's just *gossip,* Hubert, there's not the slightest chance *The Common Pursuit* is going to fold — in fact, at this very minute the Arts Council is making a formal decision to award us a substantial grant at last, it'll more than cover the debts — (*Little pause.*) *Absolutely* sure. Peter Whetworth is on the committee. You must have met him — he's an old friend of mine from Cambridge days. He teaches history at Oxford

now. The one everybody calls Captain Marvel. Yes. With the
very pretty wife, Erika, yes. Anyway, he's on the committee,
and he's virtually my representative. So, you see our survival
is guaranteed. Of course, I'm delighted you're so pleased — but
what do you say about my doing the poems. Thank you,
Hubert. You won't regret it, I promise you. Well, I'll get them
into proof this week, and I'll bring them over to you myself —
we can correct them together if you like. (MARTIN *enters*.)
What — oh right. Well thanks again, Hubert. Really thanks.
Charlotte, yes, hello, I'm sorry to have kept him so long.
Thank you for letting me talk to him. (*Hangs up*.) I've got
them.

MARTIN. What?

STUART. Hubert Stout's new poems. All six of them.

MARTIN. Well that's terrific. Oddly enough, I had a feeling
we'd have something to celebrate.

STUART. Eight years and thirty-one issues. And most of them
have been pretty good I think. Not all of them, of course. Not
even any of them completely from cover to cover. There's
always something I've let by that I didn't quite believe in. The
first poems of Dougan and O'Leary, for instance were an
unforgiveable mistake. Oh, do you know they sent some more
of their stuff just the other day? It arrived in a weird brown
parcel that looked as if it were throbbing. I thought at first it
might be a letter-bomb. From a rejected contributor. Or a gang
of Marxist critics. But it was worse than a letter-bomb. It was
the latest poems of Dougan and O'Leary. And what was worse
was that they were worse than the last bunch I sent back,
which were worse than the ones I should have never published
in the first place. But the point is — Dougan and O'Leary
aside, along with say a few doubtful short stories here and one
or two inadequate or over-written articles there — I've put out
thirty-one pretty good issues, actually discovered three, no,
two good new writers, one very decent one, but I've never
produced an issue that in my heart of hearts I consider to be
a great one. The next one will be. And right at the centre will
be Hubert's six poems. A great issue. That's my point.

Phone rings.

Oh Christ, it's either the printers, the stationers or old Giorgio.

MARTIN. Giorgio?

STUART. The landlord. I can't pay any of them. (*Answers the the phone in Irish accent.*) Good morning to you. (*To MARTIN.*) Giorgio. (*To phone.*) That's right, the offices of *The Common Pursuit,* yes. (*Pause.*) Stuart Thorne? No, I'm afraid he's not here, nobody else either. Oh, my name's Dougan, that's right Dougan O'Leary, sir. A poet from Belfast passing through London on his way to Dublin, and a great admirer of *The Common Pursuit,* sir, famed across the waters for its high critical standards and its undeniable integrity, so I dropped in on the off chance to give my salutes, sir — Oh, I'll be glad to, yes. Of course I've got a pencil, I'm a poet, fire away — uh-huh, uh-huh, Oh, eviction? How do you spell that, two eff's or one? Oh vee, right. Well, you learn something new every day, don't you? Yes, I'll leave it where Mr Thorne can see, OK. Not at all, and a good morning to you. (*Hangs up.*) Where the hell is Captain Marvel!

MARTIN. You're not worried about the Arts Council, are you?

STUART. I'm beginning to be. You know what Captain Marvel's like. He's quite capable of forgetting he's meant to be at the meeting — picking up some bloody girl on the train and bundling her straight off to bed —

MARTIN. Yes, but never when he's had to be somewhere important.

STUART. He's never had to be anywhere important before. Besides, the fact is I don't trust him to explain the value of all the stuff I gave him — when I pointed out Hubert's poems, do you know what he said? 'Oh, right.' And shoved them into that appalling calfskin briefcase of his. 'Oh, right.'

MARTIN. I don't see that that matters. I mean that he doesn't appreciate Hubert Stout's poetry — or any of the other stuff you gave him, if it comes to that. Just think of the way he got his lectureship at Oxford. Before he'd even published his first book.

STUART. His only chance of getting the lectureship was *before* he'd published that book.

MARTIN. That's exactly what I mean. He's a born hustler, and that's exactly what you need at the Arts Council. And that's why you chose him in the first place, remember? So stop worrying.

STUART. Right. Thank you. But do you mind if I worry just a little. Until he actually arrives here with the news? As my whole future depends upon it. (*Smiles at* MARTIN.)

MARTIN (*smiles back*). All right. Just a little. How's Marigold?

STUART. Oh, she's fine. A bit preoccupied at the moment. I think the teaching's getting her down.

MARTIN. Oh. And who's the girl with the Welsh accent?

STUART. I don't know. Who is she?

MARTIN. I don't know either. But when I phoned you at your flat last night, I got a girl with a Welsh accent. Very nice and talkative, but all she seemed to know was that you'd moved out and — Marigold had gone away somewhere.

STUART. Oh yes. She's gone to Tunbridge Wells for a few days. To visit her parents. One of them is ill. She's due back this morning.

MARTIN. Her parents?

STUART. Yes.

MARTIN. But I thought she only had a father.

STUART. That's right. Then that must be the one who's ill. I didn't get along with her mother either, especially when she was alive.

MARTIN. Ah. (*Nods. Little pause.*) But then who was the girl with the Welsh accent?

STUART. That must have been her flatmate.

MARTIN. Oh. But I thought — well, (*Little laugh.*) that *you* were her flatmate.

STUART. Of course I am. It's just that last week we discovered

302   THE COMMON PURSUIT

that neither of us could afford my share of the rent. So I
moved out, and Marigold got a teacher from her school to
move in. She wanted somewhere temporary to stay. It's just
until I can — I can — (*Gestures.*) I didn't notice the Welsh
accent.

MARTIN. Where are you living, then?

STUART. Here, of course.

MARTIN. Here? (*Looks around.*) But what do you sleep on?

STUART. On that. (*Indicates sofa.*) There's a sleeping bag over
there.

MARTIN. But what — well, what do you do about washing, and
all that?

STUART. Slip into the Greek place around the corner. They've
seen me around so often they think I'm one of the waiters. By
the way, I shouldn't eat there if I were you. The lavatory's
virtually attached to the oven, and I'm the only person who
bothers to wash his hands.

MARTIN. But why on earth don't you come and stay with me?
You can have either of the spare rooms. Or both of them. I
can move old Samantha back to my bed. Where she longs to
be anyway, and would be, if she didn't make me sneeze. So
why don't you move in? Tonight, if you want.

STUART. Thanks. But I'm here from strategy too, you see. I
have an odd feeling. To do with territory. That after
seven years it would be harder to get me out of here if
I've made this completely mine at last. If Giorgio does try
to evict me, he'll get nervous if he finds I'm sleeping here.
He'll start imagining me as some animal defending his lair.
A threatened lion or a trapped tiger. Or a bankrupt rat.
Anyway, something savage with teeth and jaws.

MARTIN. You know, the awful thing is, I just couldn't live
like you. I'd love to be able to. But I actually couldn't.

STUART. Oh, it's actually quite easy. All it takes is no money.

Pause.

MARTIN. Oh by the way, I haven't told you yet, have I? I'm thinking of quitting.

STUART. Quitting what?

MARTIN. My job, of course, at Haylife and Forling.

STUART. Really? Why? I thought you were doing better and better there.

MARTIN. Yes, but the trouble is the books we publish are getting worse and worse. You should see this month's list. Even the titles are ungrammatical.

STUART. Does that matter? They're books for people who can't read anyway. You know, he should have been here — or at least phoned — a good, what? — twenty minutes ago.

MARTIN. Actually, I've already made some plans. I'd like to discuss them with you.

STUART. Really, what?

Telephone rings.

Might be Giorgio again, or the printers.

MARTIN. I'll take it. (*Answering, with Irish accent.*) Hello. *The Common Pursuit.* (*In his normal voice.*) Oh, hello Erika. (*Winces at* STUART.) No, it's not Stuart, it's Martin, do you want Peter, he hasn't turned up yet, I'm afraid. Oh, you want me, do you, how nice. What can I do for you? (*Pause.*) What time precisely am I meeting him? I was just saying to Stuart, I wasn't quite sure. Ah, one-thirty at L'Epicure. Don't worry I'll be there. Oh, yes, I'm looking forward to his new title — he changes it all the time. Sex Scandals, really. (*Pause.*) Curtain rods. Right. Got that. See you soon, Erika. I've really got to go now, if I'm going to make it on time. Goodbye. (*Hangs up.*) This time, so the Ghastly Erika tells me, I'm having lunch with Peter to discuss a book I've commissioned from him called Sex Scandals In Nineteenth-Century Politics. I'm to remind him not to forget the curtain rods.

STUART. What do you mean?

MARTIN. Nothing. He's simply using me as an alibi. He does it all the time. I wish he'd warn me.

STUART. An alibi. What for?

MARTIN. Why, for coming up to London, of course.

STUART. He has forgotten.

MARTIN. What — ?

STUART. The meeting, he's forgotten the meeting.

MARTIN. How does that follow — ?

STUART. Because if he'd remembered the meeting he wouldn't need an alibi, would he? He already had a perfectly good reason for coming to London. (*Quietly.*) Do you know what my specially chosen representative to the Arts Council meeting is probably doing at this very minute? While we're sitting here waiting for him? Fucking himself senseless in a hotel room. While the Arts Council is doubtless ladling out its money to every magazine in the country except mine. I'd like to kill him. Yes. Kill him.

MARTIN. I should have told Erika the truth. She'd kill him for us.

STUART. You know what this means, don't you? Without the grant I'll have to cancel the next issue too. Making it three in a row and then go back to the usual round of begging, borrowing and stealing; and I'll have to return Hubert's poems. He won't let me hold on to them indefinitely. So. My special place in literary history is likely to be as the editor of a small literary magazine, who, through a combination of craft, bribery and moral blackmail, actually got his hands on six — six! — major new poems by a major poet. And then had to send them back because as it turned out he didn't actually have a magazine to publish them in. Have I got matters into perspective?

MARTIN. Well, not quite. Actually, you don't need the grant. That's what I was going to discuss with you. Just before Erika phoned. I want to offer you a partnership, Stuart.

STUART. A partnership?

MARTIN. I'm going to set up as an independent publisher. I've always had the capital, now I've got the experience. We'd be

partners, you see. You would commission and edit the fiction
and the poetry. I'd do the business side and any editorial
hack-work. I've learnt an enormous amount at Haylife and
Forling's, I really have. I'm ready. (*Little pause.*) And the
point is, we'd keep *The Common Pursuit* going. As our
subsidiary.

STUART. Subsidiary?

MARTIN. We wouldn't have to depend on the Arts Council. And
I know how much you'd like that. You've always said that
they only give it out so that they can take it away when it
really matters.

Little pause.

And you could move back with Marigold. The two of you
could live, well, you know, like a couple at last. As I know
you've always wanted. Especially with a baby coming.

STUART (*after a little pause*). How did you know about that?

MARTIN. Oh, well I had lunch with Marigold last week, you see.
The day after she found out she was expecting.

STUART. She's not expecting. She's merely pregnant. (*Little
pause.*) I wonder why she didn't tell me. About your having
lunch, I mean, not about merely being pregnant.

MARTIN. Actually, because I asked her not to. I wanted to know
what she thought you'd feel about the prospect of coming in
with me. But I didn't want to press ahead with you until I'd,
well, sorted a few things out. Which I now have, actually.
And was in a position to make you what they call (*Slight
laugh.*) a formal proposal. Which I now am. You see?

STUART. And what did she think I'd feel?

MARTIN. Oh, well, to be honest, she refused to say. All she said
was that it had to be your decision.

STUART. I wonder why — (*He stops.*)

MARTIN. What?

STUART. Why she told you she was pregnant. We'd agreed not to
make it public. Until we'd made up our minds whether or not
we wanted to have it.

MARTIN. No doubt because of Samantha. (STUART *looks at* MARTIN.) She's pregnant, too. Didn't I tell you?

STUART. No. Congratulations. (*Ironically*.)

MARTIN (*laughs*). Thank you. It's probably the only one I'll allow her, poor thing, before getting her fixed. She should litter in about a week. And I offered her a tabby, because she adores tabbies, as you know — Marigold, I mean. Samantha seems to adore them, too, at least the one I hope is the father. He was hanging around at the right time. A real old-fashioned Tom. A right rogue.

There is a pause.

STUART. Oh, I see. So you and Marigold were just swapping pregnancy gossip?

MARTIN. Well what actually happened was that I was rabbitting on in that boring way of mine when on cats, and Marigold suddenly, well, broke down and told me she was pregnant. And then asked me not to tell you she'd told me. Because of your agreement. To wait. So I'd rather you didn't tell her.

STUART. Tell her that you told me that she told you? But how can I? As she only told you during a lunch you told her not to tell me you were having.

MARTIN. Quite. (*He laughs.*)

STUART *smiles.*

Quite. So I suppose, under the circumstances I can't tell you how passionately she, well, seems to want to have the baby, can I?

STUART. Under the circumstances, no, you can't. But then you don't have to. As I know. These things tend to slip out, between long-established couples.

MARTIN (*nods*). Sorry. (*Little pause.*) Well then. What do you think? About our setting up as partners in publishing. Keeping *The Common Pursuit* going?

STUART. Yes, well, thanks. *Really* thanks, Martin. But I'd rather keep the magazine independent. I've always believed that editing it is a full-time job. Even when it's failing to appear. I haven't forgotten that I owe you quite a lot of money, by the way.

MARTIN. The money was a gift to *The Common Pursuit*. You know how much I want it to survive.

STUART. Yes I do. So do I. Want it to survive. But not as a subsidiary to something else, you see. It has to come first.

MARTIN. Before Marigold and the baby? Stuart, it'll break her heart not to have it.

HUMPHRY *enters.*

HUMPHRY (*enters*). Hello, what's going on? This room reeks of passion, in a famous phrase. What have you two been up to?

MARTIN. Nothing. We're waiting for Peter.

STUART. Although we suspect he's forgotten to come.

HUMPHRY. Oh. He'll turn up. Is this all there is? (*Surveying the opened wine bottles.*)

MARTIN. No, there's some there.

STUART. What makes you say that?

HUMPHRY. What?

STUART. That he'll turn up.

HUMPHRY. Because I saw him only two days ago when I went to give a paper at Oxford. I had dinner with him. And Ghastly Erika. And their babies. He boasted that he was coming down here this morning to do what he called your street-fighting for you. Why do you think I'm here, if not to observe you in crisis and triumph. You're evidently handling the crisis part badly, let's hope you come up to snuff in the triumph part.

STUART. And you in the disaster part. (*To* MARTIN.) Tell him.

MARTIN. Well, there's a possibility that Peter's merely coming to London for one of his usual — um —

STUART. Fucks.

HUMPHRY. Of course he is. He'd go anywhere and do anything for a fuck. Including even attending an Arts Council meeting on your behalf.

MARTIN. Yes, but you see — he lied to Erika about why he was coming up to London, he told her he was coming to see me to discuss a book, which isn't true, instead of saying he was going to the meeting, which would have been true, and the obvious lie to tell, because at least it would have been true, if he remembered it. If you follow.

HUMPHRY. Of course I follow. Merely because you can't speak properly doesn't mean I can't understand you. Generally well before you're finished. I suppose you got all this from Erika?

MARTIN. Well, not about coming for the fuck.

HUMPHRY. The reason he lied to Erika was that it was simpler and less fatiguing than telling her the truth. Have you tried talking to that woman recently? A simple statement from you is followed by an imbecile question from her, and she doesn't stop until your statements have become as imbecile as her questions, in a ghastly parody of a Socratic dialogue. Then as you sit drained of ideas, energy, humanity, she changes a baby in front of you. Virtually all over you, in fact. He had absolutely no right to marry her. Getting her pregnant was no excuse. We should have talked Nick into taking his place. He's got nothing particularly important to do with his life and they'd have got on perfectly. Her pathological need to ask imbecile questions would actually give a purpose to his pathological need to tell lies. (*To* MARTIN.) Do you follow?

MARTIN. I think so.

HUMPHRY. Explain it back to me, then.

MARTIN. It was easier to tell Erika he was coming to see me to discuss a book than to explain about the Arts Council, the magazine, grants, etc., and Stuart.

HUMPHRY. Exactly. Furthermore he won't let you down because a) he's a good and loyal friend, b) he actually longs to crusade on Stuart's behalf because, c) he's got nothing better to do with his life either. And he's only twenty-eight. Unlike Nick he actually had a mind, a few years back. What'll he be

like when he's forty? Probably exactly the same only less
so, having less energy to be it with.

MARTIN. Yes.

STUART. What?

MARTIN. I think Humphry's got it right as usual.

STUART. Then why isn't he here? He's now actually late. Or
why hasn't he phoned?

HUMPHRY. Wait thou child of hope. For time shall give thee all
things. Except a decent glass of wine, at least here. Ever. This
is simultaneously bland and acid, is it English?

MARTIN. Of course not, it's French. It's a Chablis. (*Checks
label.*) A vintage in fact, isn't it? At least that's what they told
me.

HUMPHRY (*going to shelf, pours himself stale wine*). How's
Marigold? Still teaching at that school?

STUART (*little pause, making an effort*). Fine, she's taken a few
days off. To go down to Tunbridge Wells to visit her mother.
Who's ill.

MARTIN. Her father.

STUART. Yes. That's right. Her father.

HUMPHRY. Odd how Martin always seems to know more about
your life than you do. (*To* STUART.) Perhaps because he
takes a greater interest. Anyway, you're all right, are you, you
two?

STUART. Which two?

HUMPHRY. You and Marigold.

STUART. Why do you ask?

HUMPHRY. Because when I phoned you at your flat last night to
say I'd be coming down this morning, I got an exceptionally
loquacious Indian girl, from the sound of her. She gave the
distinct impression that you and Marigold were no longer
living together. Although I can't be sure. Her rhythms got in
the way of her sense.

STUART (*after a pause*). As a matter of fact she's pregnant. And we're going to get married.

MARTIN *looks at him.*

HUMPHRY (*after a little pause*). Good.

STUART. Really? You don't think we have a duty to talk me out of it? Or get Nick to take my place?

HUMPHRY (*he looks at* STUART). I've got the greatest admiration for Marigold, as you know.

STUART. Why? Because she's got a fine mind?

HUMPHRY. No, she hasn't. But when it comes to the things that matter she's got a mind of her own, which is more important. Congratulations.

STUART *nods.*

And now to a vastly more passionate relationship. (*To* MARTIN.) How's Samantha? Kindly confine your reply to two sentences.

MARTIN. Oh, she's pregnant. But we're not going to get married. What about you?

HUMPHRY. I'm not pregnant. And I wouldn't dream of getting married, even if I were. My only news is that I've changed my accommodation at last. I've moved into Great Court. Your old rooms as a matter of fact, Stuart. I've always wanted them, did you know that? But that ridiculous Scotsman who lived above you took them over when he got his fellowship and so I'd given up hope. But last month he committed suicide.

MARTIN. Oh Christ.

HUMPHRY. Quite upsetting, isn't it? I mean people we convert into jokes have an obligation not to do that sort of thing. He was a mathematical genius apparently, but his creative juices dried up suddenly. As they tend to with mathematicians. They finish young. Actually he must have been rather short on real personality, in spite of his bluster, as he hasn't left the trace of a ghost behind. Even in the bedroom, where he did it with a razor. I haven't even

bothered to have it redecorated. The odd thing is that I feel
I'm finally where I always intended to be. At home, in other
words. So much so that this morning I rose at six, walked
twice round Great Court, and wrote the first fourteen and a
half lines of my book on Wagner.

MARTIN. That's marvellous, Humpty.

The door opens. NICK *enters, coughing with cigarette in
his mouth.*

NICK. That does it. (*Coughing.*) I'm giving up — (*Coughing.*) —
taxis. The way that shit of a driver took the corners, my
bum skidding, my stomach churning, my head pounding,
God I wish I'd thrown up. All over the back of his neck. It
was red, with ginger hair on it.

MARTIN. Where were you coming from?

NICK. Don't know. Earls Court it looked like. Some girl picked
me up at a publishing party last night, took me back to her
place. At least I hope it was a girl. Had her back to me when I
woke up. Had a girl's spine. Smelt like a girl. But snoring like
a man. So it was either an Australian or a hermaphrodite or
both. The haunting question is whether I poked it, I keep
recalling a brief spasm during the night. I hope it was just my
cough. News from Captain Marvel?

MARTIN. We're waiting.

NICK. Oh, well I've only a few minutes — but don't worry.
The grant's in the bag.

HUMPHRY. Nicholas's confidence is the first real alarm signal.

NICK. Hey, Humpty, what's all this I've been hearing? About
you.

HUMPHRY. What have you been hearing?

NICK. About your lethal effect on the Cambridge undergraduate
sensibility, and — (*Seeing something on* HUMPHRY's *face,
changing tack.*) other tittle-tattle, very complimentary about
you as an intellectual glamour-figure because of your
lectures and stuff, from Harrop. Nappies Harrop. He was at
the party too. The little creep is everywhere these days.

Private viewings, first nights, publishings binges, wherever I go, Nappies is already there, standing in a corner, shoulders hunched, light gleaming off his bald pate, boasting shyly about his latest triumph, and do you know what he claims? He claims his latest, latest triumph is that he's won the Cheltenham Prize. For that nappy full of homosexless verse he dropped last year.

MARTIN. Well, he has, hasn't he?

NICK. How do you know? He told me he wasn't allowed to tell anyone until the announcement.

STUART. I was one of the judges. In fact I voted for him.

NICK. You didn't tell me.

STUART. No, well I'm not allowed to tell anyone either.

NICK. But how could you vote for Nappies? You know I loathe him.

STUART. I didn't vote for him. I voted for his poems.

NICK. God, Stuart, how could you be so frivolous?

STUART. Why are you so sure it's in the bag?

NICK. What? Oh, your grant, because Captain Marvel told me so himself.

STUART. When?

NICK. Last night. He phoned to say he was coming to London for the meeting, what about lunch afterwards, along with the rest of us, but I can't make it because I'm having lunch with *Vogue*.

MARTIN. *Vogue*?

NICK. Um, uh, yes, to discuss doing a series of articles on this and that, but he said, en passant, the grant was in the bag. (*He coughs violently*.)

HUMPHRY. That's aesthetically one of the least attractive ways of killing yourself, Nicholas, why don't you stop it?

NICK. Yes. Well I will. I've got to go. Love to Peter, sorry I missed him — Oh, Martin, I think I'd better not take one of your kittens after all. For one thing they turn into cats, and I'm less soppy about those and also, I'm too young to settle down. Well, see you soon everyone. (*He goes to the door and stops.*) Oh God, I almost forgot, Stuart. *Snakes and Ladders.*

STUART. What?

NICK. My article. *Snakes and Ladders.*

STUART. Ah, yes. Well the fact is I haven't had a chance to read it properly yet. I've looked at it of course, but I haven't — (*He gestures.*)

NICK. No, that's all right, but can I have it back for a while?

STUART. Certainly.

NICK. I'm not really happy with some sections of it, especially the couple of pages on Angela Thark, for instance, I didn't know she was dying when I wrote it, don't forget. I'd like to be more — more delicate. Cut out the bit about her blood-soaked prose, etc., and get at some of the reviewers for not admiring her more — she's got that daughter, after all. Grieving friends. I'm one myself, in a way.

STUART *has gone to his desk and is looking for the manuscript.*

MARTIN. I thought you couldn't stand her?

NICK. Only when she was alive. (*He gives a little laugh.*) Death brings its own respect. (*Laughs again.*) And I always maintained that she was sexy. Anyway the point is I can't let the article go as it stands. It makes me seem a brute. Which I am, about her. But I can't afford to seem it, can I?

STUART. I can't find it. Can you work from your own copy? (*Still looking.*)

NICK. No, I can't. I destroyed it. I lost a bit of confidence in it, you see, when you went on failing to mention it every time I saw you. Not that I'm blaming you. I destroyed a lot of other stuff too. Virtually my whole life's work. Threw it all in the fire, as a matter of fact. I sometimes wonder whether you realize what an influence you have, Stuart. You've always been the reader over our shoulder. Hasn't he? Any luck?

STUART. It's here somewhere.

NICK (*conscious that* HUMPHRY *is watching him*). You know I'm beginning to wonder whether I'm really cut out for a career in literature. I find writing even more of a chore than fucking. And a lot of the people one meets are even worse. Actually, I wish I were a simple rural vicar. Riding about among my parishioners on a bike, with my dog running behind my rear wheel, my wife at home with the children. And with a little bit of faith to keep me going. Oh, and a private income too. Two private incomes. (*Laughs, avoiding* HUMPHRY's *eye*.) Any luck? (*To* STUART.)

HUMPHRY. What I can't work out is why?

NICK. Why what?

HUMPHRY. Why you're lying, Nicholas. Your motive. Or are you just keeping in practice?

MARTIN. You don't think by any chance, well, he's *sold Snakes and Ladders*? To somebody else, I mean.

HUMPHRY. *Vogue,* of course!

STUART. What?

HUMPHRY. Nicholas has sold it to *Vogue.* Well done. (*To* MARTIN.)

NICK (*little pause*). Yes, well actually what happened is that I sent a copy to my agent.

HUMPHRY. The ashes of your copy, you mean. You burnt it, remember, along with the rest of your life's work.

NICK. Yes, well — (*Gestures.*) — and she showed it to *Vogue,* without my consent, naturally, and it turned out that *Vogue* was thinking of doing a piece along those lines. So they snapped it up. Not as it stands, of course. It's got to be spiced up with more character assassinations thrown in, illustrated with fish-eye photographs. And a special cartoon of Nappies wearing his nappy. What do you think? (*To* HUMPHRY.)

STUART. And that's why you want my copy back, is it? Nothing to do with Angela Thark at all.

NICK. Well, my agent says she doesn't like the thought of it being offered to two different magazines at the same time. She says it's unethical. And I agree with her.

STUART, MARTIN, *and* HUMPHRY *laugh.*

Perhaps. But bloody hell, I'm a professional literary journalist. I live by what I sell. And you didn't bother to acknowledge receiving it, let alone let me know what you thought about it. Do you realize it's six years since you last asked me to contribute something — and the fact is, it could lie rotting away on your desk for ever. The magazine's failed to come out twice running now, and there's a decent chance it'll never come out again.

A pause.

STUART. A decent chance, is it?

NICK. According to Peter.

STUART. According to Peter when?

NICK. This morning. He stopped in for a cup of coffee on his way to the meeting.

STUART. But you were coming from an Australian or a hermaphrodite in Earls Court this morning.

HUMPHRY. Whom you either poked or coughed into.

NICK. Ahhh —! Yes. Well that must have been yesterday morning. In fact it sounds like all my yesterday mornings recently. Except tomorrow. Because tomorrow I'll have had coffee with Peter yesterday. Won't I? (*He attempts a laugh, coughs instead.*)

STUART. And what precisely did he say? About the grant?

NICK. Yes, well — apparently the whole Arts Council panel, virtually, thinks you're élitist.

STUART. Élitist.

NICK. He's going to do his best, but he reckons you haven't got a chance. But knowing you you'll struggle on for years, editing a magazine that never comes out at all. And I'll have missed the chance of getting in with *Vogue*. And I need it. Can I have the article please?

STUART. Actually no, you can't. I must have accidentally stuck it in with the material I gave Captain Marvel to show the Arts Council. So it was probably sitting in his briefcase when you had coffee with him. But don't worry, Nick, I shan't publish it. The truth is I've been wondering how to return it to you without hurting you. All you had to do was to say straight out that *Vogue* wanted it, did I mind. I'd have been delighted. It's perfect for *Vogue*. Just as it stands. But I don't think it could ever be good enough for *The Common Pursuit*.

NICK. Yes — well they're right. You *are* élitist.

STUART. Well, somebody's got to be, haven't they? Especially at a time when nobody else wants to be.

NICK. But they don't want you to be either. Do they? They're not interested in your high critical standards and intellectual rigour and traditional poetic forms — in fact, they don't want *The Common Pursuit*. The magazine's finished, Stuart. Why don't you face it and come out into the real world at last?

HUMPHRY. Where is the real world, Nicholas? Somewhere among the lingerie and perfume ads in *Vogue*?

NICK. Yes, well you're exactly like Stuart, aren't you, Humpty? You can't face the facts about yourself either.

There is a pause.

HUMPHRY. Well, go on, Nick. Help me face the facts about myself. Say them to me. The facts.

NICK *stares at* HUMPHRY.
MARIGOLD *enters.*

MARIGOLD. Hello chaps.

MARTIN. Marigold.

HUMPHRY. Marigold.

MARIGOLD. Hello Humpty. I didn't know you were coming down.

NICK. Hi, Marigold.

MARIGOLD. Nicholas.

MARTIN. How's your mother?

MARIGOLD. Terrific. Apart from being dead, that is.

MARTIN. I'm terribly sorry — I meant your father of course.

MARIGOLD. They've discovered he's got a bad heart. So he'll
have to give up all the things he really lives for; Scotch,
cigarettes and his furtive little forays up to the dirty
bookshops. To balance that, he's got to give up his job too,
but he won't mind that, as he's always hated it.

NICK. He's a doctor, isn't he?

MARIGOLD. No, a vicar.

HUMPHRY. Oh. Then, Nicholas, you should meet him. Nicholas
was just saying a moment ago he was thinking of going into
the Church, weren't you, Nicholas? He has some of the right
qualifications. He lies badly about things that don't matter.

MARIGOLD. What have you been up to this time?

HUMPHRY. Come on, Nicholas, tell her.

NICK. I'm sorry — (*Kisses* MARIGOLD's *hand*.) — I've got to go,
I'm late. See you all then. (*He goes to the door, hesitates*.)
Look. (*To* STUART.) I'm — sorry. (*Coughs slightly, goes out*.)

MARIGOLD. What's he done?

STUART. Merely withdrawn his unwanted article on
inconsequential literary figures of our time.

MARIGOLD. But that's good, isn't it? You were agonizing
over how to tell him.

STUART. It was the way he did it, Nick being Nick.

HUMPHRY. Of course you realize he only offered the article to
Vogue to spare himself the humiliation of your rejecting it.
Which he nevertheless has just managed to achieve, Nicholas
being Nicholas. Good to hear about the baby, but that
doesn't mean you have to marry him, you know?

MARIGOLD (*laughs*). Thank you. (*Looks at* STUART.)

STUART. I decided to make it official. As word seems to be
getting round anyway. (*Looks at* MARTIN.)

MARIGOLD. Ah. (*Also glances at* MARTIN.) But where's our Captain Marvel? I thought he was meant to be here by now?

STUART. We think he may not make it, but it doesn't matter, as he sent a message via Nick. We're not getting our grant. On the grounds that we're élitist.

MARIGOLD (*after a little pause*). Élitist?

STUART. All right, let's face it, or rather let me face it, at least. It's probably the right decision. The fact is that *The Common Pursuit* doesn't really matter, to anyone except me. As Nick pointed out. (*Little laugh.*) To do him credit.

MARIGOLD (*to* STUART). You're not seriously talking of giving up! Not now! You can't. He can't, can he?

STUART. Oh, yes I can.

MARIGOLD. But — but it's not fair. (*She gives a little laugh.*) After eight years, it's actually not fair.

STUART. Oh, yes it is. The printers want their money and why shouldn't they have it, they've worked hard for it. Giorgio wants his rent, and why shouldn't he have it? He owns the place. I can't pay the telephone bill, the electricity bill, I can't even pay for the issues of the magazine I *fail* to bring out. If fair means anything, it's time I was fair to them. And time I was fair to you. Especially now. Come on, Humpty. Let's hear the truth.

HUMPHRY. But you've just spoken it. Almost. Even if you get the grant you'll be having a version of this conversation a baby or two from now. (*Pause.*)

MARIOLD. You don't know everything! You don't always know everything!

STUART. Yes, well, trust Humpty to go the unpalatable stage further. But he is right. In the end the magazine won't survive.

MARIGOLD (*to* HUMPHRY *and* MARTIN). Can I — look, do you mind if I talk to Stuart?

MARTIN. I'm sorry. I didn't mean to. It just — just slipped out. I'm sorry. (*Exits.*)

HUMPHRY *goes to* MARIGOLD, *bends down, kisses her.*

MARIGOLD (*with a little laugh, hugs him*). Oh Humpty. I'm sorry.

HUMPHRY *goes out.*

There is a pause.

MARIGOLD. You're doing it because of the baby, aren't you?

STUART. No, I'm not.

MARIGOLD. I don't believe you. What would you have done if there hadn't been a baby? You'd have gone on. You know you would.

STUART. If so, it would have been out of habit.

MARIGOLD. Look — you've talked about facts. Well, you're the only fact in my life. You know you are. From the first moment we started you and the magazine came together. And the magazine has always been a part of your life. I've not just accepted that, it's how I want things to be. How I want you to be. To go on being. You won't be you without it. Oh, please, my love — please. You mustn't give up. You mustn't.

STUART. I've got to give up. I don't want *The Common Pursuit* any more. It's already in the past. Look, when I found myself announcing to Humphry that you were pregnant and that we were going to get married, well, my heart turned over. It was joy. And after that things began — simply to drop away. So that by the time you came into the room I found myself gazing on the central — well, fact in my life. Not the magazine. You. Us. It always has been. I've merely behaved as if it were the other way around. Now I see it so clearly I want to start again. From there.

MARIGOLD. I've had an abortion.

STUART *stares at her.*

I didn't go to see my father. I didn't want you to have to choose — I knew we couldn't cope, even if you got the grant. (*Looks at* STUART.) Please don't say anything. Help me. Please.

PETER *bursts into the room, carrying calfskin briefcase in one hand, curtain rods in the other.*

PETER. Sorry I'm late. Had to stop off to buy some bloody curtain rods, can you believe it, I promised Erika. (*Putting stuff down, turns.*) Anyway, SHAZAM! I've got your grant. In spades! They've undertaken to guarantee all your costs, clear all your outstanding debts, pay your rent, and provide you with a salary that will lift you at last into our lowest income tax bracket, plus bona fide expenses for the odd literary binge for African poets in transit and so forth. Which is, I think, substantially more than you expected and more than substantially more than I thought we had a hope in hell of getting, which was frankly nothing. But I did it all on my silver tongue and contents of my briefcase. Congratulate me!

MARIGOLD. Oh Peter, you've done wonderfully. Thank you! Thank you!

PETER. Oh, I know it's not enough to live and breed on, but going by my own experience, who wants to do that? (*Laughs.*) But a bit of credit to old Nick too, eh?

STUART. Nick?

PETER. They're such shits! The only thing those salaried buggers with pensions to come know about you is that you are élitist. So that was that, nothing to discuss. Until I read out Nick's article. To tell you the truth I didn't even know it was there. It just happened to be the first thing I plucked out of my briefcase, a despairing gesture, really, while I shouted angrily at them about how could they ignore the value and quality, etc. of this sort of thing, and one of them said, 'Well read it out, then. Let's judge it on its merits, shall we?' So I had to, of course. When I realized it was by Nick and knew the kind of stuff that was coming, I nearly threw up, and Christ it was awful, so of course, they loved it. All his appalling jokes about Angela Thark had them falling about. They wanted more samples of what you planned for the future, so I pulled out a sheaf of poems. That clinched it.

STUART. Hubert's.

PETER. No, those Belfast hooligans, Leary and O' — O' —

STUART. Dougan. Though actually it's Dougan and O'Leary.

PETER. Yes. They adored them for their directness, their
simplicity, their brutal rhymes and vocabulary, their — their
sing-song —

STUART. Lack of talent. They were in the wrong bundle, too. I
was going to send them back.

PETER. You mustn't. That poem about shit exploding in our
faces made up for all the Hubert Stouts. Which they loathed
on the grounds that they were — were —

STUART. Poems.

PETER. Exactly. What were they about? Must say, I couldn't
make much of them either. Perhaps teaching in Oxford has
addled my brain, eh? Anyway, the thing is — you're off and
running.

STUART. Peter. Thank you.

PETER. No. I enjoyed it. I mean, what could be nicer than
paying out large sums of taxpayers' money to one's chums.
(*To* MARIGOLD.) But God you look ravishing — And I
haven't kissed you yet — (*Does so.*) — but distraught. Are you
distraught?

MARIGOLD. No, perfectly, um, traught, thanks.

PETER. Terrific! Oh, do you mind if I use the phone? (*Goes to
telephone.*) Somebody's waiting on my call. Oh, by the way,
Humpty was up in Oxford the other evening, to give a paper,
a very short one I heard afterwards, but he came over for
dinner (*Looking for a phone number on scraps of paper taken
from his pockets.*) very relaxed and charming, anyway, for
Humpty. But then Erika always brings out the best in him,
they seem to have a rapport, partly because she doesn't think
much of his intellect, just goes on being herself, gets him to
help with the children, changes the baby, that sort of thing, he
loves it really — ah, here we are! (*Finding number.*) Oh, by the
way, who is that in your flat, is she foreign or what?

MARIGOLD. Yes, she's from Manchester.

PETER. Manchester? Really? Sounded like an Arab to me. (*Into phone.*) Joan, hello! What, yes I know, that's what I said, Jean, so hello Jean. Sorry, I'm running a bit late, I've just been pulling some chestnuts out of the fire for an old friend. What? Oh, I'm phoning from his office. *Of course* I'm alone! Anyway, look, I've booked us into the Charing Cross Hotel. (*Little pause.*) Because they know me there, it'll be a good room, we'll have post-coital views of the Strand, eh? So I'll see you in the bar in — (*Checks watch.*) in eight and a half minutes. Oh — and why don't you bring the um — you know. Right. See you, um, darling. (*Hangs up.*) Oh, has Erika phoned?

STUART. Yes.

PETER. What did she want?

STUART. To remind you to get the curtain rods.

PETER. Oh yes. Well, if she phones again remind her of my arrangement to meet Martin about the book on — um —

STUART. Sex Scandals in Nineteenth-Century Politics.

PETER. Yes. And then tell her I'll be going on to Selfridges to pick up the curtain rods, and then I'm meeting Nick and Humpty for a drink, and then I'm having dinner with you two, and I'll be back on the last train, but that I won't be able to call her probably because of the bloody disgraceful condition of the telephone boxes in London, but that she's not to worry, all my love. Right? What they call tit for tat. Not that *The Common Pursuit*'s tat. (*Laughs.*) But I'm after tit! (*Exits, with brief case, without curtain rods.*)

Pause.

STUART *walks around, touching various objects in the room. Spots the curtain rods.*

STUART. He's forgotten them. The curtain rods.

MARIGOLD. So he has.

There is a pause.

So I've been saved, then, haven't I? Just in the nick of time. So perhaps there is a God after all.

STUART. You mean the Arts Council? More like a devil, I suspect. (*Turns around, smiles at her.*) I'm not tempted.

MARIGOLD (*after a small pause.*) You're not going to accept the grant, then?

STUART. Of course not.

MARIGOLD. No. (*In despair.*) Oh why — why are you so obstinate?

STUART. I've told you already. I love you. We're going to get married. And have babies. Lots of babies. All the babies you want. And more.

MARIGOLD. Oh, my love.

Lights.

Curtain.

Act Two

Scene One

STUART's *and* MARTIN's *office. Three years later. Late afternoon.*

The office is transformed, painted and orderly. STUART still has the same desk, in the same position. Opposite is MARTIN's desk, slightly smaller than STUART's, but more antique. On both desks, a telephone. There is also a desk in the corner with a typewriter on it, a vase of flowers, some photographs propped, a secretarial desk. On the walls there are some book shelves, but now full of books, most of them evidently proofs of coffee-table style books. On the walls, covers of books on gardening, nursing, cricket, bridge, Napoleon, Hitler, Churchill, etc., some by Peter Whetworth, and a poster for the poetry reading, new, by Dougan and O'Leary.

There is a new armchair, a new sofa, a couple of hard-backed chairs, and an elegant and antique cocktail cabinet. On MARTIN's desk, and on the wall above his desk are photographs, drawings, cartoons and reproductions of paintings of cats.

The sound of footsteps on the stairs.

MARTIN increases the speed of his typing, as HUMPHRY enters. He is carrying an overnight bag. He looks around, has trouble locating MARTIN in the corner as MARTIN types.

MARTIN. Hi, Humpty. Won't be a second. (*Scribbling his signature at the bottom of the sheet.*)

HUMPHRY. Oh. Now you're being the secretary too, are you? Where's that girl of yours, what's her name, Michele?

MARTIN. Tonight's her evening class, so I let her go home early. She actually has to finish her essay on Macbeth. Actually I expect we'll have to replace our Michele soon. She's determined to go to university.

HUMPHRY. By far the best place for her. She's not bright enough to be a secretary.

MARTIN (*laughs*). Want a drink?

HUMPHRY. A small brandy, to settle the stomach. It always tends to be a bit queasy after lunch with Nick.

MARTIN (*going to the cocktail cabinet*). I've only got a classical French one, I'm afraid. Will that do? (*Extracting the bottle, pouring.*) What's he up to, we haven't seen him for a few weeks, old Nick.

HUMPHRY. You might see him later. He said he'd look in. But only if he gets his television job.

MARTIN. What television job?

HUMPHRY. Presenting the new books programme.

MARTIN. The one on the BBC?

HUMPHRY. So I gather.

MARTIN. Good God! You mean Nick might get that programme? Nick!

HUMPHRY. Might, but lots of competition, from what he says. He's particularly worried about the current front runner. The balding, portly poet, the one he calls Nappies.

MARTIN. Oh, Harrop. He's becoming quite famous — I've never understood why Nick hates him so much.

HUMPHRY. Because they're soul mates of course. Which is why Nick will kill him if he gets the job. I keep expecting you to move office. Aren't you getting cramped?

MARTIN. Well, frankly, yes. But Stuart's very attached to the place. And as a matter of fact, he got into a bit of a mess financially with old Giorgio, the landlord, which I'm still in the process of sorting out. But it's probably wiser to stay on. For the moment, anyway.

HUMPHRY. Where is Stuart?

MARTIN. At the printers. We take it in turns. He hates going but he insists on doing his stint.

HUMPHRY. Ah. And how's Marigold?

MARTIN. Oh. She's applied to be Assistant Head Mistress at her school. We're just waiting to hear whether she's got the job. The interview's this afternoon. Where are you off to by the way?

HUMPHRY. Oh, Edinburgh. To see my parents.

MARTIN. They're still in decent fettle, I hope?

HUMPHRY. It's my father's seventy-fifth birthday tomorrow, but he's OK. Thank you. And I've brought along a sweater I cut a hole in for my mother to darn. So she'll be OK too. I've also brought along a book inscribed to me by Edwina McClusky, on Plato, which they won't understand, which is just as well, as it's mainly wrong. But it'll support my boast that Edwina and I are having an affair.

MARTIN. But surely she's getting on a bit, isn't she, Edwina McClusky?

HUMPHRY. She's seventy-four, but my parents don't know that. And I hope they don't find out or they'll think there's something wrong with me. All they suspect is that she's an older woman. Which worries them a little. Which is exactly the right amount, for parents of their age, with a son of my type. And they'll be reassured by the news that I've been appointed the college's Senior Moral Tutor. Did we ever bump into one of those in our day? Apparently their job was to advise us on all our little problems, financial and especially emotional. A sort of uncle figure, with a cutting edge. I'm certainly the first Senior Moral Tutor I've ever come across.

MARTIN. But you'll enjoy it, won't you?

HUMPHRY. I'm afraid I probably will. Well, Martin?

MARTIN. How's the brandy?

HUMPHRY. I hadn't noticed. Probably a good sign. Come on then. What do you want?

MARTIN. Why do you think I want something?

HUMPHRY. Because when you phoned to ask when I was next coming down, and I said today, you said good, please come and see us. But you and I don't usually end up in the same room unless Stuart's present, do we? And as you *didn't* say Stuart wouldn't be here, it must be something you want, and don't want Stuart to know about. Is it?

MARTIN. I sometimes wonder whether you enjoy knowing so much. Yes. Have you committed your book on Wagner to a publisher yet?

HUMPHRY. No.

MARTIN. Would you commit it to me?

HUMPHRY. To make up one of your coffee-table specials. A short and breezy life padded out with photographs and facsimiles? The sort that Peter hacks out for you? (*Looking at* PETER's *book-jackets on wall.*)

MARTIN (*laughs*). I thought you'd say that. (*Small pause.*) Actually I was hoping you'd do me the honour of being our first real book. A book of scholarship, judgement and imagination. As we all know it will be. To usher in our next phase. It can be as long as you like, have no illustrations at all, if you prefer. Two, three, even four volumes. Three anyway. (*He laughs.*)

HUMPHRY. Have you discussed this with Stuart?

MARTIN. No.

HUMPHRY. Why not?

MARTIN. Because I want it to be a surprise. He'd be your editor, you see. Would you like that?

HUMPHRY. Yes.

MARTIN. Good! Then we'll draw up a contract.

HUMPHRY. No, we won't. The slight catch, from all our points of view, is that I'm not writing a book on Wagner. I abandoned it about three weeks ago, if October the seventeenth, at three in the morning, was about three weeks ago.

MARTIN. But why, Humpty? The last time I was in Cambridge I saw how much you'd done. There was what? Three hundred pages already on your desk.

HUMPHRY. You counted them did you, while I was out of the room?

MARTIN. Oh, come on Humpty. I'm a professional publisher. I could see at a glance how much you'd done. You mustn't give it up. You mustn't.

HUMPHRY. Yes, I must. I've got the scholarship, and the judgement, but not the imagination. Everything I've written about him reduces him to my own sort of size. Which makes him too small to be interesting to me. You see I've discovered I have a slight flaw after all. Moral, I think, rather than intellectual. I diminish what I most admire.

MARTIN. But — well, mightn't it help if you published *something*? What about a monograph? If not on Wagner, somebody else. What about our publishing your fellowship dissertation?

HUMPHRY. It's on Hegel, Martin. In German, mostly. I stopped believing in it before I began it. I went through with it because it would allow me to work on the things I loved. Which I want to go on loving. Which is why I won't allow my intelligence to fix on them, ever again. I don't think I can be simpler, even for you.

MARTIN. I'm being selfish. I'm sorry.

HUMPHRY. You're being selfish for Stuart, as usual. I'm sorry. I expect it's all far harder for you than for me.

MARTIN (*looks at him*). No, I'm actually very happy. (*Little pause.*) Really. If that's what you mean. Although you're right, I'm sometimes not sure what you mean, being simple. (*He laughs.*)

HUMPHRY. He doesn't know, then?

MARTIN. Know what?

HUMPHRY. Don't be alarmed. (*Little pause.*) It's not my business.

MARTIN. Thank you.

HUMPHRY. Our lives aren't dissimilar. In spite of appearances.

And reality, come to that. Can I give you some advice?

MARTIN (*thinks*). No. Really, Humpty, thanks. I respect
you far too much. I might listen to it, you see. And then I'd
have nothing. Nothing I want, anyway.

Sound of footsteps on the stairs. Coughing.

HUMPHRY. Nick. He's got the job, then?

Cough, off, followed by a sneeze.

But do we want that noise on our television screens — even
though it's livelier than what he'll have to say about books.

PETER (*enters*). Don't you ever get your bloody stairs swept?
Humpty, how are you? It's been ages.

HUMPHRY. Peter.

PETER. Stuart not here, then?

MARTIN. No, it's his turn at the printers. I didn't know you
were coming in today.

PETER. Nor did I, but I had to, as it turned out. Here you
are. As promised. Two weeks of exhaustion and only a
month overdue. (*Slapping a typescript down on the table.*)
About forty-five thousand words I worked it out at on the
train, which is only fifteen thousand fewer than we agreed. So
if we add an extra dozen pictures — who's doing the pictures
by the way? I'm looking forward to seeing what she's got.

MARTIN. Well, I think you are actually, aren't you?

PETER. Am I, bugger!

MARTIN. Yes, well that's what we usually put in the contract.
Anyway, you've finished it, wonderful.

HUMPHRY. What's it on?

PETER. The great religious leaders of world history, Mohammed,
Buddha, Jesus, you'll probably think I skimped a bit on Jesus,
just five pages or so, as a matter of fact, but then let's face it,
he's being over-done at the moment, he's always being over-
done, in fact, but I'll pad him out if you think it necessary,
and there's a whole chapter (*To* HUMPHRY.) on Wagner, in

the myth-creator section, out of deference to you. You're in
the index. And the acknowledgements, Humpty.

HUMPHRY. Thank you. Why do you do it?

PETER. What?

HUMPHRY. Go on turning out books like this?

PETER. Because I've got four children. Why do you think?

MARTIN. Um, even with pictures I've got a feeling that
forty-five thousand might be a trifle on the short side —

PETER. Yes, yes, well the thing is I've got to get on up to
Hampstead fairly quickly, there's somebody I've got to see.
Can we go into this next time I'm here, or you and/or Stuart
are in Oxford? The really crucial question is whether Erika
and I can have dinner with you tonight, preferably at your
place?

MARTIN. Oh, I'm sorry. Not really, I'm afraid. Not tonight.

PETER. Why not?

MARTIN. Because I'm going out to dinner.

PETER. We'll come too.

MARTIN. I'm terribly sorry. I'm afraid you can't. You see,
they happen to be people I don't know. Well, I mean.

PETER. Then cancel.

MARTIN. Oh no. I couldn't do that. They're an elderly couple,
you see, and they've gone to a lot of trouble. (*Little pause.*)
Probably a ghastly evening, but I can't let them down.

PETER. Oh Christ! Erika's made arrangements for a babysitter
especially so we could have dinner with you.

MARTIN. What dinner? We never discussed any dinner.

HUMPHRY. He means you were his alibi and it's all gone wrong,
at last.

PETER. Exactly. I told her I was having dinner with you and
then I'd probably stay overnight in one of your extra rooms,
as usual. But just as I was leaving she took it into her head
for the first time ever — *ever* — that she wanted to come too.

HUMPHRY *laughs slightly*.

Shut up, Humpty.

MARTIN. Well, tell her you got the day wrong. Or I did. Yes, blame me, that's the easiest.

PETER. I can't.

MARTIN. Why not?

PETER. Because she made me phone you to warn you there'd be one extra for dinner.

MARTIN. But you didn't phone me. Unless Michele forgot to give me the message.

PETER. No, of course I didn't phone you.

HUMPHRY *laughs again*.

Will you shut up, Humpty! No, of course I didn't phone you, but I had to pretend to. I was phoning somebody entirely different, of course.

MARTIN. Oh, who?

PETER. Jane.

MARTIN. Jane?

HUMPHRY. The girl he'd actually arranged to have dinner with, of course.

PETER. Of course. So I had to stand there trying to talk to Jane, with Erika at my elbow thinking I was talking to you, and hoping Jane would understand my saying that Erika was coming to dinner too meant that my dinner with her was off.

MARTIN. And did she?

PETER. No, because as it turned out, I wasn't talking to Jane at all. I was talking to her mother-in-law. Jane had already left Oxford. She's up in Hampstead now, still thinking we're going to have dinner.

MARTIN. Good heavens! What did she make of it?

PETER. Who?

HUMPHRY. Jane's mother-in-law.

PETER. No idea, as soon as I cottoned on to who I was actually talking to, I said, so we'll see you at eight, Erika's looking forward to it enormously, aren't you, darling, and hung up, but the thing is —

MARTIN. So the mother-in-law of the girl you're spending the night with in London is expecting you and Erika for dinner in Oxford. Can that be right?

PETER. Oh, don't be ridiculous, Martin, the mother-in-law hadn't the slightest idea who I was, so she doesn't know who to expect for dinner tonight, does she? So it doesn't matter. What matters is what am I going to do about Erika.

MARTIN. Why don't you phone Oxford and tell her I'm ill?

PETER. She's already left. She was catching an afternoon train.

HUMPHRY. Who is Jane, exactly?

PETER. Oh, nobody. Just the wife of a friend.

MARTIN. Anyone we know?

PETER. No, no, his name's Papworth, Roland Papworth, a theologian at New College. But what —

HUMPHRY. Does he know what you're up to?

PETER. What?

HUMPHRY. Does Roland Papworth know what you're up to? With his wife. Jane.

PETER. Of course he doesn't. I wouldn't hurt old Roland for the world, he and I have become extremely close, he gave me an enormous amount of help with *Great Religious Leaders*, for one thing. He's particularly strong on Buddha. (*To* MARTIN.) Can't you really get out of your dinner?

MARTIN. You don't mean he wrote it?

PETER. What?

MARTIN. This Roland Papworth, the theologian, did he write it? Your book? I need to know because of the copyright —

PETER (*exasperated*). No, of course he didn't write it, he merely filled in a bit of the history, background, ideas, that sort of thing. And the Buddha bits, but I did most of the last draft. Of course, he's probably expecting his name on the title page, that was one of the things I wanted to discuss with you later, and he'll want a share of the royalties, but look —

MARTIN. There aren't any royalties. You get paid a fee. Half of which you've already received, you see.

PETER. Yes, well, don't worry. I'll think up some way of sharing something with him.

HUMPHRY. Apart from his wife, you mean?

PETER. What?

HUMPHRY. I suppose Jane's good in bed, is she?

PETER. Yes, well. That's not the point at the moment. The point is Erika. I don't want her to start getting suspicious after all these years.

HUMPHRY. But does that matter?

PETER (*incredulously*). Does it matter? She'd crack up completely. We've got four bloody children. Do you think I don't care?

HUMPHRY. I know you don't care. About anything that matters.

PETER. What do you mean?

HUMPHRY. Haven't I made myself plain, even to you? That you go on spawning children and pretending to love a fatuous wife that you can't even be bothered to betray competently, while writing books on subjects that you inevitably demean.

There is a pause.

PETER *hits* HUMPHRY, *knocks him to the ground.*

PETER. What did you say that for? What did you have to say it for?

HUMPHRY (*still on the ground*). Because I've just been made a Senior Moral Tutor. It's our job to help people to see their little tangles more clearly.

PETER. But I've been a senior fucking moral what's-it for years. I don't go around insulting my friends and inviting them to hit me.

HUMPHRY. That's because you moved to Oxford. You've
forgotten how seriously we take moral matters at Cambridge.
I've got to be on my way if I'm going to just miss my train,
and enjoy an hour and a half hanging around the station
lavatory. (*He goes to the door, turns.*) I suppose I'm sorry.

He exits.

There is a pause.

MARTIN. You all right?

PETER. Yes — yes — but I — I — why did he? That I should have
hit Humpty. Of all people. Why did he?

MARTIN. I think — well, because he's so fond of you, isn't he?
Fonder than of anyone else.

PETER. But I can't spend my life being what *he* needs me to be,
can I?

MARTIN. No. You have to make your own life. I expect your
being so prolific doesn't help either.

PETER. Yes, well that's a different matter. He'd be ashamed
to have written what I've written. But then he hasn't got a
family — (*He stops.*) — I've got to get to Hampstead. Christ,
what a day, and the worst part hasn't even begun yet. Don't
you realize what's happened?

MARTIN. You've fallen in love with um, Jane, isn't it?

PETER (*nods*). It's a nightmare. But Jane isn't just another —
another of my fucks. I've got to get her out of my system.

MARTIN. I'm so sorry about dinner. If I could see any way —

PETER. No, I know. I had no right to involve you, really, had I?
But you've been such a convenient fiction all these years. I
must get going.

STUART *enters.*

STUART. Peter.

PETER. Stuart. Hello.

STUART. I didn't know you were coming down today.

PETER. No, well, actually the pity is I'm just off. I've got to be in Hampstead — oh, Christ, ten minutes ago. I dropped in to hand over the book. I've finished it.

STUART. Terrific, Peter. That's really terrific.

PETER. There are a few complications — Martin will tell you all about them — all about everything else too, I expect. (*Little laugh.*) I must really dash.

STUART. Love to Erika.

PETER. Absolutely. And to Marigold. (*Exits.*)

STUART. What book?

MARTIN. Oh, *Great Religious Leaders of World History.* To tell the truth, I'd almost forgotten we'd commissioned it. I rather wish he'd forgotten it too, as apparently it was mainly written by some Oxford theologian called Roland Papworth with whose wife, Jane, Captain Marvel is having an affair.

STUART (*clearly preoccupied, goes to his desk*). Ah.

MARTIN. Humpty passed through on his way to his father's birthday. He's seventy-five today. He's going to pretend he's engaged to Edwina McClusky, she's seventy-four. Peter took a swing at him and knocked him to the ground.

STUART. Really? Why?

MARTIN. Oh, Humphry was in a particularly provocative mood. Perhaps he'd decided that the time had come to consummate their entirely one-sided affair and that was the only way open to him. I think I've given a pretty accurate resumé of the afternoon's events so far.

STUART. Well, it all sounds very lively.

MARTIN (*looks at STUART, who is sitting at his desk evidently still preoccupied*). Oh, by the way, Peter was desperate for me to have dinner with him and Erika for reasons too boring to go into, except that they involve simultaneous enagagements with Jane Papworth and Erika naturally. I told him I couldn't because I'm already going out to dinner. With an elderly couple of my acquaintance. So could you remember that if the subject ever comes up?

STUART. Right. An elderly couple. What couple?

MARTIN (*laughs slightly*). Well, you and Marigold, I suppose. As that's who I'm actually having dinner with. Apropos, any news?

STUART. About what?

MARTIN. About whether she's been appointed Assistant Head Mistress.

STUART. Oh, well she said she'd come straight here after the interview, didn't she? So we'll know soon enough.

MARTIN. Anyway, she's bound to have got it. Even she seems to think she's got a slight chance which makes it a racing certainty virtually, doesn't it? (*Laughs.*) So let's relax and enjoy the tension, shall we? You look a bit — um — is it too early for drink, or too late?

STUART. Oh, not for me, thanks. So. (*Vaguely.*) Humphry was here, was he? I'm sorry I missed him.

MARTIN. How were things at the printers?

STUART. Mmmm?

MARTIN. The printers. Everything all right?

STUART. Yes. Well, I'm afraid I didn't go. Sorry.

MARTIN. Oh. That's all right. I can look in first thing tomorrow. (*Little pause.*) What did you do?

STUART. I went to see Hubert Stout.

MARTIN. Did he recognize you this time?

STUART. Oh, yes, straight away for once. In fact he was anxious to see me as he's written eight new poems especially for me. He's been keeping them under his mattress. He thinks the nurses or doctors will try to steal them. He's decided that *The Common Pursuit* either still exists or has been born again. I don't know quite which.

MARTIN. But eight new poems. Any chance we could publish them — with an introduction by you. We might get up quite a nice little volume — well at least a pamphlet.

STUART (*takes eight scraps of paper out of his pocket*). Yes, but unfortunately he hasn't written eight new poems. He's written eight shopping lists, or rather the same shopping list eight times. Orders for a pound of apples, a calendar, a ball of wool, knitting needles, scissors, a — a turvey drop —

MARTIN. What's a turvey-drop?

STUART. I don't know I think he's a character in Dickens. Isn't the dancing master in *Bleak House* called Turvey Drop? Anyway, the last order in his lists is for eight new poems in eight different rhyme schemes including one in terza rima. Good to know he's still experimenting with verse form. He's never worked in terza rima before.

MARTIN. Good God! What did you do?

STUART. Oh, shuffled through the bits of paper, nodding wisely until he fell asleep. Or pretended to. His eyes were shut and he made a sort of snoring noise. But there was a funny little grin under his beard, like a snarl. When I got up to go he was clutching at my coat, it turned out. I had trouble prising myself free. I think he knew perfectly well what he'd given me. I think the trouble is he's terrified of dying. And when you think of his best poems, they're mainly about death. So urbane, so wise. Especially the ones he wrote in memory of Charlotte. So seeing him like this is like a — a contamination. (*Smiles slightly.*) I'd have done better to have gone to the printers.

MARTIN. Yes. Look, I know it sounds inadequate but why don't we go somewhere special for dinner tonight? I'll book a table at L'Epicure. Marigold loves it.

STUART. Martin, I want to quit.

MARTIN *stares at him.*

Sorry. I didn't mean to blurt it out like that.

MARTIN. But you can't quit!

STUART. Why not?

MARTIN (*laughs*). Well — well, for one thing, you're our poetry and fiction editor. I can't manage without you.

STUART. Oh yes, you can. And we both know it. We never put
out more than three novels a year and they're really just a gift
from you to me. At least nobody but me seems to like them
much, not enough to buy them anyway. And as for poetry, a
few token volumes which I suspect nobody ever reads, let
alone buys — so really just another gift from you to me. Apart,
of course, from Leary and O'Dougan, Dougan and O'Leary,
whose shit is still exploding in our faces, though at least at a
profit. Oh, I'm not blaming you for publishing them, you're
absolutely right to, but the fact is I can't face reading them, let
alone editing them and that applies to almost every book
we've ever published, including — probably especially Captain
Marvel's latest. So you see —

MARTIN. But I was going to do Peter's. I wouldn't dream of
inflicting it on you. And I don't mind doing Dougan and
O'Leary either. In fact, I quite like them, not as poets I mean,
but they're great fun to take out to lunch. And you're quite
right, the main point about them is that they're profitable.
And Peter might be too, actually, come to think of it. If
Papworth's any good or we get him rewritten. Haven't you
noticed the competitions' lists? Religion's on the way
back with a vengeance. They've even started killing again
because of it. So Peter might turn out to be a blessing in disguise.

STUART. Yes, but the point is that none of that has anything to
do with me.

MARTIN. No, the point is that if we go on as we have been going
on for just a while longer — a year or two at the most — and
then consolidate, we'll be in a position to publish the kind of
book you'll be proud to edit. You should have let me keep
The Common Pursuit going. I told you you needed it.

STUART. *The Common Pursuit* has nothing to do with it. It's
me I'm talking about, as I am now — as I understand me,
anyway courtesy of Dennis.

MARTIN. Dennis? Who's Dennis?

STUART. The cat you gave us. Look, the other evening I was
sitting in the kitchen, vaguely waiting for you and Marigold
to get back from your concert. And Dennis was strutting

about on the counter. Then he did one of his things. You
know, he gathered himself together, eyed the top of the fridge,
jumped and missed completely. He caught the corner and
ricocheted off, to the floor. And then strutted away. And
instead of finding him funny and endearing, as I usually do, I
sat there loathing him. Because a cat who can't do any of the
things a cat is meant to do is really just a freak, especially
if he's been neutered. You see.

MARTIN. I'm sorry. I don't follow. You're surely not comparing
yourself to Dennis?

STUART. Well, I certainly don't do any of the things I'm meant
to do — and come on, Martin, you know why I came in with
you as well as I do. To have children comfortably at your
expense. And there's a lot wrong with that on any terms, but,
especially if, like Dennis, I can't produce any children to
justify it — justify it at least partially.

MARTIN. But you will, why shouldn't you? After all, Marigold's
been pregnant once.

STUART. Yes, well that was obviously something of a miracle.
So what we aborted might well have been the second coming.
We're not going to have them.

MARTIN. But how can you know?

STUART. I'm sterile. We had some tests done. Apparently I
produce a mere million sperm, when only a hundred million
or so will do. So her pregnancy was a miracle you see.
Medically speaking. And it's not going to be repeated, is it. Or
it ceases to be a miracle, which is what is required. (*Laughs
slightly.*) The effect of this news has been to render me
impotent as well, by the way. But that's likely to be only a
passing phase. Once I stop worrying about being sterile, I'll
probably become potent again. So they tell me. Anyway,
that's one of the reasons why things haven't been too good
between Marigold and myself recently, as you've no doubt
noticed. I know you have as you've been more than usually
terrific, even by your own high standards of delicacy and so
forth. And of course she's come to blame herself more and
more for killing off our only chance. I suspect she thinks
my present condition is God's revenge on her.

MARTIN. I'm terribly sorry, I'm terribly sorry. But I beg you, don't make a decision now. At least not yet. I'm sure we can come to some arrangement. Have you discussed it with Marigold?

STUART. Not yet. Martin, having put almost all my cards on the table, I might as well plonk down the last one. Apropos of dinner tonight, really. I should quit for your sake, too, you know. You shouldn't go on just being part of a trio living for other people. You really need to be your own person at last — you do Martin. It's time you were free of us.

There is a silence between them. MARIGOLD enters.
She is carrying a briefcase as well as a shoulder bag.

MARIGOLD. Hello, you both. You're looking very sombre, anything the matter?

STUART. Not at all. We were — just speculating about your career prospects as a matter of fact.

MARIGOLD. And did you reach any conclusions?

MARTIN. That depends rather on whether you got the job.

MARIGOLD. Ah, then you can go back to speculating, I won't know for a couple of days at the earliest.

MARTIN. I expect you need a drink.

STUART. I'll get it. I'm better at the preferred proportions. You tend to over-do the gin and under-do the lime, Marigold recently confided to me. Oh, Christ, we're out of lime.

MARTIN. I got some more, it's in the carrier bag there. And a fresh bottle of gin. But how did it go, the interview?

MARIGOLD. Oh, it was great fun. Old Miss Duffy, to whom I've addressed good mornings, polite inquiries after health, and so forth, every day for the last ten years, and with whom I've also actually organised two school concerts and three school plays, seemed rather puzzled by my identity and asked me how long I'd been a teacher there. And then Rosalind Spiggs came toddling in in a kind of pinafore and cotton stockings, looking like Alice in Wonderland. And as she had assured me months ago that she had absolutely no intention of applying, I couldn't help expressing mild surprise at finding her there. But she explained, she'd changed her mind after Headmistress, as she calls her, had said it was her duty to apply.

MARTIN. I thought 'Headmistress' said it was your duty to apply.

STUART. Yes, what the hell are they playing at? (*Bringing* MARIGOLD *a drink.*)

MARIGOLD. Oh, I suppose they just want a lot of dutiful candidates.

MARTIN. What were the others like?

MARIGOLD. Like well-established Assistant Headmistresses, it seemed to me. I think one or two of them actually were but on the whole I'd rather not relive the experience in further detail, at least not for a while, if you don't mind. I don't really want this. (*Putting drink down.*) It's still too early to eat, I suppose, where are we going to dinner? The Greek place?

STUART. Are you all right?

MARIGOLD. Yes, yes, fine — fine — just a mite peckish from nerves, probably, that's all.

STUART. Then let's go somewhere — somewhere special, what do you say to L'Epicure?

MARIGOLD. Lovely. (*To* MARTIN.) Your favourite.

MARTIN. Yes, but actually, I won't be joining you, I'm afraid.

MARIGOLD. Oh. Why not?

MARTIN. Well, because I — I — Peter entangled me in one of his alibis and before I knew what was happening I found myself having to have dinner with him and someone called Jane Papworth. Or is it him and Erika I'm having dinner with, anyway I'd better get a move on, if I'm going to make it out to — to Hampstead in time — so I'll leave you to close shop. Good night. (*Goes to door.*)

MARIGOLD (*unable to stop herself*). Don't go!

MARTIN *and* STUART *look at her, look at each other.*

STUART. Darling, what is it? Has something happened?

MARIGOLD (*takes a drink*). Sorry. I seem to need this after all.
I'm sorry. Sorry. You see — you see — Martin and I. We've
been having an affair.

STUART (*after a pause*). Yes, I've had a feeling — a kind of — of
thought at the back of my — my mind. How long has it been
going on?

MARTIN (*to* MARIGOLD). Why are you doing this?

MARIGOLD. Because I've just discovered that I am pregnant.

STUART. Of course. And you wanted to tell the husband and the
father in the same breath, so to speak. (*To* MARTIN.) Well,
congratulations.

NICK *enters. He is smoking an enormous cigar. He coughs.*

NICK. This is a mistake. My agent gets them free on Concorde,
she dishes them out as school prizes when we've done well. So
you'll gather that the answer is yes, I am about to be a
television star. You shall have the first kiss from a celebrity
soon, (*He kisses* MARIGOLD.) being my all time favourite
lady and first real love, I your chevalier. Before I break the
bad news. Nappies has got the job too. We're going to be
co-bloody presenting. Can you believe it! Apparently the BBC,
the Boring Buggers Corporation, thinks Nappies and I
complement each other, my brio striking off his lumpishness,
I assume, so it'll be over to Nappies for analysis, back to me
for liveliness sort of stuff, but once they go over to me they
won't be going over to him very often, I'll see to that. In fact
I intend to make this my chance to wipe Nappies out of public
life and back to wanking poesy, where he belongs, and I'll tell
you something else, his agent told my agent — (*He stops.*) —
Is something the matter? A death been announced, or
something? (*Looking around.*)

MARTIN. Nick do you think you could go?

NICK. You want me to go?

STUART. Yes, Nick, please.

NICK (*after a pause*). Oh. Right. (*He exits.*)

The sound of NICK *going down the stairs. A door slams. There is a pause. The phone rings.*

STUART (*lets it ring, then answers it*). Yes. Oh hello Erika. Yes, it is. No, Peter's gone, I'm afraid. (*Little pause.*) Yes, he is. (*Listens, and then to* MARTIN.) Erika's babysitter's let her down. So she won't be able to join you and Peter for dinner tonight. She's sorry if she's caused any problems. (*Into phone.*) Right, he's got that. (*Little pause.*) Very well thank you — yes, Marigold too, but Erika, I really can't talk now, we're in a — a rather important meeting. See you soon. 'Bye. (*Hangs up.*)

There is a pause. STUART *looks at* MARIGOLD, *then at* MARTIN.

MARTIN. I'm sorry.

STUART. No, you're not.

MARTIN (*after a pause*). No, I'm not. How could I be? I've never wanted anyone else in my life. From the first moment I saw her. I've never loved anyone else. Apart from you. So I'm sorry I've brought you — brought you hurt is what I meant. Of all people. If it had been yours I'd have loved it —

STUART. Shut up! Shut up! (*Moving towards him. Checks himself.*) I haven't got your capacity for decency, loyalty, etc; as it's yours I want to kill it. And you. (*To* MARIGOLD.) And you. As a matter of fact. (*Stands staring at her.*) I've no intention of letting you go. I love you too much. And we've spent far too many years — many years — (*Turns suddenly away, goes and sits down.*)

MARIGOLD (*stares at him*). Oh, my love! (*Little pause.*) Oh, my love! (*Runs to him, puts her arms around him.*)

Lights.

Scene Two

MARTIN*'s office. A few years later. Late autumn. About
6:30 in the evening. Thin sunshine through the windows. The
office door is open. MARTIN's jacket is over the back of his
desk chair. STUART's old desk is still there, but at a different
angle, no longer directly facing MARTIN's.*

*There is a bottle of whisky on MARTIN's desk, and a glass
with some whisky in it.*

NICK *is in the armchair, a drink in his hand.*

PETER *is sitting at MARTIN's desk, feet on desk, a drink in
his hand.*

PETER. What a bugger funerals are! Eh? Especially for atheists.

NICK (*after a pause*). Why doesn't somebody do 'Fear no
more . . .'?

PETER. Fear no more what?

NICK. 'Fear no more the heat of the sun / Nor the furious
winter's rages, / Thou thy worldly task hast done / Home art
gone and ta'en thy wages. / Golden lads and girls all must /
As chimney sweepers, come to — (*He wheezes uncontrollably,
starts to cough violently. Sits breathing heavily, clearly
shaken.*)

PETER. I thought you'd been ordered to stop.

NICK. Well, I still hold to my life's single principle. You don't
live longer, it just seems — (*He coughs again rackingly.*)

The sound of footsteps, coming up the stairs.

PETER. But you'll never know, will you, how long it might have
been. If you go on like this.

NICK. No. That's an extra perk.

MARTIN (*enters, in his shirt sleeves*). I was absolutely sure I
heard footsteps. And there was an odd smell at the bottom
of the stairs. Of alcohol and hospitals. Probably some old
wino staggered in for a moment, I suppose.

PETER. Or the ghost of Hubert Stout come on ahead.

MARTIN. One ghost is enough for the evening. Anyway, I've

left the door unlocked — so if he *does* turn up — he'll be able
to get in. He probably didn't even get the message on his
answering machine. He might still be in the States for all I
know. What train (*To* PETER.) are you catching?

PETER. I promised Jane I'd get the seven-forty. The ghastly
Erika's dumping the kids on us for the weekend. It's sheer
malice, as she's got nothing better to do than look after
them, which is all she's ever been up to anyway. And Jane
can't dump her lot on bloody Papworth as he's away at some
theological conference giving his now famous lecture about
me — Judas as Adulterer. I sometimes think I should get a cut
of his fees. So there are going to be seven kids — eight, with
the baby, who seems to have discovered a method of going
without sleep entirely, by the way, and what with all the
catering, the bed-making, the quarrels over sleeping bags, etc.,
Jane made me promise I'd get back on the seven-forty.

NICK. I was just saying, what about 'Fear no more . . .'?

MARTIN. What?

PETER. The dirge. From *Cymbeline*. Nick's idea is to recite the
first few lines and cough himself to death. And then we could
have a double funeral. He's got emphysema.

MARTIN. Emphysema. You're an idiot, Nick.

PETER. How do you manage to control it on your dreadful
television programme? Or do they cut to Nappies whenever
you cough? I've noticed his appearances have been getting
longer and longer.

NICK. Actually, Nappies is leaving the Boring Buggers
Corporation. He's going to be theatre critic on the *Sunday
Times*. Apparently they're impressed by his lack of
qualifications. But he's under the impression I'll allow him
back now and then as my guest, to read out some of his
wankings. We're having dinner (*He looks at his watch.*) to
celebrate. Five minutes ago.

MARTIN. I'm going to be publishing Nappies, did I tell you? His
collected poems.

NICK. Really, well he's not a bad poet, a bit derivative, but that's what he should stick to. As a matter of fact, I'll miss him. One needs someone one hates meshed into the texture of one's life.

MARTIN. Well, has anyone come up with any more ideas?

NICK. Well, we can do anything we like really these days, can't we? The last funeral I went to was my aunt's. They played a selection of ballroom waltzes. She'd asked for them especially.

PETER. I imagine she'd have to. After all, it isn't something a vicar would have the wit to think up by himself. Look, we're not really getting anywhere, and I haven't much time. Why don't we just stick to playing some Wagner and read some —

Sound of footsteps. They look towards the door. STUART enters.

STUART. Sorry. I only got in an hour ago — the flight was late as usual. And there was only half your message. Something seems to have gone wrong with my answering machine again.

There is a pause.

MARTIN. You got the bit about Humpty though, did you?

STUART. Only that he was dead. What happened? Was it suicide?

PETER. Sort of.

MARTIN. He was murdered. A young man he picked up in the Cambridge market place. At the tea-stall actually. Humpty took him back and — (*He gestures.*)

NICK. Apparently Humpty didn't put up much of a fight. Just let himself be beaten to death.

MARTIN. He was naked, apparently.

PETER. Except for a sock.

MARTIN. We'd heard what he was getting up to. The risks he was taking. We all tried to warn him, but it was almost as if he *wanted* to be murdered. Have a drink.

STUART. Thanks.

He gets a glass.

PETER. Yes, well, he certainly seems to have anticipated it. For one thing he left some stuff. In an envelope. A letter to me. And some poems.

MARTIN. Yes, there are about a dozen. Apparently he'd just started writing again. Anyway, we're meeting because of his father. The mother died last year and he's what, nearly eighty. He asked me if I'd organize the funeral. He wants to do the right thing, you see. And he wants to have something characteristic of Humphry, whom he obviously didn't know very well. He kept saying, 'the sock, I don't understand about the sock'. We've got to decide tonight as the college wants to know what we've planned. The Master and some of the Fellows intend to come to the service.

PETER. I should think so too. For a Senior Moral Tutor.

MARTIN. So far we've had proposals of a brief reading of those poems he wouldn't let you publish when he was an undergraduate — and the new poems, if you think they're any good of course. And an extract from the introduction to the Wagner book he never wrote. And — um —

NICK. The dirge from *Cymbeline*.

STUART. Surely Humphry would have wanted whatever his father would have wanted.

PETER. Well, what would that be? (*Glances at his watch.*)

STUART. I should think the traditional Church of England service in the traditional version.

A pause.

MARTIN. Yes, of course. I'm sure that's right.

PETER. Yes.

MARTIN. I suppose one of us should make a short memorial speech, though. (*To* STUART.) Will you do it, Stuart?

STUART. Well actually I think Peter should, as he's the one of us Humpty really cared about.

PETER. Yes, I had an idea it would end up with me. All right.

NICK (*getting up*). So that's settled then? Oh, by the way,

Stuart, terrific that your Hubert Stout biography is doing so
well — did you get a message from your agent about appearing
on our show — my show from now on?

STUART. Yes, I did. Thanks, Nick. Can I think it over?

NICK. Yes of course, but don't worry, I'll do you proud. I'll give
you the main slot. All I ask is that you keep it anecdotal. Your
own experience of Stout, things you found out from his
friends, his various marriages, mistresses and other messes,
his school days — that sort of thing. Most of our audience
won't know anything about his poems, but we can make them
interested in his life, if we go about it the right way. And the
thing is, it'll be a big plug for your book, won't it?

STUART. I know, and I'll certainly think about it, Nick. Thanks.

NICK. Look, let's have lunch and talk about it properly. I've
got to be off. I mustn't keep Nappies waiting more than the
usual half an hour. He might take offence and stay on the
programme.

PETER. Where are you having dinner?

NICK. Notting Hill Gate.

PETER. Good. Can I come with you? You can drop me at the
station.

NICK. Right. 'Bye Martin.

MARTIN. 'Bye.

PETER. It's a good book, Stuart. Bloody well researched too.
You really got the goods on him, although in the end I was
actually quite moved. Anyway, I wish I could write something
like that. Although I still don't understand the poems.

STUART. Congratulations on the job at Leeds, by the way. I
meant to drop you a note.

PETER. It's a dump. But at least I'll be a Professor — the fifth
youngest in the country, as a matter of fact, and I'll be
earning twice the money which I need. Oh, Erika sends her
love, by the way.

STUART. Erika?

PETER. I mean Jane, of course. Sorry. (*Little embarrassed laugh.*) So next time you're in Oxford — Leeds, that is, from next term —

STUART. Right.

NICK (*from the door*). Come on Peter, if you're coming.

PETER, NICK *exit. Sound of* NICK *coughing.*

There is a pause.

MARTIN. So how was New York?

STUART. OK. A lot of lectures, interviews, all that. Like Nick, they're not much interested in Stout's poetry. Only his life. The marriages, mistresses and messes in other words.

MARTIN. I had the impression that you didn't like him very much by the time you'd finished.

STUART. I found out rather more than I wanted to know, you see.

MARTIN. Oh. Here's Humpty's stuff. I'm thinking of publishing the poems. Perhaps you'd do the introduction.

STUART. Yes. If they're any good.

MARTIN. Right. Look, I've got to go. (*Slight hesitation.*) We're having dinner out for once. L'Epicure. Our babysitter, Michele, by the way, our first secretary, remember? — doesn't allow us out late. She's re-taking her university entrance, she very nearly got a place last time — so if you want to stay and finish your drink — and lock up after. You don't need a key — but you know the procedure.

STUART (*smiles*). How is Marigold?

MARTIN. She's fine. A bit of trouble with her father. That's normal of course. (*Little pause.*) He was caught shop-lifting.

STUART. Oh. And the twins?

MARTIN. They're fine.

STUART. Good. And Samantha and Dennis?

MARTIN. Yes. I'm afraid we've had to have them put down. The twins are asthmatic you see, and they were too old to find a new home for.

STUART *nods.*

We're moving out of here. We're looking for premises on two floors.

STUART. I'm sure that's the right thing to do.

MARTIN. Might you come and see Marigold and the twins one day? She'd like that.

STUART. Oh, one day I'm sure I will.

MARTIN *picks up his glass, holds it out to* STUART.

MARTIN. Humpty, eh?

STUART. Yes. Humpty. (*He lifts his glass. Both drink.*)

MARTIN (*little pause*). Do you think he was the best of us? I've been wondering that since it happened.

STUART. Well, he didn't mess up any lives except his own, I suppose. Except — I suppose the poor sod he probably provoked into murdering him. Have they caught him, by the way?

MARTIN. Oh, yes. Trying to sell Humpty's hi-fi and a whole stack of his records. He didn't give himself a chance. (*He drains off his glass.*) Well then, if not the best, then the first to go. If Nick doesn't look out he'll be next.

STUART. So. It happened in his rooms, did it?

MARTIN. Mmmm?

STUART. Humphry's murder.

MARTIN. Yes, in his rooms.

STUART. My old rooms, in fact.

MARTIN. So they were. (*Little pause.*) Please come and see us. She misses you dreadfully, of course.

He turns, and goes out quickly.

STUART *goes to* MARTIN's *desk, looks at it, then crosses to his old desk. He turns on the desk light, takes the poems out of the envelope, puts on his glasses, glances at the poems, still standing.*
Strains of Wagner, in full and majestic flow, towards the end side of the record from Act One, Scene One.
Lights.

Epilogue

Epilogue

STUART's *room in Cambridge. Twenty years ago exactly where it left off in Act One, Scene One. Wagner is in full and majestic flow. MARTIN is still in his intensely-listening posture. PETER is sitting, casually, looking through a pocket diary. HUMPHRY is watching NICK, who is lying on the bed, conducting and humming along with Wagner. MARIGOLD stands breathlessly at the door.*

MARIGOLD. Hello everybody.

PETER. Shazam! Where have you been?

MARIGOLD. Sorry we're late. Stuart is just coming. He's just saying goodbye to Hubert Stout. He told me to make sure that nobody had left.

NICK. Hubert Stout! Do you mean to say that while we've been seething passionately away in here, close to fisticuffs from time to time, you two have been calmly having it off with Hubert Stout! And you didn't even bring him over and introduce him!

MARIGOLD. The thing is we saw him crossing the court to one of the guest rooms. So we decided to nobble him. So we knocked on his door and when he opened it, we just barged in and Stuart began telling him about the magazine as if he'd known him all his life. The thing is, he was very, very interested. Wanted to know all about contributors, how we were going to organize subscriptions, (STUART *enters the room.*) but most of all how many pages we were going to give to poetry and he said he might even give us a poem.

STUART. Well, actually, he didn't go quite that far. But the point is, the real point is, that meeting him today seemed like a sort of omen. A portent. I told him it was going to be called

The Common Pursuit, he liked that. He's a great admirer of
Leavis, though of course he has his reservations. But he said
that it would establish what our critical standards were. That
we were serious, in other words. So he's already on our side,
you see. Oh, Marigold, have you been introduced to Humphry
Taylor, who sent in the poems I told you about. Marigold
Watson.

MARIGOLD. Hello.

STUART. And this is um, um, I'm terribly sorry.

MARTIN. Martin Musgrove.

STUART. Who's offered to take over the advertising, business,
etc.

MARTIN. All the really boring stuff, in fact, is my level. (*To*
MARIGOLD, *smiles.*)

STUART. Right. Let's get started.

HUMPHRY. As a matter of fact, I've just come to pick up my
poems.

STUART. What? But why?

HUMPHRY. Because I don't like them any more.

STUART. But they're very good. In fact, they're remarkable.
Every time I read them I find something new in them. You
must let the magazine have them.

HUMPHRY. I'm sorry. I don't want to see them published.

STUART. Look, can I talk to you about them properly? Just the
two of us. You mustn't make a decision now. Please —

NICK. There is going to be a theatre column, isn't there?

STUART. We'll get to that in due course.

NICK. Well, if we don't have a theatre page, can we have a sex
page? Marigold and I can edit together, can't we Marigold?
And we'll publish pictures of Captain Marvel having it off with
ghastly Erika. If I choose to introduce them.

PETER. You better or I won't write any more of your essays.

NICK. Is that a promise — ?

HUMPHRY. I thought this was going to be serious.

STUART. What we need to talk about now isn't simply what we want for our first few issues but our whole future. One very important thing Hubert Stout said is that, above all, we've got to be very careful. Take into account all the things that could go wrong, all the traps that other people have fallen into when starting out on something like this. That's the only way we'll survive. By knowing what it is we are about to give the world, precisely.

MARIGOLD. Absolutely.

MARTIN. Yes. Absolutely.

Lights.

Curtain.